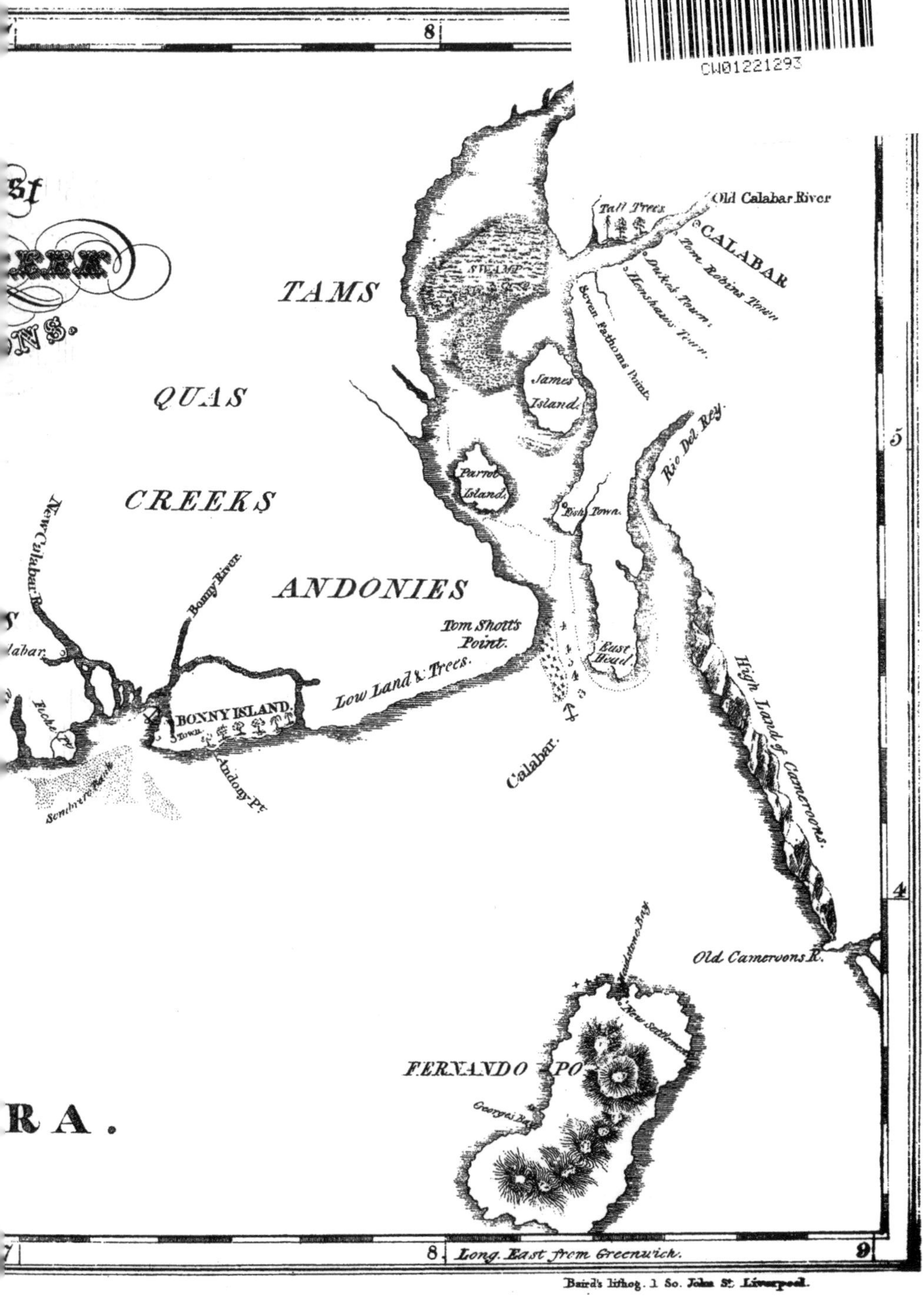

Baird's lithog. 1 So. John St. Liverpool.

The Memoirs of Captain Hugh Crow

Figure 1: Captain Hugh Crow (1765–1829). Watercolour by Albin Roberts Burt, 1820.

The Memoirs of Captain Hugh Crow
The Life and Times of a Slave Trade Captain

Bodleian Library
UNIVERSITY OF OXFORD

ARGYLL & BUTE LIBRARIES	
0404401	
HJ	26/04/2007
306.362092	£15.99

This edition published in 2007 by the Bodleian Library
Broad Street
Oxford OX1 3BG

Original 1830 edition printed by G. & J. Robinson, Liverpool.
All rights reserved

www.bodleianbookshop.co.uk

ISBN: 1 85124 321 6
ISBN 13: 978 1 85124 321 1

This edition and introduction © Bodleian Library, University of Oxford, 2007
Images ©Bodleian Library, University of Oxford, and other named copyright holders, 2007

Illustration credits
Figure 1 © National Museums Liverpool, Merseyside Maritime Museum. Reproduced with kind permission.

Figure 2 Bodleian Library. Shelfmark C17:65 e.1

Figures 3, 5 and *6*, photograph by John Pinfold.

Figure 4 Herdman Collection no. 107, 'Ranelagh Street, 1867', courtesy Liverpool Record Office, Liverpool Libraries

Endpapers 'The Coast from BENIN CREEK to CAMEROONE'. This and all other images are from the original edition (Bodleian Library of Commonwealth and African Studies. Shelfmark 710.11 r.25.)

No part of this book may be reproduced, stored in a retrieval system, or transmitted in any form or by any means, electronic, mechanical, photocopying, recording, or otherwise, without the written permission of the Bodleian Library, except for the purpose of research or private study, or criticism or review.

Designed by Dot Little
Printed and bound by Biddles Limited, Kings Lynn, Norfolk
British Library Catalogue in Publishing Data
A CIP record of this publication is available from the British Library

INTRODUCTION
Captain Hugh Crow and the Slave Trade

The author of this book, Captain Hugh Crow, was intimately involved in the slave trade for seventeen years, making thirteen voyages across the Atlantic on slave-trading vessels, the last seven of them as master. Few had greater knowledge of the practicalities of the slave trade, and his employers had such trust in him that he was specially selected to command the *Kitty's Amelia*, one of the last ships to make a legal crossing from West Africa to the Caribbean with its 'human cargo'. Crow never wavered in his view that the slave trade was an entirely legitimate form of commerce, or, even more controversially, that the slaves were treated better on the West Indian plantations than they had been in Africa. These views were undoubtedly shared by all but a very few of the ships' captains who commanded slave-trading vessels, but Crow was unique in attempting to justify his position even after the slave trade had finally been abolished in 1807. He devoted a great deal of time in his retirement to writing his *Memoirs*, and made generous provision in his will for them to be published after his death. Although clearly embarrassed by some of Crow's views, his executors carried out his instructions and the *Memoirs* were published a year after his death.

The *Memoirs* are an important source for anyone seeking to understand the eighteenth-century debate over the slave trade. The arguments that Crow puts forward in its defence seem wholly unconvincing today, but were held by a significant body of people in his own day. Moreover, his vivid descriptions of the practicalities of life at sea on a slave-trade ship provide an important eyewitness account of the conditions endured by both slaves and seamen, and should be read alongside the more pejorative accounts provided by Thomas Clarkson in his *Substance of the evidence of sundry persons on the slave trade* (London: James Phillips, 1788). A hero to some, a villain to others, Crow emerges from his *Memoirs* as a somewhat flawed character, unquestionably brave and resourceful, and in his own way a kindly and compassionate man, but too concerned to gain the good opinion of his employers to question the legitimacy of the trade in which he was employed.

He was born in Ramsey on the Isle of Man in 1765, the son of Edmund Crow (1730–1809), a 'respectable tradesman' of the town, and his wife, Judith (1737–1807). Hugh lost his right eye in infancy,[1] and nearly drowned at the age of twelve. When he was fifteen he was apprenticed to a boat builder in Ramsey, but after two years he determined upon a life at sea and moved to Whitehaven, in Cumberland, where he was apprenticed to Joseph Harriman.

Crow's first voyage was to the West Indies in 1782. He also sailed to the Baltic on a number of occasions, as well as to the newly independent United

States of America. None of these early voyages had any direct connection with the slave trade. Although he received several offers to go as second mate on ships employed in the African trade, he turned these down because of what he called his 'prejudices' against the trade.

In 1790, however, Crow changed his mind. The reasons are not entirely clear. He claimed that his friends talked him out of his 'prejudices', but the chances both of promotion and of sharing in the huge profits that could be made from the slave trade may well have played a major part in his decision. He was appointed first mate of the *Prince*, and they sailed to Rotterdam to take on a cargo of spirits before travelling on to the Gold Coast. On his fourth voyage as mate, Crow was captured by the French, and he spent the next year as a prisoner in France. Eventually managing to escape, he was able to pass himself off as a Breton by speaking Manx whenever challenged, and made his way to Le Havre, where he was able to board a neutral Danish ship which brought him to England.

On his return to Liverpool in 1795, Crow again signed on as a mate in the African trade, and after further adventures he was promoted to captain and placed in command of the *Will*. He completed several voyages with this ship, on one of them fighting an action which lasted nine hours with a French privateer. On a later voyage, when in command of the *Mary*, he fought another action, which passed into legend, taking on two English sloops of war, the *Dart* and the *Wolverine*, mistaking them in the dark for French ships. The fight lasted from 10 p.m. until daylight, and Crow only surrendered after his rigging and sails had been almost totally destroyed. He gives a highly coloured account of this action in his *Memoirs*, but this is substantiated by the entries in the logbooks of both the *Dart* and the *Wolverine*. This confirmation of Crow's veracity is significant when one considers other, more contentious, parts of his narrative, and especially those that deal with his relationship to the slaves he carried on board his ships.

In all, Crow made thirteen voyages on slave-trade ships, seven of them as captain. These can be summarized as follows:

Year	Vessel	Rank
1790	*Prince*	Chief mate
1791	*Bell*	Mate
1792	*Jane*	Second mate
1794	*Gregson*	Chief mate
1795	*Anne*	Chief mate
1796	*James*	Mate
1798	*Will*	Captain
1799	*Will*	Captain
1800	*Will*	Captain
1801	*Will*	Captain
1802	*Ceres*	Captain
1806	*Mary*	Captain
1807	*Kitty's Amelia*	Captain

In many respects Crow's career was similar to that of many other slave-trade captains. It was common for them to gain experience through serving on ships which traded directly with the West Indies before transferring to ships engaged in the slave trade, and common too for them to serve as chief mate for a number of voyages before gaining command of their own ship. On average, slave-trade captains obtained their first command at the age of thirty, so Crow was slightly older than most when he was appointed as captain of the *Will*.

Crow's background was also not untypical. Many captains were sons of small traders as he was, and a considerable proportion of them were fellow Manxmen. In fact, fifty-three of the Liverpool slave captains have been identified as having come from the Isle of Man, and these included Crow's brother, William, who was drowned at Bonny on the African coast in 1800 whilst on his second voyage as master of the *Charlotte*. His fate was a common one, as the mortality rate amongst the slave captains was very high; it has been estimated that no fewer that 27 per cent of the Liverpool and Bristol slave captains during the period 1785 to 1807 died during the course of the voyage. Hugh Crow was unusual amongst slave captains in living as long as he did, a consequence perhaps of his continual efforts to ensure the cleanliness of his ships.[2]

Crow may also have been unusual in treating his 'human cargo' relatively well. He did not overcrowd his ships, paid attention to the health and diet of the slaves, and allowed them on deck during the voyage. He records providing pipes and tobacco for the men and 'beads and other articles' for the women, and permitting them to 'dance and run about on deck to keep them in good spirits'. Perhaps most remarkably, he even employed the slaves in the defence of his ships against French privateers, and trained some of them in the use of firearms. One of the most striking, as well as surprising, passages in the *Memoirs* describes some of the slaves as 'eagerly employed in practising firing at empty bottles slung from the ends of the yard arms', a scene Crow describes as furnishing 'general merriment to all throughout the day'.

Despite this seemingly risky strategy, Crow never seems to have had to deal with a slave revolt on any of his ships, although he records this happening on other vessels.

So well did Crow look after his slaves that they had the reputation of being 'as plump as cotton bags' when they arrived in Jamaica. No doubt this contributed to his employers' profits; it also (and he is careful not to mention this) contributed to his own, for it was common for slave captains to receive a commission on the sale of the slaves they had transported. This was to compensate them for the fact that their wages were no greater than those of the other officers on board, and indeed were sometimes less than those of, for example, the ship's surgeons. We have no figures for Crow's wages, but Captain Nuttall, his predecessor as master of the *Kitty's Amelia*, was paid six guineas a month. This figure can be put into proportion when set alongside the sums Nuttall received on commission. On a voyage with the *Kitty's Amelia*, which returned to Liverpool in 1805, he claimed:

Commission on 280 Negroes
at £50 per head at 2 per cent   £280 0s 0d
Ditto 4 per cent after deducting 2 per cent   £548 16s 0d
                                                                          £828 16s 0d[3]

Looking at these figures, it is easy to see that the income from the trade that slave captains were receiving was probably equivalent to that of a small merchant.

Crow's concern for the welfare of his 'cargo' also provided him with a further source of profit, as a result of Sir William Dolben's Act of Parliament of 1788, which was intended to provide for a greater regulation of the slave trade.[4] Amongst its other clauses, it provided for a bounty of £50 to be paid to the captain of any slave ship with a mortality rate of 3 per cent or lower, and this was increased to £100 if the mortality rate was lower than 2 per cent. Crow regularly received this bounty, even when he had to fight off the attacks of French privateers. Despite personally benefiting from it, it is noteworthy that Crow criticized this measure as placing a greater value on the lives of the black slaves than of those he termed the white slaves – the sailors – who, he said, 'might die without regret' from Wilberforce and his friends. Here he undoubtedly had a point, for crew mortality was greater than that amongst the slaves on many, perhaps even the majority, of slave-trade ships. On a voyage of the Liverpool slaver *Jane* in 1786–7, for example, 16 per cent of the crew died, as compared with 8 per cent of the slaves. Even when slave deaths were high, as on the *Ellen* in 1791, when 19 per cent perished during the Middle Passage, crew deaths remained higher (22 per cent in this case).[5] This seems to be a typical pattern. Thomas Clarkson's samples of crew mortality on Liverpool slavers during the year 1786–7 suggest that 20 per cent of seamen died during the voyage, and one leading historian of the slave trade has estimated that overall one in five members of the ships' crews lost their lives in the trade.[6]

One unexpected side effect of this was that some slave captains recruited Africans to be members of the crew. They thus became participants in the operation of the slave trade themselves, and may even have been involved in efforts to put down slave revolts on board ship. A recent study has found that as many as seventy-seven Africans served on board Liverpool slavers during the period 1794 to 1805. There is no firm evidence that Crow ever recruited Africans as crew on any of his ships, although he does talk of recruiting 'both whites and blacks' when the *Kitty's Amelia* suffered many deaths through sickness. We do know, however, that when he sailed as chief mate on the *Anne* in 1795 there was one black member of the crew, whose name was Quadego, on board.[7]

Crow may well have had no necessity to recruit Africans to serve as crew members because the mortality rates on the majority of the ships under his command appear to have been well below the average. He himself attributed this to his being able to procure 'good crews' (most slave-trade ships were, according to him, crewed by 'the very dregs of the community') and through his attention to diet.

He does seem to have enjoyed genuinely good relations with many of the slaves under his care. He records a visit made by a group of slaves to him when he was on board ship in Kingston to express their good will towards him, and the *Memoirs* contain many examples of his going out of his way to help individual slaves, including diving into the sea to rescue one of them from drowning. However, the most striking instance of the regard with which at least some of the slaves regarded Crow is the song which they composed in his honour. Understandably, Crow was 'not a little proud' of this, and reproduced it in its entirety in the *Memoirs*.

Whether Crow was typical of the slave-trade captains in this regard can be doubted. Few of them recorded their views of the Africans as Crow did, but in many cases their actions spoke louder than words. Captain Collingwood of the *Zong*, for example, had no compunction about throwing 133 slaves overboard and then claiming the insurance money for 'loss of cargo',[8] and Captain Marshall of the *Black Joke* flogged a baby to death for refusing food and then forced the mother to throw the body overboard. One of the few captains about whose views we do know, James Irving, referred to the slaves as 'black cattle' in a letter to his wife.[9] This telling phrase indicates with brutal clarity the dehumanization of the Africans in the minds of the majority of the slave traders, but it is noteworthy that Crow never refers to the Africans in these terms. Indeed, his last words in the original manuscript version of the *Memoirs* are intended to show his essential good will towards them. He wrote:

> Could I flatter myself that any thing I have said would tend to place the poor blackey's character in a more favourable point of view than it has been generally represented, and thus obtained for him a more kindly consideration for my countrymen, I should feel that I had not in vain employed the leisure hours spent in committing these sketches to paper.

Nevertheless, he never seems to have seriously questioned the licitness of the slave trade, even after he retired from the sea. He thus stands in marked contrast to John Newton, the former slave-trade captain who later joined Wilberforce in campaigning against the trade. Newton, however, was very much an exception, and even he only came to change his mind some years after he had left the sea. Crow's ability to reconcile his humanity and his religious beliefs with the slave trade was typical of most Europeans of the time. As he himself put it, 'It has always been my decided opinion that the traffic in negroes is permitted by that Providence that rules over all, as a necessary evil'. His defence of the trade was essentially pragmatic and rested on the grounds that, first, the conditions under which the slaves lived in the West Indies were actually preferable to those under which they had lived in Africa. To back up this claim, he repeatedly refers to acts of human sacrifice and barbaric punishments inflicted on the slaves by their African masters, whilst portraying the condition of the slaves he met in the West Indies in a very positive light.

To understand how Crow reached this conclusion, it should be remembered that he never seems to have ventured beyond the coast of either Africa or the West Indies, so his knowledge of conditions in both locations was inevitably very partial. Most of the slaves he saw in Africa were not domestic, but criminals, prisoners of war or those who had been captured by gangs of slave traders in the interior and brought down to the coast for sale. As such, they would have been treated far worse than the domestic slaves, who had existed in African society for centuries. In addition, Crow was undoubtedly influenced by the comments made to him by the kings and rulers with whom he came into contact, that the alternative to slavery for the majority of the prisoners was death or human sacrifice.

Crow's knowledge of conditions in the West Indies was equally partial. Again he never seems to have ventured inland, and almost all the slaves he came across would have been domestic servants or artisans in the ports, whose treatment was markedly better than those employed as labourers on the plantations. In their introduction to the *Memoirs* Crow's executors attempted to explain his 'errors' in defending the slave trade through this lack of knowledge of the true situation. 'His sense of honour', they said, 'would not have allowed him to remain in any employment which he found to be incompatible with integrity and the exercise of humanity'.

Crow's argument that the lot of the slaves was actually improved by their transportation to America was one that was often employed by defenders of the slave trade. It received its most direct expression in a pamphlet by the Liverpool merchant Henry Wilckens, published in 1793. Interestingly, Wilckens had no direct or even indirect involvement in the slave trade. Born in Bremen, he had moved to Liverpool at the age of twenty-six. His primary business was in the salt trade and he owned several considerable salt works in Cheshire. He also campaigned for many years for improvements to be made to the Liverpool dock system, and he was regarded locally as 'exemplary in religious principle [and] strict in moral conduct'.[10] In writing on the slave trade he was thus able to present himself as an impartial enquirer after the truth. However, the arguments he put forward were far from impartial. He reasoned that as there had been no change in African 'barbarity' from 'the earliest accounts of history to the present day', to transport the slaves across the Atlantic was actually to benefit them by saving their lives. In return for this the slaves owed the Europeans some service, that is, labouring on the plantations. As Wilckens put it:

> The advantage which the Negroes, the objects of the slave trade, thus derive appears to me sufficient to justify the continuation of it; and that the Europeans, by preserving the lives of the slaves, are very much entitled to their services.[11]

It thus followed that:

> If this trade were ... abolished it would place Africa and the negro states in a more wretched situation than they are at present.[12]

This line of argument, specious as it may now appear to be, had a remarkably long life, and was often used by later historians to excuse the slave trade. As recently as 1957, in what was intended to be a standard history of Liverpool, the then City Librarian, George Chandler, wrote:

> In the long run, the triangular operation based on Liverpool was to bring benefits to all, not least the transplanted slaves, whose descendants have subsequently achieved in the New World standards of education and civilisation far ahead of their compatriots whom they left behind.[13]

This view, it seems, is one shared by at least some Black British or African Americans today. In his recently published history of Cape Coast Castle (the principal British slave emporium in present-day Ghana), William St Clair records some visitors commenting, 'I'm glad my ancestors were enslaved and transported, for look how much better my life is compared with the lives of the descendants of those who remained in Africa'.[14]

It seems highly unlikely that the slaves themselves shared this view of their enforced migration. Indeed, the most direct and powerful riposte to this line of argument was given almost two centuries earlier by Ottobah Cugoano, himself a former slave. In 1787 he wrote:

> Is it not strange to think that they who ought to be considered as the most learned and civilised people in the world, that they should carry on a traffic of the most barbarous cruelty and injustice, and that many ... are become so dissolute as to think slavery, robbery and murder no crime.[15]

Crow's second line of defence was that the living conditions of the slaves were better than those of many poor labourers at home. These he repeatedly referred to as 'white slaves', and on more than one occasion he included the ordinary seamen on his ships (and indeed himself in his younger days) amongst them. In one passage he even goes so far as to declare:

> I would rather be a black slave in the West Indies, than a white one at home; for there is no comparison between the comforts of one and those of the other.

He then attempted to substantiate this surprising statement by drawing attention to the appalling conditions under which many Britons lived – fishermen, miners, factory workers, those in jail or the workhouse amongst them. These he described as 'some of the greatest slaves in existence'. He also drew attention to the system under which many of the poor were shipped from the British Isles to America as indentured labour, a condition little better than slavery itself. In a striking passage early on in the *Memoirs* he described the sale in Charleston of some Irish labourers as indentured labour, with the clear implication that this was no different in essentials from the slave market.

In making this argument, Crow was once again echoing Wilckens, who, in his pamphlet of 1793, had stated that 'Great numbers of slaves in our islands (colonies) do live happier and more contented than the majority of the labouring poor in this country'.[16] Needless to say, Cugoano thought very differently, writing that 'bad as it is, the poorest in England would not change their situation for that of slaves'.[17]

Crow's third line of defence was that the prosperity of the West Indian colonies was wholly dependent on slavery. This was an argument that would be repeated many times, principally by the West Indian planters and their supporters in England, until slavery itself was abolished in the British Empire in 1833. Its proponents started from the premise that the mortality rates on the West Indian islands were very high, and thus 'a constant supply of negroes from Africa is requisite to continue the cultivation of the islands'. They were able then to argue that unless the slave trade was continued, the lot of the existing slaves on the plantations would worsen, as they would 'no longer be joined by new recruits to share and lighten their labours'. And if the labour supply dried up, the planters would emigrate and Britain would lose its colonies in the West Indies. At a time of war with France this was regarded as unacceptable by all parties. Seen in this light, of course, it was possible to argue, as one West Indian merchant did anonymously, that 'The West India planters and merchants have only been the humble instruments ... for extending the commerce and thereby adding to the wealth and strength of the British Empire'.[18]

And lastly, Crow, and many others, argued that if the British gave up this very lucrative trade other nations would not be slow to take their place, and they might not treat their 'human cargo' so well. As the same anonymous author put it,

> The result ... of the abolition of the slave trade by Great Britain alone, will be the aggrandisement of foreign merchants and foreign colonies at the expense of our own, and that the slave trade, instead of being carried on in British ships, subject to the humane regulations adopted by parliament for the accommodation of slaves on their passage, will be carried on in American and other foreign ships not subject to these restrictions, and thus the cause of humanity will be injured instead of being benefited.[19]

This line of argument, of course, has a long history, having been employed in our own time by, for example, those opposed to sanctions against apartheid South Africa, or those keen to sell arms to countries with a poor record on human rights. Crow quotes King Holiday, the ruler of Bonny, as saying 'we tink trade no stop', despite British abolition, and this did in fact prove to be the case. In the years following abolition, and indeed for a large part of the nineteenth century, the Royal Navy devoted considerable resources to patrolling both the west and east African coasts in an attempt to suppress the continuing trade in African slaves.

Today none of these arguments sounds very convincing, but in expressing them as he did Crow showed himself to be a man of his time and place. Unable to consider the slave trade in abstract terms, he looked at it simply in terms of its practical results as he saw them. No doubt, like many others in Liverpool, he saw the prosperity of the port as largely dependent on the slave trade, and would employ any argument he could to defend it. As the debate sharpened he, again like many others, became more extreme in his views and, as his executors noted in their introduction to the *Memoirs*, he would 'occasionally express himself in no very measured terms respecting his opponents'. They took it upon themselves to excise some of these 'vituperations', from the published volume. Since the original manuscript no longer appears to exist, it is impossible to say how much or what has been removed, but it seems likely that it would have included sharper and more personal attacks on Wilberforce and the other abolitionists. Crow's executors were also careful to add a number of more positive references to Africans at the end of the volume, 'inferring' that had he known of them he would certainly have included them in his memoirs.

Perhaps the most remarkable aspect of the support that even humane captains such as Crow or James Irving gave to the institution of slavery was that they had themselves suffered periods of imprisonment – indeed, Irving was himself enslaved, having been captured off the Barbary coast. Yet they seem to have been unwilling to accept that slavery or imprisonment for a European was no different to slavery for an African. Here, once again, Henry Wilckens provided a justification for them, writing:

> The assertion that slavery is not the same thing even in idea to an African as to a European is highly probable:– Many of the Negroes are born in a state of slavery; it is even interwoven in the government, customs and manners of the African Negro; he feels not the indignity, he scarcely wishes for a change in his situation; or if he would change it, he knows not how to devise advantage from it:– The European who scarcely knows what slavery is, or has only heard of it, from the dreadful descriptions of particular acts of cruelty; imagines that by opposing this Trade he is warding off slavery from himself.[20]

Nor was this an extremist view at the time. Had Crow read David Hume's *Essay on national character*, he would have found the following passage:

> I am apt to suspect the negroes, and in general, all the other species of men (for there are four or five different kinds) to be naturally inferior to the whites. There *never was* a civilised nation of any other complexion than white, *nor even any individual* eminent in either action or speculation.... There are negro slaves dispersed all over Europe, of which *none* ever discovered any symptoms of ingenuity.[21]

If a leading member of the Scottish Enlightenment could write in this way, it should not surprise us that men such as Wilckens or Crow found it easy to justify the slave trade. They also had on hand Rev. Raymund Harris, who claimed that the slave trade was sanctioned by God himself. In his pamphlet *Scriptural researches on the licitness of the slave-trade* (1788) he quoted liberally from the Bible, particularly the Old Testament, to show that 'the Slave Trade is perfectly consonant to the principles of the Law of Nations, the Mosaic Dispensation and the Christian Law, as delineated to us in the Sacred Writings of the Word of God'. Indeed, he went further: quoting Leviticus (25: 44–6), he maintained that:

> the Slave Trade has not only the sanction of Divine Authority in its support, but was positively encouraged (I had almost said, *commanded*) by that Authority, under the Dispensation of the Mosaic law.

This passage in Leviticus, which was so useful to Harris and other supporters of the slave trade, refers to the enslavement of the heathen, and Harris was quick to add that God 'does not say ... *of them MAY ye buy bond-men and bond-maids*, but, *of them SHALL ye buy bond-men and bond-maids*'; thus 'the word of God encourages the persecution of the slave trade'.[22]

This interpretation of Divine Will met with such approbation amongst the Corporation of Liverpool that they presented Harris with £100 as a mark of their appreciation.

From a modern perspective, Harris's interpretation of the Bible seems wilfully self-serving; but he was by no means the only writer to use the scriptures as a means for justifying the slave trade.[23] By far the most remarkable (as well as the most surprising) of these was Jacobus Capitein (c.1717–47), who was himself a victim of the slave trade. Snatched from his home on the West African coast at the age of seven or eight by Dutch slave traders, he was later taken to Holland and studied at the University of Leiden. There he published his thesis, the original title of which was *Dissertatio politico-theologica de servitute libertati Christianae non contraria* (*Political-Theological dissertation on slavery not being contrary to Christian freedom*). In this he argued that 'whether one is bought with money or born to slaves ... or captured in war, one becomes a slave through silent permission'. He then quoted the Second Epistle of Peter (2: 19) that 'a person becomes a slave of anything [anybody] that overcomes him'; like Wilckens, he argued that the slaves owed their masters service through having been rescued from a worse fate. Capitein's thesis, which was published in Latin in 1742 and translated into Dutch a matter of weeks later, was widely distributed throughout Europe and undoubtedly encouraged many of those engaged in the slave trade, for here was a former slave justifying their activities![24]

Although the publication of works such as these suggests that those involved in the slave trade increasingly felt the need to justify their actions to the rest of the world, within the Liverpool mercantile community participation in the slave trade was never a bar to respectability. Looking back many years later, James Stonehouse, whose father was both owner and captain of the slaver *Mary Ellen*, remembered that as a boy:

> while the *Mary Ellen* was fitting-up for sea, I was often taken on board. In her hold were long shelves with ring-bolts in rows in several places. I used to run along these shelves, little thinking what dreadful scenes would be enacted upon them.

Stonehouse went on to say about his father that:

> at the present time [he] would not, perhaps, be thought very respectable; but I assure you he was so considered in those days. So many people in Liverpool were ... 'tarred with the same brush' that these occupations were scarcely, indeed, were not at all regarded as anything derogatory from a man's character.[25]

Indeed, what is striking about eighteenth-century Liverpool is how few people felt any qualms at the town's involvement in the slave trade. Later historians have tried to redress the record by drawing attention to the group of abolitionists in the town, men such as William Roscoe, Edward Rushton, Dr James Currie and William Rathbone. Recent research has suggested, however, that their influence was considerably less than has previously been supposed, and indeed that for much of the time most of them (Rushton being a notable exception) kept their opinions to themselves. William Roscoe, for example, who as one of Liverpool's Members of Parliament voted in favour of abolition in 1807, never mentioned the slave trade during his election campaign the previous year, and included amongst his backers many who had gained, directly or indirectly, from the trade. Indeed, Roscoe's own partner in his banking business, Thomas Leyland, was one who had made enormous profits from the slave trade.[26]

Inhabiting this society, and always keen to gain the good opinion of his employers, it is perhaps hardly surprising that Crow felt little need to apologise for either his profession or his source of income. Two centuries on we might feel differently, and agree with Gomer Williams, who thought that Crow 'looked at the slave trade from one side, and that the side of self', adding that: 'Self interest evidently blinded him. The slave trade, like the Rontgen rays, caused an obliquity of vision when closely followed'.[27]

Crow's reputation amongst the merchants was so great that he was specially chosen to command one of the last slave-trade ships to sail from Liverpool. This was the *Kitty's Amelia*, whose previous master, Captain Nuttall was demoted to chief mate. This change of command is a clear indication of the confidence the ship's owners had in Crow to produce a handsome profit from the trade one last time. Unfortunately, Nuttall deeply resented his demotion, and, as Crow records, tried to take his revenge by inciting the crew 'to an almost open state of mutiny'. Having taken advice from his fellow captains, Crow then dismissed Nuttall whilst the ship lay at Bonny.

The *Kitty's Amelia* left Liverpool on 27 July 1807. The slave trade had already been abolished four months earlier, but the ship had received legal clearance to sail before the Act came into force on 1 May and this technicality allowed her to sail. In the *Memoirs* Crow states that the *Kitty's Amelia* was in fact the very last slave-trade ship to leave Liverpool, and for many years this statement was accepted at face value. More recent research, however, has suggested that at least one other slaver cleared the port at a later date. This was the *Eliza*, which 'entered pay' on 16 August, and thus sailed for West Africa some three weeks later than the *Kitty's Amelia*. However, it is perfectly possible that the *Eliza* either reached the African coast before the *Kitty's Amelia* or left for the West Indies before her, leaving Crow's ship as the last to leave with a cargo of slaves.[28] Certainly the conversations that Crow records having had with the rulers on the coast suggest that both he and they regarded his ship as the last.

From Crow's point of view, the voyage was as successful as his previous ones, although it was far from uneventful. He rescued the crew of another ship that had been wrecked, and they brought sickness with them that attacked the *Kitty's Amelia*'s crew and 'cargo'. Crow also had to cope with a major fire on board, but managed to extinguish it. On arrival in Jamaica, the first thing he saw in the newspapers was a large advertisement announcing that 'Captain Crow had arrived with the finest cargo of negroes ever brought to Kingston'. He records that 'on the fifth day after we began to sell not a single negro was left on board'.

It may seem surprising that both the *Kitty's Amelia* and the *Eliza*, and perhaps other slavers too, were allowed to sail after abolition had come into force, but one little-known fact about these final slave-trading voyages is that the British government tacitly encouraged them. This was because the government was itself one of the largest purchasers of slaves, using them as soldiers in the West India Regiment, and these last voyages were intended to allow the army to make one final large purchase.[29] Crow does not mention whether any of the slaves on the *Kitty's Amelia* were intended for the army in this way, but it is at least a possibility.

This was Crow's last voyage. He handed the *Kitty's Amelia* over to another master and travelled home from Jamaica as a passenger. The *Kitty's Amelia*

Figure 2: Part of John Drinkwater's map of the Isle of Man, 1826, showing the area to the south of Ramsey. Crow's house at East Ballaterson is clearly marked.

RAMSEY

Maughold He[ad]

Lewaigue

Balla-terson
Capt. Crowe

6
Balla fayle

Balla-Glass

Figure 3: Crowville, Hugh Crow's house on the Isle of Man, as it is today.

was later employed in trading with Brazil. She was lost in February 1809 near Maldonado (a naval station of Uruguay on the River Plate).[30]

After retiring from the sea, Crow purchased a small estate on the Isle of Man at East Ballaterson near Maughold. Typically, he renamed the house Crowville (or Crow Villa as it is called in some accounts), and set out to improve the estate. The house was reconstructed and transformed from a fairly modest cottage into a fine Georgian-style property suitable for a gentleman. With its elegant frontage, walls some three feet thick, and side and rear walls hung with slates to protect it from the weather, it remains today very much as it was in Crow's day. In 1812 he was proposed as a member of the House of Keys (the Isle of Man's parliament), but declined the appointment. His son died the same year, and Crow suffered a period of depression as a result; as he himself put it, 'After the melancholy death of my son, I continued to lay off and on, and to wander about seeking to divert my mind'. In 1817 he returned to Liverpool and spent the last twelve years of his life there. He spent much of his time in the Lyceum News Room, catching up with the news, meeting his friends and retelling old stories. He also spent many hours on the dockside, watching the arrivals and departures of ships engaged in a more legitimate form of trade than the majority of his had been. It was also during this time that Crow began to write his *Memoirs*. These were clearly intended for publication, as he left £200 to his executors in his will, with instructions that the money was to be used to pay for 'the expenses attending the preparing for printing and publication a sketch of my life and in and towards the expense of engraving plates and printing and taking of impressions therefrom illustrative of the said sketch and to accompany the same and be published therewith'.[31]

Crow died on 13 May 1829, and was buried in the family plot in the churchyard of Kirk Maughold on the Isle of Man. The tomb, decorated with Adam-style pilasters, can still be seen there. The inscription, surely composed by Crow himself, reads, in part, as follows:

> Captain Crow commanded the ships 'Will', 'Ceres', 'Mary' and 'Kitty's Amelia' with much credit to himself and to the entire satisfaction of his owners. He also fought several actions with the enemy for which he received repeated marks of approbation of the merchants and underwriters of Liverpool and London.

At the end of the inscription is the quotation:

> An honest man's the noblest work of God.

Crow's grave plot also contains the bodies of his parents and of his nephew, William Hinds (1797–1848), who inherited Crowville. In his will, Crow left money for the poor of Liverpool and of Douglas, Ramsey, Castletown and Peel on the Isle of Man. There were also legacies for the Bluecoat Hospital and the Deaf and Dumb Institution in Liverpool, the Seamen's Hospital in Whitehaven and, most strikingly, the Hospital for the Poor Black Slaves in Kingston, Jamaica. As well as his nephew and nieces, individuals to benefit from his will included John Jones, the son of the Keeper of the Lyceum News Room, and John Ratcliffe, a bookkeeper at the Liverpool Auxiliary Bible Society. His estate was valued at 'under £4,000'.[32] This term means that Crow was worth something between £3,000 and £4,000, a very comfortable sum for the time, and substantially greater than that recorded for any other known slave-trade captain.[33] His 'obliquity of vision' had certainly served him well.

Following his instructions, Crow's *Memoirs* were first published in Liverpool the year after his death. It is clear that his executors were to some extent embarrassed by his involvement with the slave trade and they edited the original manuscript quite considerably in order to present him in as favourable a light as possible. Nevertheless, as one of the few eyewitness accounts of the slave trade by one who participated in it they have ensured that Crow has not been forgotten, having been used as a source by historians of the slave trade from the mid-nineteenth century onwards.

Despite his involvement in the slave trade, Crow's reputation has remained fairly high, not least because many writers have chosen to downplay it. This was a trend that began during his own lifetime. James Aspinall, a member of one of the ship-owning families that employed Crow, remembered him later in life as 'bluff and resolute', and 'as brave a sailor and as odd and eccentric a man as ever walked a quarter deck'. Aspinall ignored Crow's role as a slave trade captain, other than to remark in passing that his famous fight with the British warships took place 'somewhere in the middle passage, which Liverpool ships were

Figure 4: Ranelagh Street, Liverpool 1867. Watercolour by William Herdman.
The Lyceum newsroom is the building on the right.

engaged upon in those times'.³⁴ And even the local author of an anti-slavery history referred to Crow's 'good mixture of fun and humour', subsequently quoting uncritically from the *Memoirs*.³⁵

In the late nineteenth century the Manx nationalist writer Edward Callow devoted a whole chapter to Crow in his history of the Isle of Man *From King Orry to Queen Victoria* (London, 1899). Unsurprisingly, Crow's involvement in the slave trade barely merits a mention, Callow preferring to concentrate on his sea battles against the French privateers and his daring escape from captivity in France. To him, Crow 'bore a high character ... for his great care of and humanity to his sable passengers', and was above all a patriotic hero and a role model to later generations of Manxmen. Callow concludes with the stirring words:

> I think that ... Captain Crow was a man that not only every
> Manxman but every Britisher ... should be justly proud of.
> Thank goodness there are many more like him both afloat and
> on shore!³⁶

By the beginning of the twentieth century some historians were beginning to look at Crow a little more critically. Ramsay Muir, in his influential *History of Liverpool*, thought that Crow's 'three cardinal virtues' were his 'resourcefulness, straightforwardness and utter loyalty to his employers', and that his treatment of the slaves was at best characterised by 'a bluff contemptuous kindness'.³⁷ This seems a fair assessment of his character. There are many passages in the *Memoirs* designed to show the good opinion his employers had of Crow, and there can be little doubt on reading them that he also possessed a very high opinion of himself. As one nineteenth-century writer put it, he 'possessed, and that very largely, the feeling of, – I am Captain Crow'; the same author also recorded that 'often did he shake hands with himself with that urbanity which always accompanied him'.³⁸

Crow has also been remembered in other ways. In 1934 he featured in a play about the slave trade by Mary D. Sheridan entitled *A City of Ships*, which

Introduction · XXI

opened at the Embassy Theatre, London, to mixed reviews. *The Times* called it a 'serious and sober reconstruction' of the slave-trade debate, which presented both sides of the argument, but 'does not do much more'.[39] It seems to have been totally forgotten since. Around forty years later there was another possibility of Crow being portrayed on stage when Nigel Kneale, author of *The Quatermass Experiment* (1953), wrote a play based on his life called, simply, *Crow*. Unable to set this up on the stage, Kneale sold the play to ATV (one of the British independent television companies of the time); within a week of filming having started, Lew Grade, the boss of ATV called a halt to the production and it was never shown.

The portrait of Crow which appears as the original frontispiece engraving of the *Memoirs* has often been reproduced. In 2004 the Merseyside Maritime Museum acquired a watercolour portrait of him by Albin Roberts Burt (1783–1842), painted whilst the artist was living in Chester in 1820.[40] Showing the Captain with his cutlass and pistols, this is an altogether more lively portrait of him.

But Crow's true memorial lies with the *Memoirs*. With his customary self-regard, he himself viewed them as 'one of the finest things of the kind ever got up by a Manxman'.[41] This assessment may seem over-generous today, but his swashbuckling account of his adventures remains a lively read and sheds a vivid light on the world of privateering and the slave trade as seen by one who was intimately involved in both activities. The book is a prime source for anyone seeking to understand both the practicalities of the slave trade and the flawed, though deeply held, justifications of it by those who engaged in it. For students of West African history, it is also an important early source of information about the kingdom of Bonny, on the Niger delta.

In the *Memoirs* Crow makes little reference to his family. It is known, however, that he married Mary Hall on 25 August 1793 at St Paul's Church in Liverpool, during the period when Crow, unusually, spent a year at home, from June 1793 to June 1794. They had one son, Edward, born on 30 May 1794 and baptized a week later at St Nicholas's, the traditional sailors' church on the Liverpool waterfront. Crow clearly had high expectations of his son, but all he received was, in his own words, 'grief and mortification'. Having failed to dissuade him from a career at sea, he used his influence to get him into the Navy. But Edward was soon captured by the French, and during his imprisonment he became 'contaminated with loose and immoral principles'. He made a courageous and daring escape from the French, but, falling in with bad company, he yielded to their 'insidious persuasions' and enlisted in the 9th Light Dragoons. Crow again had to use his influence to have him discharged, but he died soon afterwards in Lisbon in 1812, aged no more than eighteen. Crow wrote:

> Thus were my fondest hopes blasted. I am persuaded I shall carry my sorrow for that ill-fated youth to the grave, and these lines, which so vividly call to mind all he was and might have been, I write with many tears.

Figure 5: Crow's tomb in the churchyard of Kirk Maughold, Isle of Man.

He had no such words for his wife. The date of her death is unknown, although she was still alive in 1826, when she is mentioned in Crow's will. As she was entitled to an annuity of £40 per year on his death, a sum he regarded as 'ample provision for her support and maintenance', he left her only ten guineas (£10.50p) 'for mourning', a sum less than that left to his nieces. She is not buried with him at Kirk Maughold. Crow's nephew, William Hinds, continued to live at Crowville until his death in 1848. The house and farm were later sold to the Moore family, who continue to occupy it today.

The original edition of the *Memoirs* was published in 1830 by Longmans in London and by G. and J. Robinson in Liverpool. Both this and a previous reprint by Frank Cass in 1970 are now collectors' items. To mark the two-hundreth anniversary of the abolition of the slave trade, and the eight-hundreth anniversary of the granting of the first charter to Liverpool, the town Crow made his home, the Bodleian Library is now making this important text accessible to a new generation of readers.

John Pinfold
Bodleian Library of Commonwealth and African Studies
2007

Note on values

There are differing estimates on the purchasing power of the pound in the eighteenth and nineteenth centuries, but in general terms a pound in Crow's day should be multiplied by between seventy-five and eighty to give its approximate value today.

Figure 6: Part of the inscription on Crow's tomb, Kirk Maughold, Isle of Man.

Notes

1. Hence his nickname 'Mind your eye' Crow; see p.53 of the *Memoirs*.
2. S.D. Behrendt, 'Captains in the British slave trade from 1785 to 1807', *Transactions of the Historic Society of Lancashire and Cheshire*, 140 (1991), pp.87–91, 101, 111; F. Wilkins, *Manx slave traders: a social history of the Isle of Man's involvement in the Atlantic slave trade* (Kidderminster, 1999), p.87.
3. Quoted in C.R. Hand, 'The *Kitty's Amelia*: the last Liverpool slaver', *Transactions of the Historic Society of Lancashire and Cheshire*, 82 (1930), p.72.
4. Sir William Dolben (1727–1814) was Member of Parliament for Oxford University and a leading campaigner against the slave trade.
5. S. Schwarz, *Slave captain: the career of James Irving in the Liverpool slave trade* (Wrexham, 1995), p.32.
6. P.D. Curtin, *The Atlantic slave trade: a census* (Madison, WI, 1969), pp.282–6.
7. E. Christopher, *Slave ship sailors and their captive cargoes, 1730–1807* (Cambridge, 2006), pp.231–3.
8. This incident was regularly cited by anti-slave-trade campaigners as proof of the barbarity of the trade, and it seriously embarrassed the *Zong*'s owners. Fortunately for them, perhaps, Collingwood died before the case was resolved. More recently, it has formed the basis of an historical novel by Charlotte and Denis Plimmer, *The Damn'd master* (London, 1971).
9. Schwarz, *Slave captain*, p.113.
10. H. Smithers, *Liverpool: its commerce, statistics and institutions* (Liverpool, 1825), pp.433–4.
11. H. Wilckens, *Letters concerning the slave trade and with respect to its intended abolition* (Liverpool, 1793), pp.19–20.
12. *Ibid.*, p.4.
13. G. Chandler, *Liverpool* (London, 1957), p.306.
14. W. St Clair, *The grand slave emporium: Cape Coast Castle and the British slave trade* (London, 2006), p.264. I noticed similar comments when I visited the castle in 2005, although it is fair to record that the majority of the African diaspora who visit this and the other slave castles along the coast are overwhelmed by emotion when they imagine what happened to their ancestors there.

15   O. Cugoano, *Thoughts and sentiments on the evil and wicked traffic of the slavery and commerce of the human species* (London, 1787), p.112.
16   Wilckens, *Letters concerning the slave trade*, p.16.
17   Cugoano, *Thoughts and sentiments*, p.17.
18   'Mercator', *Letters concerning the abolition of the slave trade and other West India affairs* (London, 1807), pp.4, 8, 15. It has been suggested that 'Mercator' was Sir John Gladstone, the father of W.E. Gladstone, later four times Prime Minister.
19   *Ibid.*, p.15.
20   Wilckens, *Letters concerning the slave trade*, p.29.
21   Quoted in A. Mackenzie-Grieve, *The last years of the English slave trade: Liverpool 1750–1807* (London, 1941), p.33.
22   R. Harris, *Scriptural researches on the licitness of the slave trade* (Liverpool, 1788), pp.vii, 41–2. Harris, whose real name was Hormasa, was a Spanish Jesuit who had been expelled from his homeland with his Order and had settled in Liverpool. He died in 1789.
23   These included John Moore, the Archbishop of Canterbury.
24   D.N.A. Kpobi, *Saga of a slave: Jacobus Capitein of Holland and Elmina* (Legon, Ghana, 2001), pp.34–9. Capitein's thesis has been republished in Latin with an English translation as *The agony of Agar* (Princeton, NJ, 2001).
25   J. Stonehouse, *Recollections of old Liverpool, by a nonagenarian* (Liverpool, 1863), p.10.
26   G. Cameron and S. Crooke, *Liverpool: capital of the slave trade* (Liverpool, 1992), pp.54–9.
27   G. Williams, *History of the Liverpool privateers and letters of marque; with an account of the Liverpool slave trade, 1744–1812* (Liverpool, 1897), pp.649, 656.
28   Behrendt 1991, p.107.
29   St Clair, *The grand slave emporium*, pp.239–40. St Clair states that, during the period 1795 to 1808, 13,400 slaves were purchased for service in the West India Regiment at an approximate cost to the government of £1 million.
30   Hand, 'The *Kitty's Amelia*', p.79.
31   Crow's will is held by the Lancashire County Record Office, Preston (WCW 1829 CROW HUGH).
32   Probate issued 3 June 1829, Lancashire County Record Office, Preston (WCW 1829 CROW HUGH)
33   Behrendt, 'Captains in the British slave trade', pp.108–9. This gives details of the wealth of thirty-three slave-trade captains, whose estates ranged from £300 to £2,600. Crow's fellow Manxman, Captain Christian, who also owned land near Ramsey and died in 1798, left £2,500.
34   J. Aspinall, *Liverpool a few years since, by an old stager*, 2nd edn. (Liverpool, 1869), p.75.
35   *Liverpool and slavery, by a genuine 'Dicky Sam'* (Liverpool, 1884), p.91.
36   E. Callow, *From King Orry to Queen Victoria: a short and concise history of the Isle of Man* (London, 1899), pp.156–157, 169.
37   R. Muir, *A history of Liverpool*, 2nd ed. (Liverpool, 1907), p.201.
38   *Liverpool and slavery*, pp.91–2.
39   *The Times*, 15 May 1934.
40   National Museums and Galleries on Merseyside, *Annual report and accounts, 2004–2005*, p.9.
41   Williams, *History of the Liverpool privateers*, p.657.

Figure 7: [opposite] Captain Hugh Crow. Lithograph by W. Crane, Chester. This formed the frontispiece of the original edition.

Memoirs of the Late
Captain Hugh Crow
of
Liverpool

Comprising a narrative of his life, together with descriptive sketches of the western coast of Africa; particularly of Bonny; The manners and customs of the inhabitants, the productions of the soil, and the trade of the country.

To which are added, anecdotes and observations, illustrative of the negro character. Compiled chiefly from his own manuscripts; with authentic additions from recent voyagers and approved authors.

London.
Longman, Rees, Orme, Brown, and Green; and G. and J. Robinson, Liverpool.
mdcccxxx.

Entered at Stationers' Hall.
PRINTED BY G. F. HARRIS'S WIDOW AND BROTHERS, WATER-STREET,
LIVERPOOL.

To the Underwriters of London and Liverpool;

The following memoir of an individual who had the happiness, on more than one occasion,
to receive proofs of their approbation of his conduct,
is respectfully dedicated, by their most obedient servants,

The Executors.

Contents

INTRODUCTION 6

CHAPTER I 15

    Author's early predilection for a seafaring life—Bound apprentice at Whitehaven, and sails in the Crown—The impress service—A wreck at sea—Men-of-war's-men paid off—Voyage to Memel—Short allowance—Voyage to Charleston—Scarcity of water—Attempt upon the Author's life—Irish emigrants in America—Successive voyages to the Baltic, and distress at sea—Conflict between a whale and a number of thrashers and sword-fish—Ship run on shore—Shameful conduct of the captain and crew—Nearly lost on Lancaster sands—Arrival at Whitehaven

CHAPTER II 25

    Voyage to Kingston—Narrow escape from shipwreck—Serious accident—Dolphin fishing, and chowder—Author leaves the ship for another, and is consequently imprisoned—Flogging reprehended—Author compelled to return to the brig Grove—Return to England—Sea songs—Another voyage—Author's destitution—Goes second mate of the Hall—Execution of a negro—Return voyage—Cod fishing—Another voyage—In danger of foundering—Loss of the shallop—Return to Liverpool—Author rewarded by the underwriters

CHAPTER III 31

    Author's prejudices against the African trade—Voyage to Jamaica—Loss of a seaman overboard—Singular phenomenon at sea—Press tenders at Liverpool—Author induced to try the African trade—Sails for the coast as mate—Horrid custom at Bonny, on occasion of the king's death—Benin people—Voyage to Africa in the Bell—The Bonny pilot "My Lord"—Theatricals at Bonny—Punishment of a native—Voracity of the shark—Ship driven on shore in a tornado—Is got off—Author saves a black man from drowning—Regulations for the African trade, and Mr. Wilberforce—Voyage to Africa in the Jane—Mr. John Cummins—King Pepple's death—Punishment of a native accused of crim. con.—A black boy—Return to England

CHAPTER IV 41

Author captured by a French ship, and carried to L'Orient —Horrors of the French revolution—Imprisonment at Quimper—Dreadful state of the prison, and consequent mortality—Generous conduct of Lady Fitzroy—Affecting incident—Marched to the north of France—Sufferings on the road—Anecdotes—Author left at an hospital at Pontoise, whence he escapes—Rencontre with a party of French—Great humanity of a French family—Generous conduct of a Dutch captain—Arrival at Liverpool

CHAPTER V 49

Author meets his brother—Catastrophe of the Othello— Jack alias Jane Roberts—Conflict with a French schooner —Voyage in the James—Ship grounds at Bonny—Is in danger of sinking—Exertions to keep her afloat—Obliged to strand her—Is taken possession of by the natives— Grand feast of the inhabitants in consequence—Blowing up of the ship Parr—Author appointed master of the ship Will—Successful voyage—Anecdote of "Mind your eye"—Second voyage—Rencontre with a French schooner—Attempt of four French frigates to capture the Will and other vessels—Severe action with a French brig, which is beaten off—Ship's doctor killed—Author saves the crew of the Hector—Voyage hence—Plate presented to the author

CHAPTER VI 60

Voyage to Bonny in 1801—Anecdote of a black man—Predicament of the author on the death of a native—The island of St. Thomas—A shipwrecked crew taken on board—Mortality in the ship—Return to Liverpool— Voyage in the Ceres—Attacked by an Indiaman—Barbarous sacrifice of a virgin at Bonny—Visit of an elephant—Laughable anecdote of a native chief—Author chases King Pepple out of the ship—Arrival home in ill health —Obtains command of the Mary—Expense of manning African ships—Impressment—King Pepple's wives jealous of a figure of a female—Anecdote of Pepple and "Ditto"—King Holiday shot with a bottle of spruce beer—Ludicrous situation of King Pepple in tight boots —A joke played upon him—The ship Bolton blown up —Author's danger in a boat—Is saved by a tornado— Sails for the West Indies—Preparations for enemies

CHAPTER VII 75

Author practises the men at the guns on board the Mary— Competition amongst the blacks so employed—Combustible jars invented by the author, how made—Author falls in with two suspicious vessels of war in the middle passage—Observing their superior force, endeavours to avoid them—Is chased and hailed by both successively —Believes them to be French cruizers from Cayenne, and refuses to lie to—Is attacked by one of them, a heavy brig, and returns her fire—The other, a ship, also attacks him—Sanguinary engagement in the night with both vessels—Gallant conduct of the Mary's crew—The ship drops astern—Comes up again—Both again close upon the Mary—Several men killed and wounded—The Mary fights them till daylight next morning, when the author being wounded, and the ship dreadfully cut up, the officers strike—Find, to their astonishment, that they have been all the while fighting two English men-of-war —Consequences of the author's distracted state of mind —Is kindly treated by two lieutenants—Conduct of the blacks—Damage sustained by the ship—Exculpation of the author from all blame in fighting his countrymen— Jem Berry, the sailor—Certificate of the author's gallant defence of his ship—Executions at Jamaica—Capture of a Liverpool ship by a French brig

CHAPTER VIII   86

Affectionate visit from some negroes—Their lively and grateful remembrance of the author—Visit from the governor of the colony and his suite—Author's letter to his son—Negro's definition of taking an observation at sea—Negro's whimsical defence of his running away from a pugilistic antagonist—Laughable and mischievous pranks of a monkey—Departure from Kingston and arrival at Liverpool—Abolition of the slave trade—Reflections thereon—Author takes command of the Kitty's Amelia, which springs a dangerous leak whilst lying in the river—Discovered to proceed from two large auger holes having been carelessly left open

CHAPTER IX   94

Handsome letter to the author from the underwriters— Author sails for Bonny—Impressment—King Holiday's opinion of the abolition of the slave trade—Holiday's queen taken ill—Grand palaver in consequence, and extraordinary conduct of King Pepple at the meeting—Wars in Europe and Africa contrasted—Author saves a female from cannibals—Description of the author's favourite little island, the North Breaker Head—Planting of cocoanuts upon it—Dismissal of the excaptain—Dreadful weather at sea—Puts into St. Thomas—Visits the ruins of the bishop's palace there—Ship takes fire at sea—Author succeeds, at imminent hazard of his life, in extinguishing it—Monkeys on board described—Sickness again breaks out—Successful result of the voyage—Humorous conduct of negroes at Jamaica—Prize given for negroes at Bonny—Mortality in African ships accounted for— Melancholy career of the author's son—Concluding reflections

CHAPTER X 120

Reflections on African discoveries, and the resources of that Continent—Remarks on the Coast between Cape Palmas and Bonny—The Hermitan; Lahoo; (Adams' account); the Coast eastward—Loyer's account of the Africans in 1701—Acra— Ashantee— Dahomy— Ardrah—Lagos— The Formosa—Benin—Anecdote of early African commerce—Country round Benin. BONNY, town and island—Rivers near it—Causes of the insalubrity of the Coast—Houses—Polygamy—Slaves exported thence—The Eboes and Breches—Quaws— Brasses, Appas, &c.—Cost of a slave during the English trade—Anecdote of some Priests—RELIGION of the western coast—Fetiches or charms, and animal idols— Various opinions respecting—National fetiches—High priests of Bonny, and their cunning and influence over the people—Fishtown, a sanctuary for those in danger —The Iguana, the idol of Bonny—Author protects one, and is much lauded in consequence—Penance done by King Holiday—Offerings to the gods, secured by the author for the cook's kettle

CHAPTER XI 139

Bonny—Its kings and government—Revenues—War canoes —Visit of two chiefs from Benin—Dress of the natives —Ludicrous anecdotes of—Character of the negroes, and their ignorance of the resources of their country—Reflections on—Amusement, the chief business of their lives— Other employments—Dancing—Musical instruments—Propensity of the natives to beg presents—Honesty of some of the traders, and knavery of others—Diseases of the Coast—Eboe doctors, and dependence on charms— Foo-foo—Trade of Bonny—Slave trade—Language— Specimen of the Eboe—The Eboe country—Amusing anecdote—Seasons—Marriage ceremonies of Bonny— Privileged wives—Uxorial government—Mercenary cornutos—Punishment of conjugal infidelity—Conjugal fracas in high life—Horrid custom on the birth of twins —Rights of inheritance, and remarkable diversion of from prodigal freemen to slaves—Funeral ceremonies and extraordinary mourning—Land crabs despoilers of graves —Disinterment of the remains of King Pepple, and grand fete de joie et douleur—Christening of the present King of Bonny by the author—Sacrifices on the death of kings and chiefs—Eboe funerals—Female gossips

CHAPTER XII 156

Mode of swearing by the fetiche at Bonny, and taking the ordeal-draught—Astonishment of the natives on the destruction of some of their idols by Europeans, unaccompanied by any fatal result—Administration of the laws— Punishments—The palaverhouse, the repository of the skulls of chiefs taken in war—Responsibility of the relatives of culprits and owners of slaves for misdemeanours committed by them—Delay in the courts of justice —Instance of it—Singular mode of protecting property left exposed during the night, and precluding intercourse with vessels—Bedding of the natives, and annoyance from insects—The use of knives and forks scarcely known —Surprising agility in using the fingers at meals—Manner of storing property—Carelessness in storing gunpowder—Town twice burned down in consequence— Circulating medium of the country "Bars"—Term explained—Principal objects of export and barter—Maccutes, Birames, and Indian Pieces or Muleches quaintly described by an old author—Food of the Bonnian's— Vegetable productions—Description of the palm trees, from which palm oil and palm wine are extracted, and method of extracting—Fruits, pulse, &c.—The capot, an immense tree, from which canoes are formed—The mangrove—Oysters growing on trees—Beasts of prey at Bonny little known—Forbearance of the lion—Anecdote and perilous situation of some missionaries pursued by a horde of beasts of prey—Elephants—Mode of hunting and shooting them—Crocodiles— Immense size—Ludicrous incident respecting—Varieties of fish at Bonny— Sharks—Their amazing number and voracity exemplified by various anecdotes—Cattle—Dogs—Domestic and wild fowls

CHAPTER XIII   170

CALABAR—Description of the estuary—Tom Shott—Parrot island— Fishtown—Hickery Cocktown—Old Calabar described—Duke Ephraim—Mr. James Grant's sketch —Royal household—Yam chop—Duke's wives—His dress—Children—How washed—Duke's retinue—Fighting days—A dash or duchê—Manners of the natives— Petticoats sent to the duke's wives—Head dresses— Mancelas—Palm oil—Eight thousand tons imported into Liverpool last season—Human sacrifices—Curious tombs or monuments—Narrator endeavours in vain to save a female from death—Horrid manner of execution— A hundred human beings sacrificed in a day— "Grand Egbo," a minister of destruction, described—Decapitation of a fisherman—" Picaneeny Egbo"—Widows shave their heads—Drinking parties at funerals— Currency of the country—Palm oil, how sold—Chicanery both of Europeans and Africans in trade—Anecdote of the narrator—Oil merchants, how treated—An instance of cheating and maltreating the natives on the Gold Coast —Such conduct not general—Author's remarks— Reflections of the editors—Anecdotes of negroes

CONCLUSION   194

Introduction

THE Executors of the late CAPTAIN HUGH CROW, in performing the duty imposed on them by his last will, of publishing his Memoirs, feel that they are called upon to advert to the circumstances in which they found themselves placed in carrying this object into effect.

It appears that for several years previous to his decease, the subject of the following narrative had been engaged in collecting materials for a sketch of his own life. In the prosecution of this design he was assisted by a memory uncommonly quick and retentive, which enabled him to recollect, with surprising distinctness, names of persons, and dates of transactions long gone by. Frequent communication with those who had been his compeers and associates in many of his adventures served still further to augment his stock of information, of which, it may be remarked, as a fact well known to several of his friends, that so scrupulous was he in every point relative to his history, that he often, for a considerable time, suspended the insertion of a single date, name, or incident, until by personal inquiry, either *viva voce* or by reading, he had satisfied himself of its correctness. This fact alone, independently of the integrity of his character, affords strong presumptive evidence of the authenticity of the statements adduced by him in the following sheets.

The occupation of arranging these materials served, in a great degree, to divert his mind from the melancholy feelings resulting from domestic misfortunes—more especially from the premature death of an only son, in whom he had placed his fondest hopes. In directing the publication of his Memoirs, he proposed to himself two principal objects, to which he would in conversation frequently advert:—first, to leave behind him a memorial of his respect and gratitude to those excellent individuals who had proved themselves his friends during his eventful career; and, secondly, to encourage, by his example, others who were left, like himself, to weather the storms of life, to that perseverance which leads to honour and respectability.

While superintending the arrangement of the various MSS, put into their possession, and their preparation for the press, the executors felt

EXECUTORS' INTRODUCTION

that they should best discharge their duty to the deceased by adhering, as faithfully and literally as was consistent with perspicuity and propriety, to the style and phraseology of the author. They have therefore allowed him to tell his own story in his own way; and if they have occasionally indulged in any liberty, it has been that of retrenchment in cases of tautology and verbosity, defects almost necessarily incident to those not accustomed to literary composition. For similar reasons they have not considered themselves at liberty to withhold his peculiar sentiments on certain subjects, respecting which the majority of the public, in this day, entertain views of a different kind. That the deceased was sincere in his opinion of the correctness of the principles which he had imbibed will not be questioned by those who had an opportunity of appreciating his character. His general conduct was marked by a uniform simplicity, which led him directly to the point in hand, and which neither sought to deceive, nor suspected deception in others. This trait in his character was accompanied by a frankness and suavity of manners which endeared him to all his acquaintance.

In detailing the circumstances of the slave trade (so far as they fell under his own observation) the deceased appears to have been actuated chiefly by a desire to expose the unfairness of stigmatizing indiscriminately as cruel and mercenary all who were concerned in this traffic. He contended, that a participation in the trade in negroes did not necessarily imply either cruelty or dishonesty. That his individual practice and experience serve to justify such a conclusion these pages will amply prove. It will be found that he omitted no exertion to render the condition of the slaves entrusted to his care as comfortable as circumstances would permit; and, in the course of his narrative, incidents are related tending to show that between himself and those whom he had conveyed from Africa feelings of the most pleasing and gratifying kind were long after mutually evinced. It will perhaps not be difficult to account for the mental process by which the deceased arrived at the conclusion, that to the Africans slavery was to be regarded rather as a benefit than as a curse. He believed, that in being taken from Africa to the West Indies their condition was materially improved : so far, indeed, as his observations had extended with respect to colonial slavery (and they appear to have been almost entirely confined to the seaport towns of Jamaica), the lot of domestic slaves appeared to him, on the score of personal comfort, decidedly superior to that of many of our labouring population at home. He seems all along to have viewed slavery not as an abstract question, but as a matter the propriety of which was to be decided by its results. In this view of the subject he was confirmed by the concurrent representations of the African chiefs, with whom he was on terms of familiar intercourse, and who often assured him that for their prisoners of war, and capital criminals, there remained no alternative but to be sacrificed, or, to be sold as slaves.

These explanations the executors deem to be due to the memory of the deceased—as tending to show, that his errors, whatever they might be, were those of the head, not of the heart. His sense of honour, indeed, was such as would not have allowed him to remain in any employment which he found to be incompatible with integrity and the exercise of humanity. From his settled conviction of the policy of the slave trade (which he believed to be essential to the prosperity of our colonies) arose those feelings of indignation with which he was accustomed to regard every statement on the opposite side; and under the influence of which he would occasionally express himself in no very measured terms respecting his opponents. Some of these vituperations appear in the subsequent pages, while others of a more pointed and personal nature have been omitted, as their insertion, it was considered, could answer no good end. It was from similar feelings that he was led to designate the labouring classes in this country by the epithet of " White Slaves," and to insist that they were as truly in a state of vassallage as the blacks in the West Indies. The executors do not wish, by these remarks, to be considered as offering any opinion on the correctness or incorrectness of the views held by the deceased, much less as identifying themselves with his sentiments, on the points at issue: they simply discharge a duty incumbent upon them, faithfully to represent his character, and the motives by which he appears to have been actuated.

While our author regarded the existence of slavery among the Africans as a necessary consequence of their present condition and habits, he was far from espousing the opinion of those who consider the negro as occupying an inferior rank in the scale of human beings: he believed that civilization and instruction only were needed to raise him to a level with his more favoured brethren, the whites—whether as respects strength of intellect, or capacity for the cultivation of the arts and sciences. He had probably read history sufficiently to know, that among the ancestors of the present degraded race of Africans had been those who occupied distinguished places in the annals of the human race. It will be found that he takes every opportunity of doing justice to the character of the Africans; that he is gratified when any incident occurs which enables him to represent them in a favourable light, and that he uniformly treated them with a degree of condescension and confidence not always found to subsist between master and servant in civilized countries. Nor was his interest in their welfare confined to mere professions; he was always ready to prove, by acts, the deep concern he felt for their safety and preservation. A noble instance of this occurs in the circumstance of his having offered his services as a volunteer, and, at the risk of his own life, saved that of a negro who had fallen overboard on the middle passage. To this may be added his attempt to rescue (though unsuccessfully) several victims from immolation at the shrine of superstition on the coast of Africa. His kindness to the poor negroes was not unrequited: they, on more occasions than one, evinced a devotedness and attachment which were to him far more gratifying than any other recompense they could have offered.

He does not attempt to disguise the fact of the natives of Bonny and its neighbourhood being addicted to ceremonies and customs of the most cruel and revolting description. Several instances of this kind he narrates, and for the prevention of which his humanity led him to interfere as far as his influence with the inhabitants would permit. Perhaps no individual ever acquired so high a degree of popularity and influence with the people of Bonny as the author of these pages. He seems to have been an universal favourite with the kings, chiefs, and people; and he was repeatedly admitted to their palavers or assemblies for debate, as well as to their more solemn religious ceremonies. It will be evident, that to acquire and retain such a degree of confidence with a people naturally suspicious and distrustful of Europeans, he must have sustained a character for prudence and probity of which few individuals, who were similarly situated, could boast. Of a cheerful disposition, he was ever ready not only to give way to the harmless peculiarities of the blacks, but made himself so agreeable and homely, and was so fond of exciting them to innocent merriment by his jokes, that he was known in Bonny by the name of the "playman"— an appellation which, though not of the most dignified kind, sufficiently evinced the sincerity of the regard in which he was held. That he made an impression on the minds of those unsophisticated children of nature which it was not easy to efface, is agreeably testified by a letter which he received from his old friend Captain R. Pince, who had been his fellow prisoner in France, and his frequent companion at home and abroad in after-life. This document is dated "Bonny, June 7th, 1823," and contains the following passage:—

"I have great pleasure in acquainting you, that all our friends in this quarter are well, but very much disconcerted at hearing they are not to see you again. Pepple, king of Bonny, always speaks of you in terms of high respect, and the traders in general mention you with a degree of enthusiasm approaching to adoration. Pepple mentioned the circumstance of your coming into Bonny by night,[1] and says, it must have been the Jew-Jew-men who assisted you!"

It must be confessed that our author's friend, in describing the respect in which he continued to be held by the Bonnians, uses no very measured terms when he characterizes it as partaking of " enthusiasm approaching to adoration." Allowing, however, for the hyperbolical language of friendship, it appears that the favourable impression made by his character on the natives existed long after he had bidden a final adieu to their shores. He was in the habit of corresponding occasionally with the kings of Bonny; and often received from them memorials of their respect and friendship, on which he set no small value. But the most striking proof of the estimation in which he was held by the negroes consists in the fact, that not a few of them sought to perpetuate his memory by naming their children after him; and it is believed there are now living in Bonny several persons who pride themselves not a little on being called by the name of one whom their parents universally believed to be an especial favourite of their gods. It will be seen in the course of the following pages, that our author particularly prided himself on keeping what he termed "a clean ship." He was most punctilious in his attention to every thing connected with the comfort and good order of his crew, and of the Africans who fell under his charge. To such an extent did he carry this solicitude, that he did not omit constantly to write out, with his own hand, a bill of fare for the daily diet of all on board, which he caused to be put up in his cabin for the guidance of the steward and cook. By such attentions, added to his bravery and contempt of danger, it was that he succeeded in gaining so complete an ascendancy over the otherwise unmanageable crews by which African vessels were in those days generally manned; and was enabled, on occasions of emergency, to command their exertions for the defence and preservation of the ship. His presence of mind was strikingly evinced on the awful occasion of the ship being on fire, as described in his narrative, when, regardless of his personal safety, he succeeded in saving his ship and all on board. The danger was on the first alarm so imminent, that many of the bravest of his crew were in the act of lowering the boats to abandon the vessel, and commit themselves, without preparation, to the precarious chance of escape with life in the middle of the Atlantic. The three concluding chapters, which comprise the topography and productions of Bonny and Calabar, and some particulars relative to the manners and customs of the inhabitants, will, it is hoped, prove interesting as subjects hitherto very little known in this country. The executors have, in this portion of the work, ventured to make material additions to the MSS. of the author of the memoirs, and of which had life permitted they are persuaded he would gladly have availed himself. In the endeavour to supply this desideratum, they have had recourse, not only to the various publications within their reach that treat of the geography and customs of those parts of Western Africa, but have availed themselves of information supplied by several individuals whose knowledge of the country has been acquired by repeated voyages to the coast, and a residence for some years among the natives. It is, however, to be regretted, that the occupations of the deceased did not permit him to extend his observations further into the interior. His intercourse with the natives seems to have been confined chiefly to Bonny and its immediate neighbourhood; but his remarks, so far as they extend, evince a capacity for observation seldom found in individuals, like him, devoted to the engrossing duties of a commercial life; and who, through the want of a liberal education, cannot be expected to direct their attention with much ardour to subjects unconnected with their professional pursuits.

The author has very briefly adverted to the incidents of his youth; and the following circumstance, mentioned by him incidentally to one of his executors, may be considered worthy of being recorded. He related, that at a very early age, he was one day walking on the beach at Ramsey in company with his mother, when, observing several vessels in the offing, he exclaimed with much animation, pointing to one of them, " Mother! I shall one day be captain of a ship like that!" His mother of course treated the prediction as a childish whim, but he himself always entertained a presentiment that the sea was to be his element, and that he should live to attain the summit of his ambition—the command of a ship. It was this hope which buoyed him up amidst all the trials and privations attendant on his début at sea; and which carried him through a succession of hardships, while an apprentice, sufficient to have utterly disheartened one of a less ardent and enterprising mind: and it is a singular coincidence, that not many years afterwards he became mate of one of the very ships, the sight of which drew forth the above exclamation.

The result of these protracted hardships, while they eventually led to the attainment of the objects of our author's highest ambition—the successive command of not one but several ships, and those of the "crack ships" out of our port—was the acquirement of an adequate fortune.

On retiring from active service, which he did in the year 1808, it appears he had intended to spend the remainder of his days in his native isle. With this view he purchased an estate contiguous to the town of Ramsey. Here he resided for some years, during which time he turned his attention to agricultural pursuits, and by planting, draining and other improvements, succeeded in rendering his estate one of the most delightful and productive in that part of the island.

Such however were his active habits, and his predilection for the scenes in which the early part of his life had been engaged, that, forsaking his rural employments, he, in the year 1817, once more returned to Liverpool, there to enjoy the society of those kindred spirits, who like himself had been so long accustomed to a life of bustle and excitement as to find it irksome to confine themselves to the quiet and monotonous routine of a country life.

To some traits in the private character of the deceased, and which were familiar to those whom he admitted into habits of intimacy, his executors may here briefly advert. His simplicity and suavity of manners have already been noticed. The habits of punctuality, correctness, and regularity, which distinguished him in his active career, he carried with him into private life. These evinced themselves, as well in his pecuniary transactions, as in his every day proceedings. He generally rose at an early hour, and after performing the customary duties of the toilet, in which he was scrupulously particular, he would repair to his favourite haunt, the Lyceum News Room, to cull the news of the day. After breakfast, he usually took a stroll to the quays, to enjoy the exhilirating scene of bustle and activity attendant upon the arrival and departure of numerous vessels, which our river seldom fails to present in favourable weather. Some of his old friends, actuated by similar feelings for every thing connected with the element they had so long traversed, would probably be found to accompany him on these occasions. After comparing notes, and exchanging information with such acquaintances, our author would return to his residence at the accustomed hour, and having taken a frugal dinner, he would again betake himself to the News Room. The afternoon was generally devoted to the society of his friends and compeers in the African trade. At such meetings each was wont to fight his battles over again; and such was the discipline to which this knot of veterans subjected themselves, that at one of their rendezvous, it is said, the striking of a particular hour was the signal for a general separation, when they hurried out, helter skelter, often leaving even the glass unfinished, and the tale half told. At the close of the day's occupation, our author would return to his residence, either to prepare fresh materials for his memoirs, or to refresh by sleep a constitution undermined by exposure to the baneful influence of a tropical sun, and the hardships of a seafaring life. Such indeed were the regularity and uniformity of his habits, that the history of one day presents the history of the whole of his after life.

His affection for his parents is not the least interesting trait in the character of our author. The reader will perceive, from his own account, that they were placed in the humbler walks of life; and it is a circumstance that redounds in no small degree to the honour of our author, that, so soon as his means permitted, he made it a point of conscience, as well as of feeling, to contribute a portion of his funds to their support; so that the evening of their lives was spent in comparative ease and enjoyment. Never indeed, after he attained the command of a ship, did he revisit this port, without remitting to his respected parents some token of his affectionate regard.

Nor was our author devoid of the true *amor patriæ*; for it was his constant custom, when his vessel lay at Bonny, to evince his patriotism on holidays, by hoisting the flag of his native isle at the mast head, to the amusement of king Pepple and the chief men there, who were greatly diverted by the strange device of the "three legs of man!" Before his death he furnished a more substantial proof of his good will to the Isle of Man, by bequeathing the following legacies to benevolent institutions:

The freeschool of Ramsey .... £19 19s.
The poor of ditto 19 19
The poor of Douglas 10 10
The poor of Castletown.................. 5 5
The poor of Peel 5 5

In addition to these, the deceased extended his benevolence to most of the charities of this town : he also presented a sum to the Seamen's Hospital of Whitehaven, from which he had first sailed; and another to the Hospital for Slaves, in Kingston, Jamaica, his usual port in the West Indies, and where he had always been most cordially welcomed by all classes of the inhabitants.

Our author had a nice sense of the proprieties and decorums of life, and was always ready to pay "honor to whom honor is due," and to require his due share from others. His politeness and urbanity were conspicuous. He knew and was known to almost every individual of note in our town, and for each and all had, in passing, his bow of acknowledgment, or token of warmer friendship and respect. His quickness in recognising his acquaintance, whilst traversing our crowded streets, was very remarkable. Often have the editors been hailed by the gallant captain, across the street, when but for such intimation they would not have been aware of his approach— thus confirming the oftenrepeated remark of his friend, the late Mr. Aspinall, that although he had but one eye, that was "a piercer!" Nor was he too proud to notice any one, even in humble life, who would, he conceived, be gratified by his civility. This honorable feeling, as well as the interest which he always felt for the poor Africans, was on one occasion exemplified by the following circumstance. While he was one day walking with a friend in the streets of this town they were met by a negro. The captain immediately recognized, by the tattooed marks on the African's face, his tribe and country, and addressed him familiarly in his own language. It is impossible to describe the amazement which the poor fellow evinced, when thus accosted in a strange land. He appeared quite beside himself, and danced and sung about the captain for some time, with every demonstration of the most extravagant joy. The Captain, with his wonted generosity, added still further to poor blackey's satisfaction by bestowing on him, before parting, a substantial token of his regard.

The executors trust that these preliminary remarks will serve not only to obtain for the author of the following pages a candid hearing, even on the part of those who may entertain very different views with respect to the African trade, but will also tend to shew, that how far soever he may have been mistaken in his opinions, his conduct through life was uniformly regulated by an undeviating adherence to integrity, and an uniform regard to the dictates of humanity.

Memoirs, &c.

CHAPTER I

ALTHOUGH many individuals have been engaged for a longer period than myself in the bustle and turmoil of a sea-faring life, few have encountered, within an eventful career of about thirty years, so many privations and hardships, or experienced so many singular adventures. I may be permitted to say, indeed, that "I have seen a little service;" and the hope that some of the details may be found to be instructive as well as entertaining, induces me to draw up, from occasional memoranda, the following simple narrative—any inaccuracies in the diction of which, the critical reader will do me the justice to ascribe to my want of an early education.

I was born in the town of Ramsay, in the isle of Man, in the year 1765. When very young I had the misfortune to lose my right eye, an accident which rendered my identity through life the more remarkable; and, when only twelve years of age, I was nearly drowned, but was preserved by Providence to see and to suffer, through a series of years, a variety of troubles and vicissitudes. Being brought up in a seaport town, I naturally imbibed an inclination for a sea-faring life; and after I had served, for two years, to the trade of a boat-builder (which I found to be of great advantage to me in after life) I went to Whitehaven, where I was bound apprentice to Joseph Harriman, Esq. merchant. I was almost destitute of clothing, and indeed of every necessary, when I quitted my father's roof, and all I was to receive for my servitude of four years was £14, with which I had to find myself in clothing and washing during my apprenticeship. My employer, however, to his honour, paid for my education, when I happened to be in port, and by a strict observance of economy, and the kind assistance of my parents, I managed to pass my novitiate with a considerable degree of comfort.

My first voyage to sea was in the spring of 1782, on board of a large Dutch-built ship called the Crown, commanded by Captain Newton, and bound to Waterford with coals. On our passage we experienced stormy weather and contrary winds, and I, for one, was very sea-sick the greater part of the time. The ship being leaky I was kept almost constantly at the pumps, and my sensations, both of mind and body, were extremely mortifying; for my illness excited only the derision of the older sailors, who, in those days, treated the young with great harshness and severity.

At Waterford we took in a cargo of provisions for the West Indies, and proceeded to Cork to join convoy. I had now overcome my sea sickness, and soon became a favourite with the crew; the knowledge I had acquired of nautical affairs, while at Ramsay, enabling me to make myself nearly as useful as the oldest sailor in the vessel. While at Cork, to our great vexation and inconvenience, all our best seamen were impressed. The scenes of oppression and distress which I witnessed every night, arising out of the cruel system of impressment, which is alike repugnant to liberty and to humanity, it is impossible for me adequately to describe. Some of the sailors, to escape the press-gang, leaped over-board, and swam from ship to ship, or endeavoured to gain the shore: others were in danger of being smothered by stowing themselves away in confined places below decks: and those who fell into the hands of the Philistines were dragged away like felons, sometimes by the hair of the head. Our captain, after much trouble and delay, succeeded in procuring fresh hands, and we sailed under convoy, with a fleet of between forty and fifty sail, bound to the island of Barbadoes.

Some of the fleet were dispersed in a heavy gale of wind, and, one night, when our ship was gliding along under easy sail we fell in with a large dismasted schooner, apparently abandoned, and rolling about at the mercy of the winds and waves. On boarding her we found she was laden with salt-fish and lumber; and, on further search, were horrified to find the crew, nine in number, lying dead in the cabin. There was no fresh water on board, and we concluded they must have perished for want of that necessary of life. This appalling spectacle made a painful impression on our minds, as did its announcement on all who were in the fleet. Next morning the commodore ordered the ill-fated vessel to be burned.

We arrived at Barbadoes after a passage of eight weeks, and thence proceeded under convoy to Antigua, where during a stay of some months many of our people were impressed, and others ran away. One night, while I was waiting on shore, as usual, for the captain, I was suddenly seized with a raging fever, which threw me into such a state of delirium that the captain and the young men had much difficulty in securing me, and tying me, during the paroxysm, to the boat. The captain, who had seen others similarly affected, caused me to be immediately bled, and it is remarkable that in ten or fifteen minutes I had nearly recovered my wonted health. I notice this circumstance under the persuasion that many persons who are attacked by brain fevers perish for want of timely bleeding.

From Antigua we sailed for St. Martin's, where we took in a cargo of sugar for London. There, several of our seamen deserted, as well as the carpenter, whose services were much wanted to caulk the upper works of the vessel. My knowledge of boat-building, an art which is nearly allied to ship-carpentry, now became available; and I was employed as a substitute for the carpenter, and acquitted myself in a creditable manner. On our homeward passage we encountered a succession of gales, during which we were obliged to ply both pumps. My services on these occasions, in keeping the pump gear in order, were constantly called for, and duly appreciated by the captain and all on board. Towards the latter end of our voyage our provisions and water began to get short, but our minds were relieved by our safe arrival in the Downs, in January, 1783. We had let go our anchor and were furling the sails, when we heard the pilot joyfully shout that England was at peace with all the world. The delight which this intelligence diffused amongst us was extreme, although we were, at the time, suffering severely both from cold and hunger.

On our arrival in London I lamented to observe the abandoned and profligate conduct of the sailors in that vast metropolis; for government was then paying off the crews of the men-of-war, and many of those ill-starred thoughtless beings, after squandering their hard-earned gains with reckless and wasteful precipitancy, were reduced almost to a state of beggary and starvation. While at London we were visited by our owner, Mr. Harriman, of Whitehaven, who was pleased to compliment me highly for my services to the vessel in the West Indies, and on the passage home.

In April following we sailed for Memel, where, while taking in our cargo, outside the bar, I was nearly drowned by falling under a raft of timber, but was rescued by the great exertions of my shipmates. On our homeward passage, when off the coast of Norway, the ship, which was very crank, owing to the weight of timber on her decks, was, in a sudden squall, thrown on her beam ends and nearly upset. All hands got upon the weather side of the vessel, with scarcely a hope of being saved; but when the squall subsided, and some exertions were made to lighten her, to our great relief she again righted. On nearing the Orkneys, and while sailing with a moderate breeze, but surrounded by a dense fog, we suddenly found that we were almost bows on a dangerous precipitous point of land. We saw nothing but death before us, and even the captain was so panic-struck that he fell prostrate on the deck. By extraordinary exertions, however, in backing our sails, and towing with the boats, we got the ship clear off, as by a miracle. One foggy night, some weeks after this (for our passage was prolonged by contrary winds), the look-out a-head alarmingly sung out that they saw the land close to us on either bow. We instantly let go the anchor, which brought the ship up "all standing;" and at daylight, we found, to our terror and surprise, that we had come to anchor when on the very point of running on shore on Fair-head, a dangerous part of the north coast of Ireland, and that a few minutes longer run would have whelmed us in inevitable destruction. We arrived at Whitehaven after a tedious passage, rendered the more irksome by a scarcity of provisions. Merchant vessels were, at that time, but indifferently found, and the privations and fatigue I had endured had made me, to use a homely phrase, "as thin as a lath." After discharging we sailed for Liverpool, and took in a cargo of salt for Charleston.

We sailed in October, 1783, and were not long at sea before several of our water casks got stove by the rolling of the vessel in a gale of wind, so that we were put upon short allowance. Never shall I forget our sufferings on this occasion. Night after night, when I ought to have been at rest below, have I stood on the deck, with my blanket extended, to catch, if possible, a little rain water, to quench my intolerable thirst. To obtain a temporary relief, I frequently chewed a piece of lead, and often, in the height of my distress, I apprehended that I should lose my senses. To add to my misfortunes I very nearly lost the sight of my remaining eye, but through a benevolent Providence I recovered the use of that invaluable organ.

When we arrived on the coast of America, it one night came on to blow a kind of hurricane, accompanied by the most awful thunder and lightning. So great, at one time, was our alarm, that we all lay down on our faces on the quarterdeck, for the lightning seemed completely to envelope the ship. None, indeed, but those who have experienced such a visitation can imagine the horrors of the impending scene. The sea broke wildly over the ship, and several of our sails were blown to atoms in the fury of the gale.

Some time after this I was in imminent danger of losing my life. A fellow apprentice (one of the vilest wretches I ever knew) and myself, were sent aloft to hand the main-topgallant sail. When we got on the yard and began to furl the sail, some words occurred between us; and he being on the weather side instantly let go the sail, and sprang over to me, on the lee side. The ship was lying over very much at the time, and the sail flying over my head, I was unable to give any alarm: in this situation the villain exerted his utmost strength to throw me off the yard into the sea. I was fain to exert every nerve in self-preservation, and, at length, wearied by his diabolical efforts, he desisted, and we handed the sail; but so faint was I after the struggle, that it was with difficulty I could regain the deck. Before we got down the fellow began to reflect on the atrocity of his conduct, and stung with remorse, as well as apprehensive of punishment, I thought he would have thrown himself overboard; but I had given him my word, in the maintop, as we descended, that I would say nothing about his unwarrantable conduct. I have not a doubt, that many lives have been lost, in the darkness of the night, through the malice of villains of the same vindictive disposition.

After a boisterous passage of ten weeks, and with the most of the crew in open mutiny, we arrived at Charleston. There the wretch who had nearly succeeded in effecting my destruction, became alarmed lest he should be brought to punishment, and absconded from the ship. While we lay at Charleston, several vessels arrived from Ireland crowded with poor labourers, who were to be sold for so many years, by the captains, to defray the cost of their passage out. Amongst these were many half-starved poor creatures, who were advertised to be sold to the highest bidder; and many ludicrous jokes were played off by the blacks who attended the sale. While the whites were bidding, one of these sable humourists would cry out "One dollar more for'em da; I have'em, negra buy buckra now!" another would say "Three bit more for 'em da; I have 'em, negra buy buckra now!" while the poor Irishmen, whose bodies were thus exposed to vendue, would imploringly repeat "Och! masters! Och! Jewels! don't let them blackamoors buy us at all, at all!"

Although peace had been declared with America some months before our arrival in Charleston, there was still a little of the leaven of national animosity working in the minds of the Americans, and one night, when I had just landed to look at the town, I became a victim of the political jealousies of the times. I was apprehended by the police, and thrown into a filthy prison, amongst hundreds even more wretched than myself; and for three days I endured all the miseries of hunger and cold. The winter was so unusually inclement that the inhabitants used to remark, that the place must have removed several degrees to the northward of its original latitude. The captain, at length, found me out, and I was released on payment of three pounds of jail fees—an extortion which nearly absorbed the amount of my hard-earned wages.

That the credulity of some of the Americans is equal to that of any other nation, the following fact will exemplify. One night, in the house of a respectable person in Charleston, I overheard a conversation relative to my native island, to which I naturally paid every attention. One of the speakers expressed his assurance that the isle of Man turned right round every seven years, and that unless a fire were kept burning in it night and day it would certainly sink! This relation excited much wonder and amazement amongst the company, and I was not a little amused to find so romantic an idea of my native land entertained in a foreign country.

With a cargo of rice we sailed for Liverpool, where Captain Newton, with whom I was always a favourite, was succeeded by a Captain B——. Our next voyage was to Danzig; on this trip I again experienced the protecting hand of Providence. One morning I had been employed in sending down the maintop-gallant-yard, and was called down to the deck. I had no sooner got to the maintop than away went the topmast overboard. Had this accident happened a moment sooner I should have been precipitated along with it into the sea. On our return voyage we had a narrow escape from being run down by a large ship, which came close upon us, in the night, before we saw her. The water from her bows, such was the rapidity of her course, dashed over our decks, and how we were saved from destruction God only knows. After our arrival at Whitehaven the ship was laid up for the winter, and I availed myself of the opportunity of acquiring a knowledge of navigation.

Our next voyage was to Drontheim in Norway, under the command of Captain M'C——, whom I shall have occasion to notice hereafter. We lost our mizen-mast in a gale, and, the pumps being choked, had a dreadful time of it in bailing out the ship, which was very leaky, by means of barrels. Our hands became chapped and raw by the constant action of the salt water and the friction of the sandy ropes, and the arduous duty afterwards devolved upon me night and day of attending to the repairs of the pumps. Owing to the neglect of both captain and mate, who were generally drunk and fighting, we overshot our port, which we reached with difficulty, and then proceeded with a load of timber to Belfast.

CHAPTER I

Our next voyage was to Memel, in 1785. One morning during a calm, when near the Hebrides, all hands were called up at three in the morning to witness a battle between several of the fish called *thrashers* and some *sword-fish* on one side, and an enormous *whale* on the other. It was in the middle of summer, and the weather being clear, and the fish close to the vessel, we had a fine opportunity of witnessing the contest. As soon as the whale's back appeared above the water the thrashers springing several yards into the air descended with great violence upon the object of their rancour, and inflicted upon him the most severe slaps with their tails, the sound of which resembled the reports of muskets fired at a distance. The sword-fish, in their turn, attacked the distressed whale, stabbing him from below, and thus beset on all sides and wounded, when the poor creature appeared, the water around him was dyed with his blood. In this manner they continued tormenting and wounding him for many hours, until we lost sight of him; and I have no doubt they, in the end, accomplished his destruction.

At Elsineur our captain, who had acquired a ruinous habit of drinking to excess, to indulge further in this propensity brought on board a number of kegs of brandy and gin. In his infatuation he neglected to procure a pilot, and madly weighed anchor when the night was coming on, and when most of the crew were in a state of intoxication. He, in consequence, shaped a wrong course, and about ten at night we ran on shore on a small island, which is nearly opposite to Copenhagen. In place of using every exertion to get the ship off, his first act was to call the mate and all the sailors down to the cabin to drink, leaving us apprentices, five in number, and the cook, to manage matters as well as we could. I being the oldest apprentice the others cheerfully obeyed me. We handed the sails, got out the long boat, and dropped an anchor, with a stream cable, right astern. On this we fixed a purchase, and to lighten the vessel threw overboard part of the ballast. We laboured thus by turns for fortyeight hours, while the captain and his associates continued their uproar and revelry in the cabin. I at length ventured amongst them, and stated that we were confident that, with their assistance, we could get the ship off. I was nearly being roughly handled for my interference, but was protected by the captain. The whole of them were at this time mad with liquor, and the store room skuttle being off, the captain suddenly exclaimed, addressing the boatswain, " George, don't you see that black fellow coming up from below?" "what black fellow?" said the boatswain in alarm, "why the old fellow!" replied the captain, on which announcement a panic seized the whole party, and they all ran to their berths, leaving us on deck still toiling to get the ship afloat. The natives now came down in crowds to the beach, with intent no doubt to plunder us; but by help of a strong gust of wind from the land, and the rising of the tide, we fortunately got the vessel off. After this conduct on the part of the captain all subordination amongst the crew was at an end; and in a state of the utmost confusion we sailed to Copenhagen to supply the loss of our ballast. We thence proceeded to Memel, where having occasion to go aloft, and being blind of my starboard eye, I accidently fell out of the foretop; but my fall was luckily broken by some ropes, and I was but little hurt. Much time having been lost by the improper conduct of the captain, in order to "make up the lee way" he took a large quantity of timber on deck. We had not been long at sea when we were overtaken by a dreadful gale, and being unable to get the deck timber overboard, or to pump the ship, she lay so much over, we became water-logged, and had well nigh foundered. We with difficulty reached Elsineur, where we learned that several ships and many lives had been lost during the storm. Here the captain disposed of his deck load, and took gin and brandy in payment. The sailors also provided themselves with each his half-anker of gin, and we sailed with a fair wind, but were soon after driven into a port in Norway by an adverse gale. There the captain, the mate, and finally all the sailors gave a loose to intoxication; and all was confusion and riot. The snow that fell in the night was often several feet deep on the deck, and the day generally commenced by disputes between the watches, as to whether one or both of them should throw it overboard. A general battle frequently ensued, in which the captain, the mate, and all hands were engaged, pummelling and rolling each other amongst the snow.

We lay for about eleven weeks in different ports of Norway, and were near losing the ship several times. On one occasion she broke from her moorings while I and another young man were at some distance in a small Norway skiff. The ship was fast drifting out to sea, and before we could reach her we were so benumbed with cold and fatigue that we could hardly move a limb. In a gale that followed the sea made "a highway" over us, so that our cabouse and every thing on deck were washed away. The captain, mate, and sailors went as usual down to drink, leaving me and my fellow apprentices to manage the ship, which had then five to six feet of water in the hold. The captain and crew would give us no assistance; stupified with drink they became callous to all around them, and God only knows

CHAPTER I

how we young men contrived to keep the ship from foundering. When the gale abated the captain and his associates, who had in some degree recovered their senses, were ashamed to look any of us in the face.

We got in safety to Broad bay, in the island of Lewis, where the refractory mate and crew, after a general battle, in which many hard blows were exchanged, took the boat and left the ship. The captain was at his wits' end, and I—being so great a favourite with him that he had frequently said that he had but one daughter and I should have her for a wife if I liked her—advised him to proceed to Stornaway, whither the crew had most probably gone. He agreed, and my conjecture was right. The run-aways, finding their complaints to the magistrates unattended to, returned to the ship, which, owing to the still prevailing drunkenness on board, was once on shore, and several times exposed to the danger of being lost. We at last arrived at Whitehaven, in February, 1786, after a disastrous and tedious voyage. Indeed I have often remarked to my friends that had the brandy and gin lasted we should never have got home at all.

We were ordered round to Lancaster to discharge, and it being late when we reached the N. W. buoy, off that port, we then came to anchor. In a gale, which soon after came on from the westward, we parted both cables and were driven on shore on Lancaster sands. At daylight, the ship being left almost dry by the retiring tide, the captain and the sailors went on shore, leaving me and the other apprentices behind. I wished to stick by the ship to the last; but with the return of the tide the gale which had somewhat abated again increased, and the vessel rolled and struck so heavily that we wished we had consulted our own safety by starting along with the rest. We determined to leave the ship as soon as possible, lest we should be driven to sea in a helpless state; and after dusk, to our great joy, we saw some lights on the shore, and, the tide having fallen, made our way towards them. On our way we had to wade through pools of water intersected by beds of quicksand, which rendered our progress difficult and dangerous; so that it was late before we reached any house, exhausted with fatigue and faint with hunger. We next day found the captain and the sailors at a place called Sunderland point, and while we were walking on the shore, lamenting our disaster, to our astonishment and joy we saw the ship drifting up with the tide, within about sixty yards of us. She was quite waterlogged, and we immediately made our way on board, and found her only occupant my faithful dog "Boatswain" standing at the gangway eager to welcome our return.

After waiting behind, according to instructions from Mr. Harriman, for some days, to look after the anchors and cables we had left at the N. W. buoy, and to transact some other business at Lancaster, I repaired to Whitehaven, where I was received with every mark of kindness and attention.

CHAPTER II

I HAD now completed my apprenticeship, and my two old masters, Captain Newton and Captain Burns, who had vessels of their own, were each anxious to engage my services. I gave the preference to Captain Burns, who commanded a fine new brig called the Grove, then bound to Jamaica by way of Waterford. As I was considered expert as a carpenter, it was stipulated that I should be liberally paid for acting in that capacity, and I was moreover promised the earliest possible promotion.

Having taken in a cargo of coals at Waterford, we sailed in April, 1786. On this voyage we twice narrowly escaped destruction. One night while scudding in a gale we so nearly came in contact with a French brig that our yards struck hers. On another we were almost on shore on a dangerous group of low uninhabited islands called the Salvages. I was the first who heard the dashing of the breakers amongst the rocks, and saw the dangerous shore; for though I was bereft of an eye my sight was remarkably acute. One day, too (for I was fated to be seldom out of danger), a blundering fellow having let go the peak halliards in place of another rope, the gaff fell with such force upon my head that I was knocked senseless on the deck, and did not for several weeks recover from the effects of the blow.

While running down the trade winds, I often amused myself striking the fish that came round the ship, particularly the dolphin—an exercise in which I became so expert, that when any fish were seen the cry would be, "call up the harpooner—Hugh the *'mugian!'*" The Bermudean, or, as our sailors called them, the *Burmugian* fishermen, are said, as soon as they see a dolphin, to put the pot on the fire to cook him, so sure are they of killing the fish; and hence my skill obtained me the name of the "*mugian.*" On the homeward passage, when passing through the gulph of Florida, my services in securing many a supply of dolphin, which were very acceptable as a change of food, and an addition to our stock, were most thankfully considered both by the captain and crew: and we frequently served up a mess called *chowder*, consisting of a mixture of fresh fish, salt pork, pounded biscuit and onions; and which, when well seasoned and stewed, we found to be an excellent palatable dish.

During our stay at Kingston, and on other occasions, I was laboriously employed in my capacity of carpenter, and the captain expressed his entire satisfaction with my exertions. We arrived at Lancaster after a successful voyage: we afterwards made several trips to Ireland; and I was at length enabled to save a little money, with which I purchased myself a quadrant and some articles of clothing. After another voyage to Kingston, and thence to Waterford, we again sailed for the former port, in March, 1787. For sometime previously I had felt aggrieved at the conduct of Captain Burns, who, contrary to his former promises, placed, in promotion over me, a second mate, a person who was certainly not better qualified for the situation than myself. This sense of injustice working in my mind, and being convinced that his motive in retaining me to act as carpenter was merely to save money (for he paid me for my extra services only in expressions of satisfaction), I determined to leave him; although while I served my time under him I regarded him more as a father than as a master.

I soon procured a situation as second mate of a fine ship bound to Honduras, and contrived one night to leave the Grove—taking with me my quadrant and chest. Captain Burns, however, who had suspected my intention, and who valued me too much to lose me so easily, discovered my retreat, and attended by bailiff, constables, and soldiers, boarded my new ship, and after a skuffle with the crew, who wished me to escape his search, I was discovered in the pump well, nearly suffocated with filth and heat. When dragged upon deck he threatened to cleave me with the cook's axe, which he brandished in his hand, if I made any resistance. After being tightly handcuffed I was bundled into the boat without any clothes but the shirt and trowsers I had on. I was taken on shore and thrown into a noxious prison, amongst a number of dirty runaway negroes. There I lay, without any food, and tormented by rats for forty-eight hours. It is but a grateful acknowledgment on my part to state, that many of the poor negroes shed tears on seeing my distressed situation.

To this place of misery the captain sent to know if I would beg his pardon and return on board. I indignantly replied that I would rather die where I was. He then sent me to the workhouse, about a mile distant. I suffered excruciating pain from the tightness of the handcuffs, and the blacks, both male and female, commiserated my condition as I passed along the market place. When I reached the work-house I was kindly

CHAPTER II

treated by the keeper, and my employment, the picking of oakum, was the lightest he had power to impose. Mr. Everett, the gentleman in whose employ I had proposed sailing to Honduras, had spoken in my behalf to the keeper, and interested himself to procure my liberation, but Captain Burns rendered his endeavours unavailing by patching up against me a bill of costs, which deeply involved me in debt.

While thus confined I frequently saw poor creatures brought into the yard to be punished, and, being laid down, receive thirtynine severe lashes, for perhaps a very trifling offence; and I have often heard them curse "the law for floggey negro man and poor woman, and poor buckra sailor, and red-back soldier man." This flogging was, however, quite equalled in barbarity by what I saw inflicted on board the Lynx, seventy-four, when she lay, as a guard ship, in the cove of Cork. Severity however, if not cruelty, which will admit of no palliation, must be employed to keep *slaves* in order and subordination, whether they be black or white; and there is not, in my opinion, a shade of difference between them, save in their respective complexions. In those days corporal punishments were inflicted without much regard to humanity; but, thank God! this detestable system, with many others of the kind equally arbitrary, is rapidly dying away.

After a lapse of some days Captain Burns and Mr. Hind, the merchant to whom we were consigned, and who afterwards became my warm friend, came to the prison and strove to persuade me to return to the vessel. This I firmly declined, and did not fail to express my opinion of the captain's injustice towards me. At length the brig went down to Port Royal, ready for sea, and the captain sent two men with handcuffs to bring me on board by force. Mr. M'Clean, the keeper of the establishment, and some other compasionate gentlemen, having learned their errand, entertained the messengers with some refreshments while they privately ordered a gate to be opened, through which I ran with all possible speed towards a place called Springpath. I was immediately pursued, and cries of "stop thief!" with an offer of a dollar reward, brought across my path a stout fellow armed with a hoe, who threatened to "make my yie run water" if I did not surrender; but seizing an opportunity, I made a sudden spring at him, and planting a violent blow in his breast, I threw him groaning and roaring on the ground. I ran on, but my pursuers being at hand I desperately threw myself into the middle of a prickly pear bush regardless of the pain I should endure. My retreat was, after a short search, discovered, and I was dragged out in so lacerated a state that my shirt was literally like a cake of blood.

I was taken on board the vessel almost destitute of clothing, although I had left a good supply in the ship from which I had been forced; and so much did the unworthy treatment I had experienced prey upon my spirits that I frequently thought of putting an end to my sorrows by jumping overboard. On the homeward passage the vessel sprung a dangerous leak, and after I had been, day after day, slung over the ship's side by a rope, and almost under water, I was fortunate enough to discover it. For my exertion on this occasions Mr. Hind became my undeviating friend. The captain, however, continued, throughout, to render me as miserable as he could; and when we reached Lancaster, the place of our destination, instead of making me any recompense for my services he brought me into debt for prison expenses at Jamaica, and fairly cut me adrift without a farthing in my pocket, and with scarcely an article of clothing on my back. He was never employed by the house of Hind afterwards; nor did he ever forgive himself for his treatment of me. Often, when years had elapsed, have I seen him shed tears when he recurred to it; although I endeavoured to cheer him by telling him it was perhaps, in the end, one of the best things that had happened to me; for a check in youth is frequently useful in after life. In my case, however, his conduct was unwarrantably vindictive.

When I left the ship, some of the crew observing my destitution, generously assisted me with a small contribution of money and clothes; and my friend Mr. Hind recommended me to his brother, who had a ship, the Big Nancy, Captain Davies, bound to Kingston, whither I particularly wished to return to recover my chest and quadrant. The sum of one penny was required for my passage, as at that time a sailor (though a passenger) might claim wages if something were not paid for such consideration. We sailed finally from Cork in December, 1787, and experienced a succession of dreadful gales, which greatly disheartened the crew: and many a stormy night did I endeavour to rally their drooping spirits by singing sea songs, which I managed pretty tolerably in those days. One of the most popular of these was Ye gentlemen of England, who live at home at ease, How little do you think of the dangers of the seas, &c.

A song that should be sung by every seaman who loves his country; and which I always found to have an animating effect on my shipmates, particularly on dark and stormy nights.—On this trip a young man fell from the foretopmasthead into the sea; but, by a sort of miracle he was got on board unhurt; and it is singular that when crossing the line, we were under courses, in a severe gale, a circumstance of rare occurrence,

CHAPTER II

and which I never knew but on that occasion. On my arrival at Kingston I found that my excellent friend Mr. Everett was no more: and my chest had been plundered of its contents, so that I was again cast adrift without anchor or cable.

At this juncture I fell in with my old friend Captain Ward, of the firm of Birch and Ward of Liverpool. He now commanded a fine ship, called the Hall, and with him I engaged as second mate. Mr. John Brown was chief mate.

It is a singular coincidence that in 1828, while I am writing this, which is just forty years from the time I joined the Hall, Mr. Ward, Lieut. Brown, Joseph, Birch, Esq. the owner of the vessel (now M. P.), and myself, are all four, thanks be to Providence, in good health, steering a steady course in mid channel, heaving the lead, giving true soundings, going large, and paying our way. Perhaps no other four individuals in England can boast of such a similarity of fortune after so long a lapse of eventful years.

The Hall proceeded to Montego bay to load, and I was appointed to go in the shallop, a fine boat, to different parts of the coast for sugars. While waiting one day at a place called Lucia, for a load, I attended the trial of a negro for murder. He was found guilty, and sentenced to be immediately hung, and his body to be afterwards burned. He was an Eboe man, and as the people of that nation believe that they return (as in life) to their own country after death, the latter part of the sentence was intended to strike terror into their minds by conveying an idea of the utter annihilation of the culprit. I saw the unfortunate man led out to the gallows. After being allowed to drink a quart of rum, he confessed the crime for which he was about to suffer, and pointing to a woman in the crowd, exclaimed "That is the woman who has brought me to this!" His Eboe friends continued to cheer him with the hope that he would return to his own country until he was turned off the scaffold. After the body had hung for some time it was taken down, and being placed on a pile of wood, was reduced to ashes. This shocking spectacle made a painful impression on the minds of my young crew and myself. We afterwards learned that the woman was as guilty as the sufferer. She was the wife of him who had been murdered, and had assisted in the perpetration of the deed.

My new employment in the shallop was extremely arduous, and attended with many difficulties, but I had the good fortune to give entire satisfaction—and having completed our loading we sailed for England in June, 1788. When we got to the banks of Newfoundland we were sometime becalmed, and, although I am a Manksman, I never saw such a quantity of fish as we took in a few hours. They literally covered our main deck. We reached Liverpool in August—whence we again sailed for Montego bay in November. Another deck had been previously put upon the ship, which greatly impeded her sailing; and the hawseholes being, through the carelessness of the carpenters, left in a dangerous state, the water, in a tremendous gale in the night, rushed in upon the main deck, and we had the utmost difficulty and toil to save her from foundering. I was on the main deck, up to the knees in water, toiling and cheering on the men; and Mr. Brown was slung in ropes over the bows, endeavouring to stuff up the hawseholes: Captain Ward's energetic conduct was beyond all praise, and we finally weathered the storm.

One night after our arrival in Montego bay I saw, on looking over the stern, a large fish swimming towards us. A hook and bait were instantly thrown out, which it greedily swallowed. We found it to be an enormous shark. By help of a tackle we got the monster on deck. On cutting it open many large and small bones were found in the stomach, which we had little doubt were of human beings.

It was my misfortune when on that coast, to be one day appointed to go with the shallop with supplies, to a place called Maribana, when owing to a gale, and a heavy sea, we were dashed upon a reef of rocks. The little vessel and most of the cargo were lost, and though we narrowly escaped with our lives, and no blame was imputable to any of us, the accident was for a long time very painful to my feelings. The captain, however, whose confidence in me was unabated, afterwards retained me in the same department.

On the homeward passage I was for some weeks dangerously ill, but happily recovered while at sea, and we arrived at Liverpool in August. Some days afterwards, a fine new ship, the Elizabeth, belonging to the employ arrived from Jamaica, and on coming into dock she took the ground, and in spite of every precaution fell upon her side. We mustered all the strength we could command, and lightened her in a remarkably short time, so that she took little or no injury. This was considered a smart achievement, and as a reward for my exertions, Joseph Birch, Esq. the owner, presented me with a sum of money granted by the underwriters, with which I bought the first respectable suit of clothes I ever possessed.

CHAPTER III

I HAD at this time several offers to go as second mate to the coast of Africa, but like many others I had not overcome the prejudice I entertained against the trade: I had an abhorrence of the very name of "slave," never thinking that at the time I was as great a slave as well might be; and I agreed, though with fewer advantages, to embark as second mate of the Elizabeth, the first ship bound to Jamaica.

We sailed in November, 1789, under the command of Captain Innes. During a gale in going down channel, and while we were sending down top-gallant yards, about two o'clock in the morning, one of our seamen, a fine young man named M'Cauley, was thrown from the topgallant crosstrees into the sea, which was then running high. The ship was sailing very rapidly; and amid the roaring of the wind and waves we could distinctly hear the poor fellow's drowning cries. The distressing state of our feelings may easily be conceived; for it was impossible for us to render him any assistance, owing to the darkness, and the violence of the gale.

After we had crossed the bay of Biscay, the weather, all at once, became quite calm, attended with torrents of rain. On the rain ceasing, all hands were called on deck to witness one of the most wonderful phenomena I ever beheld. The surface of the sea, as far as the eye could reach, was like a sheet of fire. No one on board had ever seen this remarkable appearance before, and we concluded that it was produced by the action of the very heavy rain falling upon a glassy sea.[2]

The temper of my new captain I did not find so agreeable as that of my friend Captain Ward, although I did every thing in my power to render myself useful. I had a short but effective method of reproving such of the sailors as were backward to perform any hazardous or difficult duty aloft. When I saw them hesitate in reefing topsails I sprang to the masthead myself, and went down by the lift:[3] of course, "lie in, and no grumbling" was then the word. This manner of reproof has more effect on the minds of sailors than even punishment itself; for although there are many stubborn beings amongst them, taken generally, no class of men are more open to the generous conviction of a superiority in others, or more ready to follow its example. Such means of exciting them to activity were in those days the more necessary, as the second mates generally lived in the steerage amongst the people, and the familiarity that naturally arose between them was unfavourable to the maintenance of a proper subordination.

Our stay in Jamaica presented nothing worthy of remark. On the homeward passage I happily succeeded in gaining a share of the good graces of the captain, which was to me a source of great satisfaction. When about making the land near Cape Clear, we learned from a brig of war that England was on the eve of going to war with Spain: we were therefore apprehensive of being impressed. We came to anchor at the N. W. buoy early in August, 1790, after a short passage; and there, in the greatest hurry and confusion we took to the boats to avoid those land-sharks, the pressgang. Some of the men having got half drunk we were as nearly drowned as possible, by running aground on a bank on the Formby side, in the night. There were at the time several tenders in the river, with their holds crammed full of poor impressed sailors and landsmen. These press rooms were little better than pigsties: yet hardly a word was said, or a murmur raised, by our great statesmen, about the pitiable condition of those who crowded these receptacles of misery. All the talk, all the commiseration of the day, was about the black slaves: the white slaves were thought unworthy of consideration, although I cannot help thinking that the charity of those who held such "palaver" ought in justice to have begun at home. On this occasion we had the good fortune to escape the pressgang, and I once more found myself safe and sound in Liverpool.

I still dreaded the words "slave" and "slavery;" but my friends at length overruled my objections to an African voyage. Indeed, had I not gone to the coast I should, probably, have been a *white slave* to this day, or perhaps have found a berth in a prison or a workhouse. I was appointed chief mate of a beautiful brig belonging to J. Dawson, Esq. called the Prince, Captain H——, a promotion for which I was mainly indebted to the recommendations of the two captains with whom I had last sailed; and, in that capacity I made my

First Voyage to Africa.

We sailed in October, 1790, for Rotterdam, to take in a cargo of spirits,

CHAPTER III

&c. for Annamaboe, on the Gold Coast. After leaving Holland we were long buffetted about by gales of wind, and the vessel was frequently in danger of foundering, her deck being almost constantly under water. Our captain became dispirited, and exposed his apprehensions of the worst to the crew. This imprudent conduct could only aggravate the perils of our situation; and I strove to counteract its effects by encouragement and example.

The weather at length grew favourable; but our captain became ill, and the management of the vessel devolved almost entirely on myself. We put our little bark in fine order; and having mounted eight three-pounders we had in the hold to set her off, she cut a very dashing and rakish appearance. Meantime the captain recovered slowly, though not entirely: and his temper was so intolerable that he made himself miserable, as well as all those around him.

We came to anchor at Annamaboe in December, 1790, after a passage of seven weeks. We lay there about three weeks without transacting any trade, the king of that part of the coast having died some time before, in consequence of which all business was suspended. According to a barbarous custom of the country on occasion of the decease of a prince twenty-three of his wives were put to death while we remained; and many no doubt had met with a similar fate before our arrival. Yet to become the wives of these great men was considered, by the parents of the females, a high and honourable distinction. It was stated to me that the late king of Dahomy, a great kingdom in the interior, had seven hundred wives, all of whom were sacrificed soon after his decease; and Captain Ferrer, a gentleman of talent and observation, who happened to be at Dahomy during the perpetration of this horrid butchery, afterwards testified the fact in the British House of Commons. His evidence was, however, of little avail, for Mr. Wilberforce and his party threw discredit upon the whole statement.

After some delay at Annamaboe (where I first became acquainted with my excellent friend Captain Luke Mann), we proceeded to a place called Lago, with negroes, and thence to Benin. We traded between both places for several months, so that I acquired a considerable knowledge, as a pilot, of that part of the coast. I was much pleased with the gentle manners of the natives of Benin, who are truly a fine tractable race of people. When they meet an European they fall down on the right knee, clap their hands three times, and exclaim "Doe ba, doe ba;" that is "We reverence you!" They then shake hands, in their way, by giving three fillips with the finger.

The agents who were employed on different parts of the coast by our owner, Mr. Dawson, having all fallen victims to the climate in a few months after their arrival, in order that we might convey to him the melancholy news as soon as possible, we took in a quantity of ivory and other articles and sailed from Benin. We arrived at Liverpool in August, 1791—where after my recovery from an attack of jaundice I engaged to go as mate in a fine ship called the Bell, Captain Rigby, belonging to Wm. Harper, Esq. and bound to Cape Mount, on the windward coast of Africa.

We reached our port in safety, and there took in thirty negroes: we thence proceeded to Bissaw, where we received thirty more, and thence to New Calabar. When near our port we took on board "My Lord" a black pilot, so called by the natives, on account of his deformity, a defect rarely to be observed in that part of Africa. "My Lord" considered it indispensable to the safety of the ship to perform certain ceremonies before we got under weigh. Solemnly addressing the sharks, which are objects of worship at Bonny, he prayed that we might pass in safety over the shoals: at the same time throwing into the sea brandy, beef, and bread, as a propitiatory offering. He at length gave the word to weigh anchor, and took us safely to New Calabar.

One day, when I was on shore, I was surprised to see some of the people from the interior of the country perform a sort of play, which they had got up, considering all things, in a very creditable manner. Several of them appeared as goats, tigers and other animals, whose habits and dispositions they imitated with astonishing acuteness and accuracy. I also observed numbers of young men earnestly engaged at a game much resembling the casting of dice—so that they reminded me of some of our young bloods at home; for many persons in Africa pursue gambling to a ruinous excess.

While we lay here one of the natives was tried by the Jew-Jew-men, or priests, for some misconduct, and though his crime was not proved, he was sentenced to swim across a narrow creek, near the town, and in which there are always great numbers of sharks, which in that country are preserved with greater rigour than even the hares and pheasants in England; for these formidable enemies of the human race being (strange inconsistency!) worshipped by the natives, it is certain death for any one to injure them. The unfortunate man was soon brought out, attended by

CHAPTER III

an immense number of priests and natives, I being the only white man present. After some ceremonies were gone through, he was compelled to swim off, while I stood in breathless apprehension of his speedy destruction. The spectators shouted vehemently as he swam along, and to the great astonishment of all, and my no small delight, the poor fellow reached the opposite shore in safety! Even his enemies now considered him perfectly innocent; he had passed unhurt the fearful ordeal from which perhaps none had ever before escaped; and he was brought back in triumph by his friends. It was indeed most wonderful that he was not devoured, for the sharks were regularly fed in the creek by order of the priests, and were thus trained to dart upon their human prey with voracious activity.

I one morning went on shore with a party to procure water. We had scarcely reached the well, ere we saw an enormous shark furiously swimming towards a man who was bathing his little son near the shore. We instantly cried out as loud as possible, to give him the alarm, and ran towards the spot. The man perceiving his imminent danger— for the shark was now so near him, and he could wade out so slowly, that he had no hope of escape— threw the child, with all his might, towards the shore, determined, if possible to save its life, if he lost his own. By this time we were close to him, when the shark, in his eagerness to spring at the man threw himself into shallow water, where he lay flapping and writhing about to regain the vantage ground, till the man caught up the child and reached the beach. The feelings of the parent on this narrow escape I shall not attempt to describe.

Having got our old pilot again on board, after patiently waiting the termination of his usual preliminary ceremony of conciliating the sharks in our favour, we weighed anchor at a late hour in the evening. Soon after, we were overtaken by a tornado, attended with thunder, lightning and rain, and before we could take in sail, or let go the anchor, we were driven on shore. The pilot fell on his knees on the quarter-deck, and uttered a number of prayers not unmingled with reproaches to his "Jew-Jew, for make ship go for shore." Our captain was at a loss how to act; while I, assisted by my friend Mr. Cummins, our second mate (and now captain) encouraged the people until we got the sails handed. The storm and the darkness of the night made our situation truly awful. To lighten the ship we employed gangs in starting the water casks and heaving the firewood overboard. Meanwhile the cries of the poor blacks below were most distressing.

The ship, at length, began to lie over, almost on her beam ends, and dreading that the blacks might be suffocated, though at the risk of our lives, we permitted them all to come on deck. They, at this time, outnumbered us by more than ten to one. Our only dependence was on the good disposition of the sixty whom we had shipped on the windward coast, and who were of a race superior to those of New Calabar: nor was our confidence misplaced. They perceived our danger, and were so active to assist that I do not hesitate to say they were mainly instrumental in saving the ship.

When the storm had ceased, we saw several large canoes hovering about us, full of men, who designed, as we suspected, to cut us off. Observing, however, that we had so many windward coast men on board, they did not dare to attack us, but remained at a short distance, singing their war songs. We continued our exertions to lighten the ship, and having got an anchor out we succeeded, with the flood tide, in getting her afloat. Having grounded on soft sand, she had sustained little damage. The old black pilot strenuously insisted that to his idol, the shark, and to that alone, we owed the preservation of the ship and cargo.

Our chief mate was but ill qualified for his situation; and our captain himself had neither the firmness nor the tact to keep others in subjection. After much entreaty on the part of the latter I consented to act as chief mate for the remainder of the voyage, a situation in which, under the circumstances, I had a delicate and a difficult task to perform. I had not only to order the man who had been my superior officer, but to revive amongst the people, who through his neglect and the captain's weakness had become insubordinate, a strict and wholesome discipline. I must say, indeed, though it may sound like vanity, that but for the attention of Mr. Cummins and myself the voyage would have been unsuccessful and ruinous. This credit at least we may be allowed to assume, for we never received one farthing in the way of reward for our unremitting exertions.

We at length sailed from the coast, and in about fifteen days touched at the Portuguese island of Annabon, which is inhabited entirely by blacks who speak the Portuguese language. There we procured a supply of provisions, and continued our voyage.

A few days after one of my windward coast men, who was assisting to wash the decks, fell overboard, and the studding-sails being set below and aloft, and the ship running at the rate of seven or eight knots, it was some time before we could bring her to. Anxious to save the poor fellow,

CHAPTER III

if possible, I prevailed upon four of the crew to accompany me, and we started in a leaky boat towards the place where we thought he had fallen, and continued to pull about in search of him for about an hour, but in vain. Our hopes were also lessened by the approaching darkness. At last, when we were about to give him up for lost, we discovered him, when he was on the point of sinking, in helpless exhaustion, to rise no more. How he managed to keep above water for so long a time, in so rough a sea, God only knows. We soon got him into the boat, and pulled towards the ship, which we could distinguish by the lanterns, which—the crew having lost sight of us, and being alarmed for our safety in so crazy a boat —had hung out on the weather side. Before we reached her the boat was nearly half full of water. Two of the men were constantly bailing, two pulling, as for their lives, myself steering, and the poor black lying on the stern seat nearly dead. Through the goodness of Providence we at length got alongside, to the great joy of all on board. This circumstance rendered me a still greater favourite with the crew and the blacks.

We arrived at the island of Dominica, after a passage of seven weeks, and soon disposed of our cargo to advantage. We then took on board a number of invalid soldiers and their wives, and we found that it was more difficult to maintain order and decency amongst these whites, and particularly amongst the females, than amongst the blacks. We sailed for England, and had not been many days at sea when the weather became stormy, and the vessel shipped so much water that we could not keep the hatches off—so that the poor invalids were in danger of being suffocated. Captain Coombe and Lieut. Loftus, their superintending officers, and indeed every one in the ship, paid them all possible attention; yet many of them, before reduced by disease, died during the storm. We at length made the land of Ireland, and soon after, while I was writing the log in the half deck I happened to look through one of the ports, and perceived, with dismay, that we were on the point of running upon a sunken rock, about twenty yards distant. I rushed upon deck and gave the alarm, and the wind being partly from the land we contrived to escape our imminent peril. The rock was one of those inside the Saltees, and had I not chanced to observe it, the ship might have been lost and no one left to tell the tale.

We arrived at Liverpool in April, 1792, after a boisterous passage of six weeks. I had the pleasure of dining frequently with Captain Coombe[4] and Lieut. Loftus.[5] The former wished me to accompany him to London, where he had some friends connected with shipping: and Lieut. L. was also profuse of his attention and kind offers. My great aim, however, was to get into the very respectable employ of W. Boats, Esq. and to my great satisfaction I was appointed second mate (equal to chief mate in any other employ) of his ship, the Jane, Reuben Wright, master, bound to Bonny on the coast of Africa.

There were in 1792 many laws made for the better regulation of the African trade, of which every person acquainted with the business heartily approved. One of these enacted that only five blacks should be carried for every three tons burthen; and as Mr. Wilberforce was one of the promoters of these very proper regulations, I take this opportunity of complimenting him for the first and last time. His proposition, however, that badges should be worn by African captains, who toiled at the risk of their lives for the accommodation of our colonies, and that he and others might enjoy their ease at home, was impertinent as well as ungracious; and his regulation that £100 should be given to all captains, and £50 to all doctors who should land their cargoes without losing a certain number of *black* slaves, was absolutely ridiculous. Not a word was said about the white slaves, the poor sailors; these might die without regret. But, could any one in his senses suppose, that after paying perhaps £25 for a negro, their owners would not take especial care of them, and give them those comforts which would conduce to their health? Many a laugh I and others have had at Mr. Wilberforce and his party, when we received our hundred pounds bounty. And with respect to the insinuation thrown out, in this country, that African captains sometimes threw their slaves overboard, it is unworthy of notice, for it goes to impute an absolute disregard of self interest, as well as of all humanity. In the African trade, as in all others, there were individuals bad as well as good, and it is but justice to discriminate, and not condemn the whole for the delinquencies of a few.

We sailed from Liverpool in June, 1792, having forty hands on board, all in good health and spirits, and arrived at Bonny after an unpleasant passage of nine weeks. Just on our arrival old King Pepple died. Three months elapsed before the chiefs and priests agreed on whom they should appoint as regent until the son of the deceased came of age; and who, as one of his duties, should "break trade," a ceremony always performed either by the king or the regent. Old Bonny, a very clever chief, being chosen for the office, went through the prescribed forms of the ceremony. On the king or regent first coming off from the shore, we always hoisted

CHAPTER III

the colours and fired seven guns, and those in the royal canoe, on coming alongside, after some forms and mutterings, broke an egg against the ship's side. They then boarded and took the customs, (which at Bonny were about £400 for each ship) after which we were allowed to trade and barter for anything we wished.

While we lay at Bonny, I was, for three months, so ill, that I feared I should lose the use of my limbs, and be thus left a destitute cripple. I was several times given up by the doctors, and owed my un-expected recovery, in a great measure, to the un-bounded kindness of the captain. The following circumstance occurred during our stay: The head man of a leading trader in the town, who had a number of wives, was suspected of intriguing with some of them, and was brought before a meeting or "palaver" of the great men, headed by the high priest. The trial lasted for several days, and the accused was found guilty, and sentenced to be tied to a log of wood in the middle of the river, so that he might fall a prey to the sharks, which always keep near the surface of the water at the highest and lowest of the tide. The sentence was put into execution, and the poor fellow must have suffered dreadfully, as the greater part of his body was out of the water when the sharks fell upon him. I saw him in this horrible state, and was afterwards told that his innocence had been proved, and that his master had one of his ears cut off for preferring a false accusation. Another painful instance of the relentless voracity of the shark soon after fell under my observation. One morning, two Eboe women, who attended the cook, by some means got overboard to swim ashore. They had scarcely been a minute in the water, and were only a few yards from the ship, when they were torn to pieces by the sharks! It was appalling to see them in their dreadful torture; and their agonizing shrieks seem still to ring in my ears.

Having completed our cargo of about four hundred blacks we set sail, after a stay at Bonny of five months, during which we lost several of our crew, and some slaves. We proceeded towards Dominica to receive orders, but just before we made the island we were brought to by H. M. frigate Blanche, and informed that England was at war with France, and had taken the island of Tobago. We therefore lost no time in getting our guns, twelve in number, on deck, and having abundance of ammunition we were soon in a condition to defend the ship, should she be attacked by the French privateers.

From Dominica we proceeded to Montego bay, where we disposed of our cargo. Having procured some additional guns, and made the ship look as dashing as possible, we sailed for England in April, 1793, and came through the gulph passage without molestation. We had on board a fine black boy, brought from Bonny, named "Fine Bone," about fifteen years of age. When we got further north, the cold began to pinch him severely; and being very fond of me he one morning came shivering to the side of my cot, and said,—"Massa Crow, something bite me too much, and me no can see 'im; and me want you for give me some was mouth, and two mouth tacken." I knew that "wash mouth" meant a dram; and he soon gave me to understand by getting hold of my drawers, what he meant by "two mouth tackin." I furnished the poor fellow with the needful, and as he had shoes, stockings and jacket before, he was quite made up. We arrived at Liverpool in June, after a tedious voyage out and home of twelve months. I had the pleasure to give general satisfaction, and continued to remain in the same employ.

CHAPTER IV

AFTER remaining at home for twelve months I was appointed chief mate of a fine ship, mounting eighteen six-pounders, called the Gregson, Captain W. Gibson, bound first to Guernsey for a cargo of spirits, and thence to Cape Coast, on the coast of Africa. We sailed towards the latter end of June, 1794, and met with no interruption until three days after we left Guernsey, when we were attacked by a large French ship, the Robuste, mounting twenty-four long twelve-pounders, and carrying a crew of about one hundred and fifty men. To these we were opposed with our little crew of only thirty-five; and, indeed, it was almost madness to contend with so superior a force. We, however, engaged them vigourously for nearly two hours, when much of our rigging being cut to pieces, and several of our people being severely wounded, we reluctantly surrendered, as to continue the action would only have been to throw our lives uselessly away.

The boat in which I and some others were taken to the French ship would certainly have swamped, and we should all have perished had not the captain, a very good man, sent us immediate assistance. We were allowed to retain our clothes, and were treated with every kindness and attention. In three or four days both vessels put into L'Orient, where we remained prisoners of war for some weeks, and had no reason to complain of our treatment, which formed a remarkable contrast to that which we afterwards experienced in the interior.

The inhabitants of L'Orient and indeed the mass of the French population, were at that time in a state of political frenzy, which bursting all the bonds of forbearance and humanity that usually knit society together, rendered them regardless of their own lives and of the lives of others. Even wives informed against their husbands, if they but suspected them to be disaffected to republicanism; and husbands, equally disregarding all family ties, reported their own wives to the murderous tribunals which had then seized the reins of government. Hundreds of thousands were thus consigned to merciless destruction; and though, being a prisoner, my observation of these tragical scenes could be but limited and casual, I myself saw many wretched victims dragged to the guillotine like beasts to the slaughter. One Sunday in particular I and my fellow prisoners saw one hundred and fifty fine-looking women, who had been caught with a priest at prayers in a field, brutally driven into the town, where, without even the mockery of a trial, they were handed over to the public executioner.

From L'Orient we were marched to a place called Quimper, about forty miles distant—where we arrived about the middle of August. We found here between three and four thousand prisoners of different nations huddled indiscriminately together, and destitute of what are considered the common necessaries of life. To convey an adequate description of the misery we endured in this horrid place is a task far beyond my abilities, but I shall relate a few particulars, from which the reader may form some conception of our aggregate sufferings. The prison on our arrival was in a deplorable state, owing to the great numbers of the sick, to whom no medicine was dispensed, or nourishment given, beyond the prison allowance, which few of them could even taste. Our bread, which was black and clammy, was so execrable that we could hardly endure the smell of it. In addition to a pound and a half of this disgusting stuff we were each served with two very small fish called "sardaigns," which hardly made a mouthful; and this was all our allowance for twenty-four hours, The French commissary, who superintended this wretched establishment, was little better than an unfeeling madman, He would sometimes come into the building at four o'clock in the morning, attended by a guard of soldiers, who with their bayonets and bludgeons, would, without a moment's warning turn to and drive the whole of us from our rooms, pell mell, down stairs into the yard. Many hundreds of us were obliged to run out with our clothes and shoes in our hands. In this situation we would sometimes be kept in the open air till three or four in the afternoon. Owing to this treatment, together with the badness of the provisions, and the consequent want of nourishment, the number of the sick increased in an alarming degree. Great numbers were taken ill of different complaints, amongst which fever and dysentery raged with uncontrolled violence. Besides these, a dreadful and uncommon disease broke out amongst us, which produced so hideous a swelling of the head that those afflicted with it could hardly see. So poor and scanty, too, was the prison allowance, that those poor fellows who happened to have no money to purchase some

CHAPTER IV

additional supply suffered a sort of famine, and became filthy in their persons to such a degree, that their clothes were covered and even their flesh eaten by vermin. Amidst these accumulated miseries all discipline was entirely lost. Stealing and plundering became the order of the day, and there is no saying to what excesses desperation and distress might have driven many of those wretched beings, had not some of the oldest sailors, for the general protection, formed themselves into a police, by means of which order was, in some degree, restored.

Amongst the prisoners was the crew of a Dutch twenty-gun ship, who suffered much; for the poor fellows had, when captured, been plundered of almost all they possessed. The prison in which we were immured had been a convent, and the small bedroom of a single nun was all the space allotted to no fewer than seven prisoners. One night a poor Dutch sailor, finding our room door ajar, and its occupants asleep, contrived to carry off some articles of clothing belonging to me. The police, in the morning, soon discovered the thief, and he was sentenced to receive six dozen lashes. When, however, he was stripped, preparatory to punishment, the horrid appearance of his back, which was excoriated by vermin, won at once my forgiveness and my pity, and I succeeded in begging him off with only three lashes.

Meantime the sickness continued to increase; so that twenty, and sometimes twenty-five died in a day. The unfeeling commissary, who could not be blind to the ravages which disease, famine, and the want of every comfort, were making amongst the prisoners, ordered, as a generous indulgence, in his eyes, an old brewing pan to be placed in the yard, that some soup might be made for us. Into this utensil were thrown quantities of unwashed cabbages, and filthy horse beans, full of grubs. When the water began to boil some dirty hogs' lard was added; and this mixture, with the worms and maggots floating on the top of it, was served out to those poor creatures who could, or would, go for it. But even this boon was continued for only a short time.

Deplorable, however, as was the general condition of the inmates of that prison, disease would have been yet more fatal amongst them had not fortune thrown some good Samaritans in their way, who were, like themselves, aliens and prisoners. Lady Fitzroy and her brother, the Hon. Henry Wellesley, (sister and brother of the present Duke of Wellington) having been captured on their passage home-ward from Lisbon, were also prisoners at Quimper. Lady F., much to her honor, often sent into the prison soups and other articles of nourishment to be served among the sick, It was a most fortunate circumstance, and the saving of the lives of many hundreds of prisoners, that neither the captain nor any of the crew of the vessel in which that excellent lady and her brother were taken, had been plundered of their money—of which, I believe, they brought some thousand pounds with them into prison. I luckily succeeded in obtaining £20 on my note of hand, which, with the little I had saved of my own, was assuredly the saving of my life. The greater number of those who had money weathered out the storm; while most of those who were less fortunate perished of want or disease.

A most affecting circumstance took place, one morning, in that miserable prison.—A shipmaster, who had with him his two sons, fine lads of about fifteen and sixteen years of age, became much distressed in his mind about his family. He and one of his sons were seized with a raging fever; and, one night, the afflicted father, in a fit of delirium, threw himself from a window of the prison, three stories high, and was killed on the spot. The son—who had been ill—died on the same night. Both corpses, with about twenty others, were put into the dead-house, and, in the morning, a scene presented itself which would have drawn tears even from a savage. Over the dead bodies of the father and child lay the surviving son, totally deprived of his reason—now moaning piteously, and now uttering the wild laugh of the maniac.

The sight of an English newspaper, which we sometimes procured, was at this time a temporary solace to our sufferings, and we devoured the contents of even such papers of a late date as fell into our hands with an avidity, heightened by all our remembrances of home, which is scarcely conceivable. We found, from these, that the feeling of the day was exclusively devoted to the melioration of the *black slaves*, of whom those who spoke the most probably knew the least; while not a word was said about the sufferings of the *white slaves*, who, it was notorious, were daily dying, by scores, in the prisons of France. Often, in our indignation at this partiality, and indifference to our fate, did we wish that our colour had been black, or anything else than white, so that we might have attracted the notice, and commanded the sympathy, of Fox, Wilberforce, and others of our patriotic statesmen.

The sickness continued to rage, and, at length, began to affect the inhabitants of Quimper, numbers of whom sought security from its ravages by deserting the town. Our distress was, moreover, aggravated by the want

CHAPTER IV

of fuel, and we were compelled to tear up the boards of the upper rooms of the prison for fire-wood. The bread supplied us became every day worse and worse: the smell of it was scarcely endurable; and I have sometimes seen hundreds of loaves thrown out into the prison yard— being found, even by the half-famished inmates, unfit to be eaten. During this dreadful time several poor fellows were shot, in mere wantonness, by the sentinels; and most of our valuable policemen having died, all good order was again at an end. During the height of our miseries the most seditious pamphlets (translated from the French into English) were sent to the prison, and industriously circulated amongst us. The object of these was to persuade us that we were badly governed in England, and that our condition was even worse than that of negro slaves; and they generally concluded by recommending us to follow the example of the French people, and join, heart and hand, in the cause of liberty and equality. Few amongst us, I am happy to remark, embraced these pernicious doctrines.

Towards the middle of November, 1794, the number of prisoners who had died from the time of our arrival having amounted to nearly two thousand, those who were at all able to walk were marched in gangs of fifty, under guands, to the north of France. Our sufferings on the road were dreadful. The weather was piercingly cold: so severe a season, indeed, had hardly ever been known before in that country; and our scanty clothing and stinted provisions but ill served to defend us from its inclemency. Sometimes, at the close of a toilsome day, we had to sleep in the ruins of churches and noble-men's houses; and at other times in dirty stables. Our food was restricted to one meal a day, and our ranks were continually thinned by the fatal ravages of privation and fatigue. One day we would march twenty or twenty-five miles, and, on the next, owing to the disturbed state of the country, be obliged precipitately to retrace our steps. For about a fort-night we were shut up in a miserable prison at Rennes, in Brittany, where we had only straw to sleep on, and no fire but such as we purchased. Here, in a small prison, five hundred of us were crammed, captains, officers and men, indiscriminately, so that our condition was truly miserable. The straw which we had for fuel being frequently stolen in the night, I ordered Donald, a simple Irish lad who had attached himself to us as a servant, to sleep upon it as a security. One morning before daylight the poor fellow came to me crying "Mr. Crow, by the holies! the boys have done it." What have they done, Donald? said I:—"By the powers, sir, they have burned the fingers of my foots!"

Some wicked villains, disappointed of their usual booty, had set fire to the bundle of straw on which the poor fellow was sleeping; and his toes were scorched so severely by the flames that we were obliged to send him to the hospital, and leave him behind.

The weather having moderated, we were again marched in parties of a hundred each. The sailors, amongst whom no subordination was observed, at this time, took great liberties with their captains and officers. If we happened, for instance, to sleep in a church, which was often the case, one of the most forward would get into the pulpit, attended by a second as mad as himself, to act as clerk; and by way of preaching would utter a rhapsody of abuse, mingled with oaths and imprecations against us officers.

After marching five or six hundred miles, during which many of our number died, and others were left behind in hospitals, it was at length my fate to be included amongst the sick who were unable to proceed. I was placed in an hospital at Pontoise, in the latter end of February, 1795. Being extremely ill, I was put into warm water, and bled in the upper part of my feet. It was the first time I had ever seen such an operation, and its good effects were exemplified by my speedy recovery.

At Pontoise I found a number of English prisoners, amongst whom was the mate of a ship, named Disney, who gave me great assistance in acquiring a better knowledge of arithmetic, and of navigation by means of logarithms, which I found to be of the greatest benefit to me in after life.

My spirits now began to rally, and I went to work to plan my escape. With this view I formed a vocabulary, in my mind, of all the French words I could pick up, and about the beginning of May, 1795, when the weather had become fine, I contrived to elude the vigilance of my keepers, and, having first fixed in my hat a large tri-coloured cockade, I took the road from Pontoise, my object being to gain some port whence I might find a passage to England. I made a pretty favourable departure; but next day, when I had proceeded about fifty miles on my way, I was intercepted at a bridge by an officer and a file of soldiers. I was strictly interrogated, but in my confusion I had forgotten nearly all my French, and stood mute. The officer followed up one stern inquiry by another, but all to no purpose. At length, as a random expedient, I bolted out all the words of the different languages I could remember, and of which I had obtained a smattering in my different voyages, mingling the whole with my native language, the Manks, with a copiousness proportioned to my facility in speaking it. The

CHAPTER IV

Frenchman was astonished and enraged, and as he went on foaming and roaring, I continued to repeat (in broken Spanish) "No entiendo!"—until worn out of all patience, he swore I was a Breton, and giving me a sharp slap with his sword, he exclaimed "*Vat en, coquin!*" I thanked him over and over again, as loud as I could, in Manks, and I assure the reader never were thanks tendered with more sincerity.

After this escape I became more cautious, and resolved henceforward to travel only by night. With the dawn I looked out for a place of shelter and repose, and every morning, as I lay down to rest among the green bushes, my drooping spirits were not a little animated by the delightful notes of the thrush and the blackbird, that emerged from their nests to enjoy the wide freedom of the air, while I, to preserve myself from a prison, sought covert from the beams of day. I continued to pursue this plan for some days, but, at length, becoming impatient of delay, I resolved again to venture a journey during the day. I therefore one morning set off at daybreak, full of spirits and buoyed up with the hope of making a good run before nightfall. Unfortunately, however, I missed my way, and wandered several miles from the direct road. All at once I found myself close upon a large camp of soldiers. Here was I, as it were upon the lee of an enemy's shore, and in the greatest alarm tacking and retacking to avoid the danger. By great exertions I happily got clear off. I was so much exhausted and fatigued that I boldly made for the nearest house I saw, for I had walked and run at feast sixty miles from the time I set out in the morning; and my poor hull was in so sad a condition from stem to stern, that I resolved, at whatever risk, to put into the first port, were it even an enemy's. I gave the people of the house to understand who I was, and submitted myself to their mercy. These kind creatures, after giving me some brandy, put my feet into warm water, but such was the effect upon my worn-out frame, that I fell insensible across the tub. I was instantly put to bed and furnished with every nourishment the house could afford. I slept soundly, and at four o'clock in the morning was awakened by these hospitable strangers, who gave me a hearty breakfast, for which, and for all their kindness, I paid them in thanks, which were all they would accept, and nearly all I had to give. They then directed me into a private road to Rouen, and with many good wishes for my safety bade me adieu. The generosity of these good people made an impression upon me which can only be obliterated by death.

I reached Rouen without interruption, and thence proceeded to Havre de Grace, where I arrived after a two days' journey. I fortunately obtained a passage to England with a friendly Danish captain, who shewed me much kindness.

On landing at Deal I kissed the soil of my native country, grateful for my return after so many hardships. I had only a few shillings left, and the generous Dane insisted on paying my fare to London. After partaking with him of a hearty breakfast at the Hamburg coffee-house we parted to see each other, I fear, no more. I have only to say that if that man be still living—may God bless him!

I luckily obtained £10 on my note of hand from a friend, which enabled me to start for Liverpool, where I arrived in great spirits, after having been absent, in a French prison, for about twelve months.

CHAPTER V

THE first person known to me whom I saw in Liverpool was my dear brother William; and our feelings on so unexpected a meeting may be easily conceived. He had latterly gone out as chief mate of a fine ship called the Othello, Captain Christian, to Bonny. While there the ship one night caught fire, and before any thing effectual could be done to extinguish the flames, she suddenly blew up, and of several whites, and about one hundred and twenty blacks, who were on board, a few only escaped destruction. Amongst those lost was a brother of King Pepple. The captain, to whom a second similar and more fatal accident occurred in a subsequent voyage, and my brother had scarcely left the vessel when the awful explosion took place.

After a short stay in Liverpool I shipped as chief mate of the Anne, a fine ship mounting eighteen guns, commanded by my old master, Captain Reuben Wright, and bound to Bonny. While we lay in the river Mersey a number of men one day came on board, and amongst them was a prepossessing young sailor of apparently about eighteen years of age, named Jack Roberts. This youth drank grog, sang songs, chewed tobacco, enjoyed a yarn, and appeared in all respects, saving the slenderness of his build, like one of ourselves. In a few days, however, we discovered that Jack's true name and designation was *Jane* Roberts, and a very beautiful young woman she was. She was landed with all possible gentleness, and, I was informed, soon after married a respectable young man. It is remarkable, that about this time several handsome young women committed themselves in the same way, and some probably succeeded in eluding all discovery of their sex, and made a voyage or two to sea.

We sailed for Bonny with the ships Old Dick and Eliza, but soon after parted company in a gale of wind. When off the Cape de Verde islands we were becalmed for about a month, and suffered much for want of water. We at length reached Bonny, where, to our astonishment, we saw the two ships we had parted with, come to anchor about a quarter of an hour before us. We thus all arrived at nearly the same moment, after being separated, at sea, for upwards of fourteen weeks. The town being full of slaves we soon completed our cargo, and after a stay of only three weeks sailed to the westward, in good health and spirits.

When about three days' sail to windward of Barbadoes we fell in with a brig belonging to Lancaster, which having through stress of weather parted convoy, now joined us as a means of protection. Soon after daylight next morning we saw a French schooner, full of men, almost within hail of us, and immediately ordered all hands to quarters. The enemy came up on our starboard side, and after reconnoitring to ascertain our strength, poured into us three or four broadsides. He, however, met with a warm reception. We had prepared, as a substitute for grape shot, a quantity of broken copper dross, made up in bags, which did terrible execution amongst his men. He did every thing he could to cut away the Lancaster brig from our protection, and would have captured her, had we not stuck to him gallantly—so that he was obliged to drop astern to refit. After continuing the action, off and on, for nearly five hours, the Frenchman at length hauled his wind and made off. The brig kept close to us all the while, and it was fortunate for her owners that she fell in with us at the time. Our damage in this action was considerable. We had several whites and blacks wounded: our main and foretopgallant masts were shot away, our foremast was almost gone, and our sails and rigging nearly cut to pieces. Having put all to rights as well as we could, we reached Barbadoes in two days after— where every man and boy, worth taking from us, were immediately impressed—a galling reception after the manner in which we had defended ourselves and the Lancaster brig from the enemy. Having repaired damages we sailed for the Danish island of Santa Cruz, where we speedily disposed of our cargo. We thence proceeded to the neighbouring island of St. Thomas, where we loaded and, in due course, arrived at Liverpool.

My next voyage was as mate, in the James, an eighteen gun ship, commanded by Captain Gibson, one of my old masters. I was to receive liberal wages, besides a gratuity of £100, and was promised a ship on my return. We sailed in October, 1796, but, through the carelessness of the pilot, the ship got on shore on the Cheshire side. We next day, however, succeeded in getting her off, and so much pleased were the owners and underwriters with my exertions on the occasion that they sent on board to signify their approval of my conduct. On this voyage we had

CHAPTER V

the misfortune to lose our second mate, Mr. Hayne, who was washed overboard, and drowned, though every possible exertion was made to save him. We narrowly escaped running upon a sunken rock among the Cape de Verde islands— and afterwards met with a misfortune which entirely defeated the object of our voyage. After taking in a cargo of blacks at Bonny we weighed anchor on the 15th January, 1797, but had scarcely proceeded five leagues when the ship grounded at half ebb on a bank; the tide was running strong, and the ship struck and strained so violently that we soon had six or seven feet water in the hold. The tide at length drove her over the tail of the bank, and we came to anchor in deep water. We had about four hundred blacks on board, and only forty whites to superintend them. The ship continued to make water; and the captain, leaving me in charge of her, to do the best I could, set off in the boat to Bonny for assistance, promising to return with all possible expedition. Both pumps, meanwhile, were kept going; but, as the water gained upon us, the spirits of the people began to sink, and what with fatigue and apprehension they could hardly hold up their heads. At last I went down with the carpenter into the hold, and, searching for the leak, heard the water rushing through the bottom of the fore peak, where, it appeared, a splice had been made in the keel. We got all the pieces of beef we could muster, and crammed them into the leak; and this expedient we soon found had a good effect. The blacks had by this time got themselves out of irons, and I determined to let a dozen of them come on deck. Having unlocked the hatch, to my surprise they all gathered round me, shook me by the hand, and begged that I would permit fifteen of their best men to come up to assist us. This was readily agreed to, and the number mentioned went to work most cheerfully at the pumps. The night had now set in, and we showed lights in different parts of the ship, that the captain and his expected party might discover us from the boat; and, with the same view, a signal gun was fired every half-hour. The captain, however, did not make his appearance until early next morning, when, to our great joy, for we were exhausted with exertion, we saw several large boats pulling towards us. We had for a time succeeded in keeping the water from gaining on us, by the assistance of the blacks, but it was evident that we could not long keep the vessel afloat, and having now sufficient assistance we ran her in for the shore, and were finally obliged to strand her in Bonny creek—she being then half full of water.

It was nearly dark when we took the ground, and we sent the greater number of our blacks on board of other vessels. When the night set in, the natives went on board, and considering the ship as their lawful prize, began the work of plunder. I had previously stowed all my own articles on the booms, and having furnished myself with scores of six-pound shot, I defended myself stoutly against all attempts of the assailants to dislodge me. At length Kings Pepple and Holiday came alongside and commanded their people to desist. I was rejoiced at the truce, for although my ammunition was not yet expended, so desperate and destructive was my defence, that had my assailants not been called off, they would, in revenge, certainly have killed me in the end. Many whites and blacks were wounded on both sides. The ship, in a few days, was literally torn to pieces, and a demand was even made for half the number of the blacks we had on board.

The fatigues I had undergone brought on a severe illness, which continued for several days. On my recovery I was invited by the kings and the great men to spend some time with them on shore. When I reached the town all classes were lavish of their presents to me (for I was always on good terms with the inhabitants), and even the children, amongst whom I was well known, sang after me in the streets. A grand ceremony afterwards took place, and I was sent for to attend the Palaver-house, where I found both the kings and all their great men sitting, attended by crowds of priests and people. The priests proceeded to lead to the sacrifice hundreds of goats and other animals, and the kings were very active in performing the part of butchers on the occasion. All the musicians in the town were in attendance, and a horrible discordant din they made. I was given to understand that during the ceremony I must neither laugh nor smile, and I believe I kept my instructions by maintaining a suitable gravity of visage. The day was afterwards devoted to feasting and revelry, and this grand *doment* was intended as a thanks-offering to their god, for his goodness in casting our ship upon their shore.

From Bonny I took my passage to Kingston, and thence to Liverpool; where, notwithstanding the unfortunate issue of our last voyage, I met with a most friendly reception from my employers.

I afterwards agreed to go mate of a ship called the Parr; but had cause to change my mind: and it was well I did so; for that ship was blown up at Bonny on the same voyage. She had, at the time, her full complement of slaves on board, most of whom as well as the whites lost their lives, and of the number was Captain Christian, whose former ship the Othello, it will be remembered, was also blown up, and he and my

CHAPTER V

brother were amongst the few survivors.

At length, as the old proverb goes, "long looked for come at last"—I had the good fortune to be appointed to the command of a very fine ship called the Will, belonging to Mr. W. Aspinall, one of the most generous merchants in Liverpool. She was about three hundred tons burthen, carried eighteen six-pounders, besides small arms, and was manned by fifty men. The instructions I received were most liberal, and as a young man on my first voyage as master of a ship, I could not but be highly gratified by the friendly and confidential language in which they were conveyed.

We sailed for Bonny in July, 1798, and arrived safely after a fine passage. One of our first occupations was the construction of a regular thatched house on the deck, for the accommodation and comfort of the slaves. This building extended from stem to stern, and was so contrived that the whole ship was thoroughly aired, while at the same time the blacks were secured from getting overboard. These temporary buildings would cost from £30 to £40, according to the size of the ship. We soon procured a cargo, and after a pleasant run arrived at Kingston in good health and spirits. Our voyage proved to be most successful. I sold nearly £1200 worth of return goods, which I had saved from my outward cargo, and received the bounty allowed by government for the good condition of the slaves on their arrival.

We sailed for England with the fleet, from which we parted in a gale of wind; but ours was nevertheless the first ship that arrived at Liverpool.

Mr. Aspinall, my owner, who was fond of a good joke, happening to meet one evening with old Mr. Hodson, merchant, commonly called Count Hodson, their conversation turned upon the voyage we had just accomplished. Mr. Hodson observed—"I give my captains very long instructions, yet they can hardly make any money for us"—adding to Mr. A. "What kind of instructions, Will, did you give your captain?"—"Why," replied Mr. A. "I took him to Beat's hotel, where we had a pint of wine together, and I told him—CROW! MIND YOUR EYE! *for you will find many ships at Bonny!*"—Mr. Hodson immediately said, "Crow! mind your eye!—Will, I know the young man well, he has only one eye."—"True," said Mr. A.— "but that's a piercer!" The joke travelled to London, and I could hardly cross the 'change there afterwards without hearing some wag or other exclaim, "Crow, mind your eye!" It is very probable that Mr. Aspinall had, in joke, told some of them that these words were the only instructions I had ever received; and as such a fancy on his part was complimentary to me, I may here state, that I should have been as proud of that laconic injunction, and acted as faithfully for his interests under it, as under the lengthened instructions which he penned, in his proper anxiety as a trader who had much at stake.

We again sailed for Bonny in July, 1799. When off Cape Palmas, a fast-sailing schooner brushed up alongside of us, hoisted French colours, and began to fire. We cooled his courage with a few broadsides, and he sheered off before the wind. We lay in the river Bonny for about three months to complete our cargo, when my brother William, then captain of the ship Charlotte, arrived, bringing intelligence that three French frigates had been seen on the coast, and would probably pay a visit to Bonny. I therefore got all ready to put to sea next morning at daylight. Just as we were about to trip the anchor, we saw three large ships and a schooner coming down before the wind. One of them, in particular, stood in so near that we thought she had struck on the bank called the Beleur, which, with some other banks, fortunately lay between us. After coming to anchor three or four miles from us, they got out their large launches, full of men, and prepared to attack us. We accordingly made ready to give them battle. Luckily for us, the tide, at the time, was about half ebb, so that when they got near the top of the banks they were afraid to push over. They, however, began to blaze away with their long guns, and we at them, and we thus maintained the action for about two hours, until slack water, when we cut the cable and got back to Bonny, fortunately without having sustained any material damage. The captains of the vessels then in the harbour, having heard my report, called a meeting, at which it was agreed, for mutual safety, to sail in company, and we appointed Captain Latham of the Lottery to act as commodore. As we mustered, in all, nine sail of fine ships, we ventured to drop down, and come to anchor, in a line, within four or five miles of the Frenchmen. There we lay seven days without their daring to attack us. They at length weighed anchor, and stood from the coast, and when I thought all was clear I put to sea, having parted with my brother, alas! to see him no more— for he died soon after.

On this voyage, while in the latitude of Tobago, the 21st February, 1800, we saw two brigs standing to the southward, one of which tacked and stood towards us. Having made all ready for action, I continued my course, and kept all sail set, trusting that should she be an enemy we

CHAPTER V

might make a running fight of it. It was evident as she neared us that she was a large armed vessel, shewing ten ports of a side, and her deck covered with men, and that the other brig was her prize. He came up athwart our bows, and, rounding to, gave us two broadsides. He shot close up on our starboard quarter, and after a loud yell, the word was given to *board* us. We, however, returned his fire with compound interest; and our guns being well loaded with round and broken copper dross, a most destructive shot, we did such execution that, in a short time, he sheered off, and continued his fire at a greater distance. After fighting off and on for about two hours, he came up a second time, close on our starboard side, and in good English ordered me to strike, or he would sink us. I replied that I scorned his threats: that we should defend the ship to the last, and that sooner than strike to such as he, we would go down with her. This answer, while it gave new animation to our crew, exasperated the Frenchman to such a degree, that snatching up a musket, he fired at me several times with his own hand. Another yell was uttered, and another attempt was made to board; but it happily failed, for just as he neared our starboard bow, we put the helm a starboard, and away the brig shot ahead of us, but not, however, without carrying away our flying-jib-boom and its rigging. Before the enemy had time to recover himself we poured three broadsides into his larboard quarter, which produced much havoc and confusion amongst his men. The French had, at that time, a dangerous custom of loading their guns from the outside of the vessel, and we saw several poor fellows, so engaged, fall overboard on being wounded. By this time many of their sails had come down, and they dropped astern to refit—after which they came up a third time, very fiercely, and the action was stoutly maintained on both sides for about two hours longer. They did not, however, again attempt to board us, and at length, after an action, in the whole, that lasted about nine glasses, they sheered off, leaving us in a very shattered and disabled condition—all our top-gallant-masts shot away, our sails cut up, and our topmasts wounded; three shot in the mainmast, four in the mizenmast, our main cross-trees shot away—our hull much injured, and our rigging so much cut up that we had hardly a brace or a stay standing. One of the enemy's nine-pound shot went into the men's room below and wounded twelve blacks, two of whom died in consequence next day, and two others had their thigh bones broken. A shot also entered the starboard bow gun-port, and wounded three men and dismounted the gun. We lost our main-topmast studding sails, the

Figure 8: 'The Will of Liverpool, CAPT. CROW, beating off a French Privateer, 21st Feby 1800'.

halliards being shot away. Under all these circumstances, and considering, too, that we had only one or two shot of made-up copper dross left, I was heartily glad that the affair thus terminated; for had the Frenchman continued the action for half an hour longer, he would certainly have taken us. As soon as we had finally beaten him off I went into the cabin to return thanks to that Providence which had always been so indulgent to me in all my dangers and troubles. When the black women (who had rooms separate from the men) heard that I was below, numbers of the poor creatures gathered round me, and saluting me in their rude but sincere manner, thanked their gods, with tears in their eyes, that we had overcome the enemy. My officers and the ship's company conducted themselves throughout the action with the greatest coolness and determination, and we found a young black man, whom we had trained to the guns on the passage, to be both courageous and expert.

In a few days after this rencontre we arrived at St. Vincent's, where we refitted, and proceeded to Kingston. We had scarcely let go the anchor at Port Royal when no fewer than eight men-of-war boats came alongside, and took from us every man and boy they could find. The impressment of sea-men I have always considered to be, in many points of view, much more arbitrary and cruel than what was termed the slave trade. Our great statesmen, however, are regardless of such evils at home, and direct their exclusive attention to supposed evils abroad.

CHAPTER V

The 12th of April being held in Jamaica as a day of festivity, in commemoration of Rodney's victory, every ship showed her colours, and, it was customary, on hauling them down at sunset to fire a gun. On that day a large sloop lay near us, manned chiefly by negroes, and the master being on shore, these fellows must needs fire a gun along with the rest. They omitted to draw the charge with which it had previously been loaded, and whilst our doctor and mate were taking coffee on the quarter deck, a double headed shot from their gun took off the thigh of the former, and his immediate death was the melancholy consequence. Owing to this unfortunate accident the firing of guns on the same occasion, at Kingston, was from that time entirely discontinued.

I was received with great hospitality by the gentlemen of Kingston, and particularly by M. Atkinson, Esq. a gentleman distinguished for urbanity of manners, and highly respected in his official capacity under the Government of the island. Our voyage proved very sucsessful, and the blacks were so healthy, and so few deaths had occurred amongst them, that I was, a second time, presented with the bounty of £100 awarded by government.

We returned home under convoy; and, on our arrival off the N. W. Buoy my owner and his brothers paid me the compliment of coming out to meet me. To add to my satisfaction Mr. Aspinall appointed a fine ship, the Lord Stanley, to sail with me on the next voyage. To Mr. Kirby, my mate, was given the command of that vessel, and she was placed in every respect entirely under my orders.

Both ships, together with some others that were to join us, being fitted for sea, and with valuable cargoes, I received my instructions, which were of the most liberal nature, and we sailed in October, 1800, for the coast of Africa. We encountered some severe gales of wind, and did not reach Bonny till after a passage of ten weeks. There, the ship Diana, having been cast ashore and become a wreck, we received on board the captain and crew. After completing our cargo we sailed in company, all in good health, and arrived at Jamaica without losing a man. Indeed my friends at Kingston used to say—"Crow has come again, and, as usual, his whites and blacks are as plump as cotton bags" Having concluded our business, we sailed from Port Royal on the 21st of May, 1801, under the convoy of the York sixty-four, Commodore John Ferrier. The Will was appointed a pennant ship, and, at the same time, one of the whippers-in of the fleet.

On the second day after our sailing a signal was made, at daylight, for our ship to bear up and assist a strange vessel which was observed to be in distress. We found that she was a large ship, called the Hector, belonging to Liverpool and bound to London. When we came up to her, she was in a sinking state. It blew very fresh at the time, and before we could take a single man from on board she upset. While she was in this state the people jumped overboard from the stern, which they had no sooner done than she went down, bodily, in a moment. By great exertions we succeeded in saving them all, except one gentleman, a passenger, who went down with the vessel. Several of them I rescued personally when they were sinking; one of them, a Swede, was only saved by being caught hold of with a boat-hook. He had on a pair of heavy half boots, and was moreover loaded with a quantity of doubloons sewed up in a belt. This fellow, when he came to himself, without thanking God, or us, for his preservation, only made anxious inquiry if his money were safe! The Hector, Blackie, master, had sailed from Port Royal on the 21st, all well, but on the following morning had sprung a leak, which continued to increase in spite of all exertions. The crew, consisting chiefly of Spaniards and Portuguese, together with the captain, I sent on shore in their own long-boat. These particulars I communicated by letter to the Commodore, who expressed his gratification —and I had afterwards the honour of frequent invitations to visit him in his own ship. We remained at Port Antonio three days to collect the homeward bound vessels that were to rendezvous there; and we finally sailed with a fleet of one hundred and sixty-four ships, which, when all under sail, presented a most beautiful appearance. We had a fine passage, and in two days after parting with those of the fleet that were bound to St. George's Channel we reached Liverpool, where I was most cordially welcomed by my owner Mr. Aspinall.

Soon after my arrival I was presented by the Merchants and Underwriters of Liverpool with a handsome Silver Tray, for my conduct in regard to the three French frigates at Bonny. This splendid present bore the following gratifying inscription :

THIS PIECE OF PLATE IS PRESENTED BY THE
MERCHANTS AND UNDERWRITERS OF LIVERPOOL
TO CAPT. HUGH CROW, OF THE SHIP WILL,
IN TESTIMONY OF THE HIGH ESTIMATION
THEY HAVE OF HIS MERITORIOUS CONDUCT
IN THE RIVER BONNY,

CHAPTER V

ON THE COAST OF AFRICA,
ON THE 16th OF DECEMBER, 1799,
WHEN MENACED BY
THREE FRENCH FRIGATES.

The underwriters of Lloyd's Coffee-house also presented me with a sum of money, and an elegant silver cup, for my successful exertions in beating off the French brig. This handsome piece of plate was valued at no less than £200, and bore the following inscription :

PRESENTED BY
THE UNDERWRITERS OF LLOYD'S COFFEE-HOUSE,
TO CAPTAIN HUGH CROW,
FOR HIS GALLANT CONDUCT
IN DEFENDING THE SHIP WILL AGAINST A FRENCH
PRIVATEER, ON HIS VOYAGE FROM AFRICA
TO THE WEST INDIES,
21ST FEB. 1800.

In addition to these testimonials an enthusiastic friend presented me with a poetical eulogy, which was afterwards inserted in the newspapers; but as it was of a nature too flattering to one who had only done what England expects every man to do— "his duty," I refrain from laying it before the reader.

CHAPTER VI

AFTER discharging the ship I was commissioned, as on former occasions, to select in London two African cargoes for the employ. Mr. Aspinall afterwards purchased a fine ship—the "Young William," of about 500 tons burthen, of which he wished me to take command; but I was so much attached to my former ship, the Will, that I declined the offer, though at a sacrifice of some hundred pounds of commissions.

We again sailed for Bonny in November, 1801, and made a fine run until we arrived off Cape Palmas, when we were for some time becalmed. While we were thus detained near the land, a circumstance occurred which places in a strong point of view the high estimation in which a good name is held by the poor Africans. A black man and his son came off to us in a small canoe, and after swallowing a dram, or *washmouth* as he called it, he with great self-satisfaction presented to me some certificates of his good conduct, which he had procured from captains who had at various times employed him. These certificates the blacks usually carry in a wooden box suspended to their necks, lest they should be lost in the event of their canoes upsetting—a casualty to which they are frequently liable. When my visitor handed me the papers which he so much prized, I determined to amuse myself at his expense; and though I found their contents highly favourable to his character, I returned them with affected coldness, and, looking him sternly in the face, said—that Tom Goodhead (which was his name) was a very good man with strict looking after; but, on the other hand, he might be a great rogue and a villain. The poor fellow on hearing these words was, for a moment, petrified with astonishment, and then sprang over the quarter-deck rails, right overboard. After swimming under water to some distance from the ship, he raised his woolly head, and anxiously cried out,"Capy! booky speaky that mouth?"—meaning "Are such in reality the contents of my certificates." Fearing that what I intended as diversion might lead to something serious, I set about redeeming my rashness, and with some difficulty composed his wounded feelings. The poor little boy had kept the canoe close to his father, and when the latter had regained it I persuaded him to return on board: I soon made friends with him, and having given him a small present, away he paddled in high spirits for the shore.

Soon after we reached Bonny a native named Jugboy, with whom I was acquainted, was taken ill, and I was requested to go on shore to see him, and to take the doctor with me. We found him in the height of a fever, sitting at a huge fire, with his wives and friends. The doctor gave him some medicine; but we had scarcely returned to the ship when I was again sent for, with intelligence of his death. Apprehensive that his friends might ascribe his sudden decease to the effect of the doctor's prescription, I immediately returned on shore; and found, to my horror, that his people had put to death one of his favourite male domestics—and a second soon after met with a similar fate. This barbarous custom of sacrificing servants on the decease of their masters was, I lament to say, frequent at Bonny, as well as many other observances equally abhorrent to every principle of reason and humanity, but from which I and others had ever found it impossible to dissuade them. Few who had not been regarded most favourably by the natives, in general, would have ventured amongst the friends of the deceased, at a time when, in their grief, they were naturally ready to impute the fatality to some of those who had latterly been about him. I had, however, always found that boldly facing those from whom danger was apprehended, went a considerable way in disarming them of their resentment; and on this occasion, to my no slight gratification, the effect of my immediate presence was such, that no blame whatever was attached to the doctor or myself. I was received with the most marked attention, and my condolence for my African friend, which was really sincere, confirmed the good opinion in which I had been held by all of his acquaintances.

We sailed from Bonny with a cheerful crew, and our complement of healthy negroes. My first object was to reach the beautiful Portuguese island of St. Thomas, at which African ships may be supplied with all kinds of refreshments. While working the vessel in the night into the bay, the young man (Mr. Gutteridge, one of my mates) who was stationed in the chains giving the soundings, having neglected to secure himself by the breast rope, fell overboard, and before we could lower the boat he was torn in pieces by the sharks. Next morning, on going on shore, I discovered that the John Bull, a brig belonging to Liverpool, and last from

Africa, had been wrecked on the coast, and that the crew and the negroes were wandering about the island in a destitute and deplorable condition. Having seen the master (whose name was Wright) and some of these poor fellows, I resolved, if possible, to save their lives; and I succeeded, with the concurrence and assistance of the governor, in collecting and conveying on board the greater part of the crew and about sixty of the negroes. The captain, who like most of the others, was emaciated by famine and sickness, accompanied them, and after we had procured the necessary supplies we proceeded on our voyage. I had however cause to repent of this well meant endeavour to relieve my fellow creatures in distress, for we had scarcely been a week at sea before sickness broke out amongst both whites and blacks, which I could not but conclude was brought on board by the poor fellows whom we had taken from the island. Many of them, including the captain, were for days in a state of insensibility, and disease and death began to rage throughout the ship. We at length reached the island of Barbadoes, where I had to call for orders. We there landed Capt. W. and most of his crew, but, notwithstanding every attention, nearly all of them died in a few days after. Having refreshed our crew and cargo, during a stay of a week, we sailed for Kingston, taking St. Vincent's and Crooked Island in our way, for orders. We arrived safely, and great as had been our sufferings we made a successful voyage.

On our homeward passage to Liverpool we had a narrow escape from shipwreck on the coast of Wales, during a gale; and, on my arrival in October, 1802, I found, to my regret, that the ship "Young William" belonging to our employ, had a few days before been driven on shore near Holyhead, and had gone to pieces. At this time I received the painful intelligence of the death of my younger brother, for whom I had procured a good situation in Jamaica, in which, had he lived, he might soon have realized an independence. He was, with five other individuals, unfortunately drowned by the upsetting of a boat, while on a party of pleasure near Kingston.

The "Will," after discharging, having been repaired and laid up, I obtained command of the Ceres, a fine frigate-built ship of 400 tons—well armed and manned. We were bound to my old place Bonny, and had a fine run of it until we neared Cape Palmas, when the weather became hazy and the wind foul. While plying along the coast we saw a very large ship between us and the shore, and almost within hail of us. We observed that they hauled up courses and heard them beat to quarters, and though

CHAPTER VI

the vessel was a castle compared to ours, we were not behind hand in preparing for action. To our surprise they instantly down courses and made sail from us. During the following day and night the weather was still foggy, and though we frequently crossed each other, our antagonist appeared shy to engage, and shewed no colours. On the third morning he had got to windward of us, and seeing that we could not escape, I determined, in the event of his proving to be an enemy, to give him battle rather than remain at his mercy. We hauled up courses and hoisting our colours fired a gun to leeward. After some hesitation he bore down, and fired upon us for some time—till we both found that we were friends and not enemies. The ship was the Marquis Cornwallis, an Indiaman of the first class, carrying fifty-six guns and a crew of between four and five hundred men. This vessel and another Indiaman had, some time before, fallen in with a French corvette the "Uncle Toby," which had captured the latter vessel, and the commander's excuse for firing upon us, though he must have seen our colours, was that he did not like our appearance, and apprehended we were French.

On the day of our arrival at Bonny I had the misfortune, while getting out the boats, to receive a severe cut in the thigh, from which the blood flowed so copiously that I had scarcely a hope of recovery; and, taking the doctor by the hand, I requested that he would see me laid by the side of my late brother William. After a lapse of some hours, during which I was insensible, the bleeding stopped of itself, and I gradually recovered.

While at Bonny a distressing ceremony took place, which occasioned some delay in the shipment of our cargo. It was the custom there, once in seven years, to sacrifice a virgin, of fifteen or sixteen years of age, as a propitiatory offering to Boreas, the god of the north wind. For some weeks previous to the sacrifice, the female selected is led through the town, attended by numbers of priests, visiting every house, rich and poor, and whatever she fancies is immediately granted her. When the poor creature is satisfied with her booty, and (strange infatuation!) expresses her willingness to die, she is placed, with all the articles she has collected, into a large canoe and taken to a place about twenty miles from the town, where, together with her booty, she is thrown into the sea by the priests, and is instantly devoured by the sharks. While the preparations for a repetition of this sacrifice were going on I made repeated endeavours to persuade the great men and priests to abandon their cruel intention; but, unhappily, my expostulations were in vain, and another young woman was added to the list of those who had fallen victims to the ignorance and superstition of their tribe.

The painful impression made on my mind by this barbarous ceremony was yet fresh, when a Quaw chief, being taken in battle, was sent from the interior to King Pepple, and the great men at Bonny, to be eaten at a grand feast. In this instance, too, I did my utmost to dissuade the king and the priests from their horrible purpose, and I offered them the price of three slaves to save the life of the captive, who was a fine looking man. Neither arguments nor money, however, could avert his fate. He was put to death, and those who had feasted on his body afterwards boasted of the delicious treat they had enjoyed!

One day a large elephant swam across the creek from the main land to Bonny, and the inhabitants, who had never seen or heard of such a visitor before, were thrown into a state of bustle and confusion. The principal men proposed putting it to death, but this the king strenuously opposed—for the noble animal was so docile and harmless, permitting even the children to sport round it, and play with its tail, that he believed it was sent on a friendly mission amongst them by their gods. An acquaintance of mine, however, named Tom Crown, a native, who was reported to be one of the greatest warriors in the country, to shew his superior boldness, ventured, contrary to every admonition, to fire a musket at the unoffending stranger. He paid dearly for his temerity, for, in an instant, the enraged animal knocked him down and tore him to pieces. The elephant, without seeking any further revenge, then swam quietly back to the main; his stay in Bonny, which he would probably have protracted had he been kindly treated, being prescribed to only a few hours.

Before we completed our cargo a troublesome sore broke out in one of my legs, and I was otherwise seriously affected. Ill as I was, however, I was diverted by the following ludicrous occurrence:

A ship from Liverpool having gone on shore on one of the inner banks near Bonny, all the great men who could muster canoes set about plundering the vessel. My friend Jue Jue House, a native merchant, was one of the foremost in this marauding excursion, and, amongst other articles, he took possession of several puncheons of brandy. He and his companions having drunk abundantly of that potent beverage started in high glee for the shore. On their way they observed a cask, as they thought, of spirits floating at some distance, and not content with what they had already purloined, they resolved to add it to their stock: but while taking it

CHAPTER VI

in the canoe upset, with the puncheons of brandy under her. Several of the crew were devoured by the sharks, but Jue Jue House, with some others, succeeded in getting upon the bottom of the canoe. Imagining that the accident was the act of his god, and that a more fearful punishment, for his conduct, was still impending over him—as every surge of the sea made the puncheons beat up against the bottom of the canoe, he kept crying in a most subdued and pitiful tone, "YaYa, what me do to me god!—puncheon of brandy go away! I no want you, puncheon of brandy! go away! I no want you at all!" At last Jue Jue and the survivors took to the water to swim to the shore. Before they reached the land they got amongst a shoal of porpoises, and it being now dark, Jue Jue believed these fish, as they puffed and blew behind him, to be the puncheons of brandy, animated by his avenging deity, and rolling after him in relentless pursuit; and as he swam on with a speed accelerated by fear, he ever and anon repeated his exclamation, "Puncheon of brandy I no want you! puncheon of brandy! go away, I no want you at all!"

A few days before we left Bonny King Pepple came on board one afternoon considerably flushed with palm wine, of which he was very fond, and of which he usually carried with him a plentiful supply. After drinking more of that intoxicating liquor, he began to boast of the great services he had done me, adding that to him I was indebted for the speedy completion of my cargo. I acknowledged his friendly conduct, but the more I thanked him the more urgent he became in preferring his claims to my gratitude, which nothing I could say or do was at length sufficient to satisfy. All this while I lay in great pain upon a mattrass, and restrained my impatience as well as I could. At length Pepple worked himself into such a rage that, coming up to me, and holding up the two fore-fingers of his right-hand (which the natives consider a great insult) he began, knowing me to be a Manxman, to utter all manner of abuse against the isle of Man, which he denounced as every thing that was little and despi-cable, and at length roared out that we were a miserable race of people, as poor as rats, and unable to support a king. Although I cared little, indi-vidually, for these reproaches, I considered myself in honour bound to defend the reputation of my native little island, and springing up, I seized a stick, and exclaiming, "You villain how dare you abuse my country!" I followed him on all fours, and fairly pursued him out of the ship. As he left the side he reiterated "Poor boy! you cant havey king." When he became sober his accustomed good humour and friendship towards me were immediately resumed, and he often reverted with laughter to the day when he was chased out of the ship, for his wanton abuse of the "leely isle of Man."

We made a fine passage from Bonny to the island of Dominica, and had the good fortune to dispose of our blacks to advantage. We there received a cargo of sugar and coffee, and sailed for Liverpool in December, 1804. In eight or ten days after we lost sight of land, we were overtaken by a dreadful gale of wind from the W. N. W.; and it continued to blow gale after gale for ten or twelve days successively. The sea ran mountains high, and we were often obliged to lay to, lest the ship should be pooped. One morning, as we were scudding under a reefed foresail, a sea struck us on the larboard quarter, which broke up the mizzen channel bend against the ship's side, and carried away all the iron stanchions on the larboard gangway. A part of this tremendous wave went as high as the maintop, which it literally dashed in pieces and carried away. Our maintopmast went overboard with a crash, and the ship's waist being deep, and holding much water, one poor fellow was washed away and perished, and several others were with difficulty saved. Another sea carried away our quarter deck rails and bulwarks, and a fine New-foundland dog was washed overboard. How we escaped foundering God only knows, for, at one time, our main deck was breast high with water, under the weight of which the ship staggered, with scarcely any power of buoyancy. Some of the guns also broke loose, and, before they could be secured, were dashed from side to side and did a great deal of damage. A quantity of water likewise got below and did considerable injury to the cargo. The main-top being gone, some days elapsed after the gale had somewhat abated before we could get up a jury topmast, and our crew was so much exhausted by fatigue, privation of proper diet, and long exposure to the storm in their wet clothes, that they had scarcely strength to work the ship. Our situation during the gale was at one time so perilous, when the sea broke wildly over the decks and through the rigging, that we could not look back upon it without thinking of "The sweet little Cherub that sits up aloft, looking out for the life of poor Jack." In the height of our distress I often called to mind the 107th psalm, which so beautifully expresses the feelings by which we were impressed in the hour of danger.

We at length cast anchor in the Mersey, and on leaving the ship to go on shore, my crew gave me three hearty cheers, a spontaneous tribute of respect which, in those days, was rarely paid to any master of a vessel. Meantime, my leg continued in a bad state, and I repaired to Manchester for relief.

CHAPTER VI

Figure 9: 'Storm encountered in the CERES, CAPT. CROW, on the passage from Dominica to Liverpool, 1804.

There one of the principal surgeons advised the amputation of my limb. I told him we had sailed too long together, and had been too warm friends ever to part. I was afterwards confined to my house in Liverpool for twelve months, before I recovered, and the torture I endured was indescribable.

I had no sooner got upon my legs again than I obtained command of a fine new ship, called the Mary, belonging to my old employer Mr. William Aspinall. This vessel was nearly 500 tons burthen, and carried twenty-four long nine-pounders on the main deck, and four eighteen-pound cannonades on the quarter deck. We were manned by between sixty and seventy men, thirty-six of whom were qualified to take the wheel, being an uncommon proportion of able seamen, at a time, when it was difficult to procure a good crew.

The expense of then manning an African ship was excessive. The wages given in the Mary was ten guineas a month to the carpenter, nine to the cooper, seven each to the boatswain and gunner, six each to the quarter-masters, and six to every able seaman. Besides these expenses, three to four pounds were given as "crimpage" for able seamen.

We sailed for Bonny in July, 1801, in company with several other well appointed vessels. On the eve of our departure I looked at my instructions, which had, on former occasions, been, as the Ameicans would say, "considerably lengthy," and to my surprise they were nearly in effect as brief and pointed as

Crow! mind your eye!

We were buffetted about in the channel for some days by contrary winds, and, when at length a fine breeze sprung up from the north east quarter, our little fleet dashed along, with all sail set, in gallant style, every one on board enjoying a delightful flow of spirits, in anticipation of a favourable voyage. Our exultation was however of short continuance; for, when we got about mid-channel, between the Old Head of Kinsale and the English side, at day-light one morning, we had the misfortune, for so I must term it, to fall in with His Majesty's frigate Amethyst, from Cork, bound to Plymouth, with a small fleet of transports under her convoy. The frigate having hoisted English colours and fired a gun, we took in our small sails and in gallant style rounded to our little squadron, in expectation of being merely hailed and suffered to proceed without molestation. But when we were boarded by the boats of the frigate we were soon undeceived: for they wantonly took from each of us a number of our ablest seamen, although we had a protection for our crew, and had a few days before paid to their friends an advance of three months' wages each, at the rate of six pounds a month. The impressment of these men by a frigate, which I have since ascerained was full of men, was nothing less than a robbery of our merchants on the high seas by parties from whom we had a right to look for protection. This was not, however, the only instance in which the merchant service, from which the riches of the state and her best defence are derived, was wantonly crippled and distressed; and that our merchants tamely suffered themselves to be so much oppressed is only to be accounted for on the supposition that no general effort was resorted to, to counteract the grievance, and individual representation would have failed to obtain redress. Lieut. Hill, who boarded us on the disagreeable duty of impressment, I found to be a gentleman whose conduct was an honour to the navy; and I did not scruple to tell him that I lamented, for the credit of my country, to say, that our little squadron would rather have fallen in with a French frigate of the same class than with the Amethyst. The impressment of these men so completely damped the spirits of our crews, that had an enemy attacked us they could not, in their grief and impatience, have been roused to that energetic defence which is expected from those only whose national liberties are duly regarded by the government under which they live. Indeed I have always considered the impress service as a thousand times worse than any negro trade whatever. The whole system is disgraceful to an enlightened country; and it is high

CHAPTER VI

time some mode should be resorted to of raisng men for the service, without injury to the merantile marine.[6]

Two days after our crews being thus reduced we spoke a brig from Jamaica, and I embraced the opportunity of transmitting by her, an account of our treatment to our owner Mr. Aspinall, upon which he instituted an action to recover the amount of the impressed seamen's wages; but owing to a misnomer of the commander of the frigate, he was nonsuited, and left without any means of redress.

We arrived at Bonny after a pleasant passage, and I found my old friend King Pepple rejoiced to see me. To gratify his majesty I brought him a beautiful figure of a female, about five feet in height, a present with which he was much deighted. Some masters of vessels then at the port, became jealous of the favour by which I was distinguished by Pepple, and were disposed to annoy me as far as they could; but he soon gave them to unerstand that if they offered, in any manner, to interfere with me, they should experience his utmost resentment. The king's wives did not at all relish the female figure. They had been told by some of these masters that it would in a short time come to life; and as Pepple when elevated with wine would often take it in his arms and embrace it, their jeaousy was strongly excited, and had I not been a favourite amongst them, they would probably have sought some desperate revenge. Besides the addiion of the female figure to the seraglio of the king; I brought him, from England, according to his own order, a handsome bed, which cost upwards of sixty pounds, and I shall never forget the rage he flew into when on reading over the bill of parcels of that splendid article of furniture I came to the words "To ditto—ditto." Whether "ditto" had any proximate or remote resemblance to some word in his own language that conveyed an abhorrent idea, or that he thought it an ugly word of no intrinsic meaning, I know not, but I verily believed he would have gone mad when I repeated it.[7] After a volley of abuse against the isle of Man, he directed his rage at the unfortunate "ditto," exclaiming, "What be dat ditto ? Can I eat 'em—or drink 'em—or wear 'em ? I think he be some thief man and big rogue that make that thing ditto." It was a long time before I could pacify him, and persuade him to give an adequate price for the bed. The bargain was at length closed, and he ordered his purchase to be put into his canoe. Just as he was setting off I could not resist crying out after him "Ditto—ditto"— which again roused his passion, and he swore he would bring back the bed : so that I was fain, lest he should keep his word, to conciliate him by such an apology, at the gangway, as I should certainly never make excepting to a king.

Soon after this I was honoured with a visit from the other sovereign of Bonny, King Holiday, who came on board to amuse himself—for such were my efforts to divert the natives who fell in my way, whether of high or low degree, that I obtained amongst them the name of "the playman." On the day in question we had been brewing spruce beer, which was, at the time, in a state of strong fermentation. Several of the bottles had burst in the lockers, and the king hearing the noise sprang from his seat wondering what it might be. I took one of the bottles, and having cut the string that secured the cork, I levelled it at Holiday's head, and striking the bottom smartly with my hand, out flew the beer with a report like a pistol, and lodged in snowy froth on the king's woolly pate, which it metamorphosed into the semblance of a large boiled cauliflower. Thus crowned, the king stood for several seconds completely stunned by the force of the explosion. When he recovered from the shock, he returned my frothy fire by a volley of curses and imprecations, with here and there a violent stamp on the floor, by way of great gun, which he followed up by exclaiming, "You no play man no more, you devilly man, Crow, you have quite spoil the king!"—and before I could apologize for my treasonable assault upon his person, or had time to wipe the froth from his dripping head, he sprang out of the cabin in a royal rage, and regained his canoe. Perceiving that I had carried the joke beyond all kingly endurance, I hastily followed him, and by entreating his pardon and promising him some presents, his anger gradually subsided. Having at length prevailed upon him to return on board, we shook hands, and, once more restored to princely favour, I resolved never again to shoot at a sable monarch with such an air-gun as a bottle of spruce beer.

Shortly after this visit from King Holiday, I witnessed a laughable scene at the house of his co-partner in the throne of Bonny. Capt. C——, with whom I was acquainted, had arrived from Liverpool in a ship belonging to Messrs. John and James Aspinall. One day while we were together I found that he had on board a drum of figs, a fruit very rarely seen in that country, and I intimated that I should have a piece of fun with Pepple at his expense. C——, however, had gone on shore before me, and our first visit was usually paid to the king's house. When I arrived there, to my surprise I found Pepple and C—— in the heat of a quarrel and about to fight. They did not know each other well, and being both

CHAPTER VI

of hasty temper, an altercation had ensued which roused his majesty to wage instant war with the offending European. Pepple was at the time considerably flushed with wine, and he wore a pair of red morocco boots, which were hauled up tight about six inches above his knees—probably the first pair of boots that had ever enclosed his royal legs. They were so tight, that when I saw him he was like a poor fellow in irons; he could only straddle, without bending a knee, after the fashion of a pair of tongs; and in this dilemma he called lustily to his wives to pull off his boots that he might fight Captain C——. The women rushed in with knives in their hands to avenge the cause of their lord and master; but when they saw that I was present they refrained from violence, and soon after retired, saying, "No fear—it be Capt. Crow palaver!" It was fortunate for C—— that I happened to make my appearance at the time, otherwise they would in all probability have taken his life. Pepple, in the mean time, continued to vent his rage against him, and, at length, addressing himself to me, he inquired, "Crow! what debble man send this hard and sauce mouth fellow to Bonny ?" I replied—"Pepple, his ship belongs to the Aspinall's, and they have sent out some most beautiful things among the cargo—such as were never before seen at Bonny; and this is what makes the captain hard mouthed and saucy. They are such things that if he but show them he must get all the trade in the river to himself, to "the ruin of me, and all the other traders!" At these words his resentment gave way, and he remarked "I think that make 'im sauce Crow!" He then fell on his right knee, and taking hold of C——'s leg,[8] he intimated that he must have " all dem new things" himself. In endeavouring to rise from his humble position, being cramped by the tightness of his boots, he rolled over upon his back and lay for some time struggling and flapping with his red flippers like a turned turtle, so that I had much ado to preserve my gravity. When we got him on his legs he strenuously urged me to tell him the names of the articles I had alluded to, and to back his suit he first offered me an elephant's tooth weighing about a hundred weight, which I was foolish enough to decline accepting; then a beautiful Benin cloth, and finally a quantity of goats, fowls, and other stock. I had, however, nothing to tell him about, except the figs, and his expectations were too great to be satisfied with them, so that I was glad to get rid of him for the night by feigning that if I divulged the secret I should never again get a ship out of Liverpool. Before daylight next morning he despatched his large canoe to convey me on shore to confer further with him on the subject. I again urged my former plea with the most serious countenance I could assume; but as he still thought he could worm the secret out of me, he ordered more presents of goats, fowls, &c. to be sent on board, so that on the whole, though my character for veracity with Pepple was in great jeopardy, I was a considerable gainer by the frolic.

During my stay at Bonny, on this trip, a dreadful catastrophe took place in the harbour. Amongst twelve or fourteen sail of vessels that lay in the river was the ship Bolton of Liverpool. She had on board about a hundred and twenty negroes, and these men not being properly guarded contrived to free themselves in the night from their irons, and rising upon the officers and crew they took possession of the ship. Unfortunately the trade powder, in quantity about two hundred barrels, was stowed in the fore peak, and to this the insurgents, in their rage for mischief, soon found access. At daylight, by which time the circumstance became known, the several masters of the vessels in the river held a meeting to determine how the ship and cargo might be redeemed. The result was that I and some others were appointed to go on board the Bolton, and endeavour, if possible, to save the blacks from that destruction to which, in their ignorance, they were so fearfully exposed. They consisted chiefly of Quaws, a most desperate race of men. Before we got on board they had brought up many barrels of the gunpowder, which they had started and spread all loose between decks. It would have been madness for any of us to go below amongst them, for a single spark thrown by one of them amongst the powder would have involved us in instant destruction. We prevailed upon a few Eboes[9] to leave the vessel, and these, with all the women, were taken on board of some of the other ships. The Quaws were deaf to all our entreaties and warnings—until towards evening, when a number of them also gave themselves up, observing, probably, the danger to which they were exposed. The ringleaders, however, to the number of about a dozen, obstinately remained amongst the loose powder, so that no one had the hardihood to venture amongst them. In this situation they remained until the afternoon of the next day, when we observed the ship to be on fire, and as she was the headmost vessel in the river we manned all our boats in order, if possible, to tow her off, lest she might fall amongst us. We had been but a few minutes in the boats when, with all the unfortunate creatures on board of her, she blew up with a tremendous explosion. I was in our boat with eight or nine of my best men—and only about a hundred yards from her when

CHAPTER VI

the catastrophe occurred; and such was the violence of the shock that the poor fellows fell down in the bottom of the boat. The smoke, the pieces of the wreck, the clothes, and other articles of trade, that flew about in every direction, presented a scene truly awful. Several of the latter fell into our boat, and many articles were afterwards found blown as far as the town of Bonny. After this misfortune it became necessary to be more watchful of the blacks, and particularly of the Quaws, who, instigated by the example of their insurgent countrymen, had already begun to exhibit an impatience of restraint.

A ship having arrived with news that a French frigate had been seen on the Gold Coast, we prepared to give her battle should she attempt to run in and attack us. We mustered fifteen sail of fine ships, all well armed and manned, and could certainly have coped with a considerable force; but to our disappointment no Frenchman made his appearance. My ship was at this time so well manned that on getting under way we were able to run up the three topsails together: and having carried away our foretopsail-yard, in less than half an hour we had another rigged in its place, the sail bent, and the ship under way, a feat which few merchant vessels could boast of in those days.

We sailed on the 20th October, 1806. After clearing the shoals of Bonny, I went, about dusk, in the pinnace to take soundings at some little distance. We had not long left the ship when the boat was carried away by a violent current towards a dangerous headland called Andonny Point, where many unfortunate sailors had from time to time been lost, or, if wrecked, put to death by the natives. Finding ourselves rapidly drifting on, we came to anchor, at about four miles distant from the ship. The wind blew fresh, and we lay in the most perilous situation in which I was ever placed, from nine o'clock at night until two in the morning, when, by the blessing of Providence, a tornado, which, in that part of the coast always blows from the land, happily drove us from a shore which had been fatal to many Europeans. The people in the ship had providently hung out lights, and continued to fire signal guns for our guidance, and we, at length, got alongside to the infinite joy of all on board, many of whom had given us up for lost. Often have I ardently wished to meet with the poor fellows who were with me on that fearful occasion, for they conducted themselves like gallant seamen, and should never want a penny if I had it in my power to assist them.

We again got under way, and in five or six days came to anchor at the beautiful island of St. Thomas, from whence, after purchasing some refreshments, we proceeded on our voyage to the West Indies.

CHAPTER VII

It was my constant practice to keep the ship in a state of readiness to receive any enemy we might chance to meet, and particularly when we drew near to the coast of Cayenne, which I had learned, by dearly bought experience, was infested by French cruizers. To this end my crew were frequently trained to work the great guns and small arms, and on the present voyage I selected several of the finest of the black men to join them in these exercises, as well as in passing along the powder, and in other minor duties that might become requisite in the hour of action. The blacks, who were very proud of this preferment, were each provided with a pair of light trowsers, a shirt, and a cap; and many were the diverting scenes we witnessed, when they were, in a morning, eagerly employed in practising firing at empty bottles slung from the ends of the yard arms. Being but indifferent marksmen few of their shots took effect; and the falling countenances of those who had just missed formed a ludicrous contrast to the animated features of the next sanguine competitors. The first who struck a bottle was presented with a dram and a new cap. This small reward excited a strong emulation, and the morning's sport furnished matter of exultation to the victors, and of general merriment to all throughout the day.

Meantime we made a rapid run to the westward, and though my confidence in my crew was such that I thought very few French or other privateers, or even sloops of war could successfully cope with us single handed, yet as I one day paced the quarter deck ruminating on the chances of being attacked by probably an unequal force, a project came into my head for the greater annoyance and destruction of an enemy, of which I determined, if occasion required, to make experiment. Having got my plan to bear in my own mind, I sent for the gunner and the armourer, who were both clever men, and having expressed to them the great satisfaction I had all along derived from the good conduct of the officers and crew, I informed them that I had before had two actions off the coast of Cayenne, and that as there was a probability of our soon falling in with some powerful French privateers from that quarter, I had resolved, being so well manned, should any one attack us, not to give them much chance at long bowls, but to slap them right on board, if possible; and to run them down rather than expose the lives and limbs of my crew by a long action. I then desired them to take half a dozen of two gallon jars, of which we had a number on board; and, first, to put about two quarts of powder into each, and the same quantity of small flints; over these an additional quantity of powder; next about two quarts of pepper, and then to fill up with powder and cork them up: they were finally to insert a tin tube with a good match through the middle of the cork, to cover the jars with canvas, and coat them thickly with a composition of powder, brandy and brimstone. Each jar was to be put into a loose sack that it might be hauled up into either top when wanted; "And," I concluded, addressing myself to the armourer, "as you are the strongest man in the ship, your station will be in one of the tops, with a lighted match, so that you may, on the word being given, heave these destructive jars right on board of any enemy that may dare to come to close quarters." The gunner, on hearing these injunctions, exclaimed—"Sir, I have seen a deal of service both in men-of-war, and in privateers, but I never heard of, or saw, so deadly a contrivance before; and if any French or Spanish privateers venture to come alongside of us, they will never be able to get away again." He did not probably exaggerate the effects of these *infernal* bombs if thrown upon the crowded deck of an enemy's vessel; for as the jars would burst into sharp and irregular fragments, they would cut and mangle with as much execution as the flints; and the burning pepper, which was to be kept in a blaze by the combustible covering, no one could abide in the heat of action. This contrivance was, I confess, destructive, if not wicked; but when I recurred to the horrors of a French prison, I should not have hesitated, rather than run the hazard of undergoing a repetition of my sufferings, and involving my crew in a similar misfortune, to resort even to more desperate means of disabling an enemy, if occasion required.

Although the course of events did not, happily, require my deadly invention to be put in practice, it was not long before we were imperiously called upon to try our utmost strength in the Mary. On the 1st December, 1806, while we were in the latitude of Tobago, and in longitude about 53°, with a fine breeze and all sails set, the man at the mast-head sung out that he saw two sail a long way ahead standing to the northward. From the square appearance of their rig, and their being so far to the eastward of our own colonies, I naturally concluded they were none other than French cruizers from Cayenne, the coast of which lay directly to the south of us. Had we continued our course we should have come right upon them : we therefore took in all our studding-sails, and other fair weather sails, and hauled our wind to the southward, thinking, as they stood on the opposite tack, to avoid, them. On observing us, they both tacked, and gave chase under a heavy press of canvas. I could soon, by help of the glass, distinguish them to be powerful vessels of war, with whom it was not our policy to contend. We, therefore, continued to carry all the sail we could until six P.M. when night came on, cloudy and dark, with heavy squalls and rain. We then made every thing snug, and I thought it prudent to tack ship to the northward to keep clear of the suspicious vessels if possible; at the same time, thinking they might possibly stand on different tacks, and that, if we fell in with one of them only, we should not be apprehensive of the result, as we considered ourselves a match for any single-handed French privateer. At about nine P.M. the look-out ahead saw a sail to windward, which I made certain was one of those in chase, and we therefore bore away to the westward, and made all sail to avoid him. He immediately stood after us under easy sail, and made signals to his consort, whom, however, we could not see in the increasing darkness. Finding that, in all probability, we should have to stand by our guns, I called all hands to quarters, and addressed them in nearly the following words :—

"Sailors and shipmates! You are aware that I have done every thing in my power to keep clear of these Frenchmen, but all, as you observe, in vain. Your conduct, on all occasions since we have been together, has been noble and brave; worthy, indeed, of the high character of true British seamen; and I hope and trust you will stand by me this night: for rather than be taken and sent to a French prison, of which I had enough some years ago, I am fully determined to defend the ship to the last, and even to go down with her sooner than strike."

To a man they cheerfully expressed their willingness to stick by me to the last, and I concluded by saying, "commend yourself, my brave fellows! to the care of Providence; let us have no cursing or swearing, but stand to your quarters; and such is my opinion of your abilities and courage that I have no doubt but that should even both vessels attack us, we shall triumphantly beat them off; and woe be to them if they attempt to board us.!"

We were not long left in that silent and intense anxiety that immediately precedes an engagement at sea, for I had scarcely uttered these words when the vessel we had last seen, and which loomed large in the obscurity, came up astern and hailed us, ordering us, in the same breath, to bring to. I was too well aware that the French cruisers had a trick of hailing in English when they thought the deception would favour their purpose—to obey this command, under all the circumstances; and I calmly replied that I would not, and that no one should bring us to, in those seats, in the night. He thereupon fired two shots, and we returned him one. In a few minutes after, I saw a ship close to us with her starboard tacks on board, evidently the consort of the other. She passed under our stern, and also hailed us, but I could not distinctly hear, or understand, the words that were spoken. I answered, at random, and as loudly as I could that we were the Rambler, off a cruize, and bound to Jamaica, repeating that no strange vessel should bring us to, in those seas, during the night. The ship held on her course, and having as I conceived spoken the other vessel, which was now some distance astern, they both made sail after us. The vessel that first hailed us came up very fast, and though the night was very dark I perceived she was a large brig. She again hailed us in English to the same purport as before, but the words were so imperfectly heard amid the jabble of the sea, and the murmurs on board of both vessels, that it was impossible to distinguish whether they were pronounced with a foreign accent or not; and I made the same answer as before. She then rounded to, and poured a broadside into our starboard quarter. We resolutely returned her fire, at close quarters, for some time. She then took her station at some distance, and we fought for about one glass, when (about ten P.M.) her consort, the ship, came up on our larboard side, and they both closed, and simultaneously engaged us.

We had now, it must be allowed, got into a warm berth, but I was no whit dispirited, and we continued to blaze away upon them as quickly as we could load and fire. I was busily employed, animating the crew by all the cheering language I could muster, and in giving directions for the skilful elevation of the guns, so that every shot might tell. While thus engaged I received a violent blow from a splinter on the left arm, near the shoulder, which staggered me a good deal, and disabled me for some time; but this none of the crew observed in the darkness of the night, and I did not mention it, for I knew that in my safety, during the conflict, they conceived their own, in a great measure, depended.

Meantime the balls of the enemy continued to whistle about us in

CHAPTER VII

Figure 10: 'Action in the night, between the MARY of Liverpool, CAPT. CROW, and Two British Men of War, Decr 1 1806'.

every direction, occasionally carrying away some of our rigging, and flying through our hull; and to all appearance the conflict was only to terminate with the entire expenditure of our ammunition. The flashes from the enemy's guns on either side, which we at first saw with some natural apprehensions, became quite familiar; and we grew callous even to the occasional crash of a ball through the ship's side. On looking round, after a broadside from one of our antagonists, I saw the man at the wheel desert his post and run forward, as if for safety. I instantly sung out, "What! is it possible that we have a coward in the Mary?" The poor fellow no sooner heard this expression of reproach than he resumed his station as speedily as he had left it, and said he hoped I would excuse his alarm at the time. Indeed, when I came to know the fact, I could scarcely blame him: he had been stunned by the wind of a large shot which struck the afterpart of the mizzen-mast just over his head. All hands, but he and myself, being at the main deck guns, he had not one to assist him in attending to the ship and the wheel, and in his solitary and exposed situation the shock naturally staggered his resolution. Companionship, I conceive, lessens the sense of danger, and inspires fortitude; or in other words frequently "screws the courage" of those which would otherwise waver, "to the sticking place."

While all were thus engaged on deck, I did not forget to station the stout armourer in the main-top to be in readiness to haul up the combustible jars, wherewith to confound our enemies if they attempted to board us : I continued to move from place to place giving instructions, and animating my crew, who boldly stood to their quarters and fought like heroes. It was now past midnight, and the firing of the enemy and our own kept up a constant din like the bursting of continued peals of thunder. I began to marvel that no fatality had yet occurred amongst us; and the thought had scarcely struck me before a large shot, entering a gunport, took off both the boatswain's thighs. Another entering the men's room below, wounded a great number of blacks, five of whom soon after died. The cries of the dying and the wounded were truly pitiable; and the feeling of resistance by which we had throughout been actuated, was now mingled with a desire to avenge their sufferings. Several of my brave crew were soon after wounded, but though we were between the fire of both vessels, we continued to blaze away with unabated animation. At length, after having been engaged for nearly six hours, to my great joy I saw the ship all at once back her topsails and drop astern. In my satisfaction I sung out—"I think, my brave fellows, we have sickened them both, and your names will be honourably mentioned by our friends in Liverpool for your resolute conduct in this action!" At these words they wished to give me three cheers, but this I overruled, and desired that they would all return to their quarters, which they did; for what I had said was rather in encouragement lest we should again be attacked than in anticipation that we should he suffered to proceed, so unequally matched, without further molestation. The result proved that I was not too sanguine. The ship had not continued long astern before she made sail, again came up to us, and resumed the action as fiercely as ever. We engaged them both, tooth and nail, until the grey of the morning, when I was struck so violently on my left side by a splinter that I fell breathless, and for a time senseless, on the deck. The man at the helm, on seeing me fall, sung out that the captain was killed. Brave as my fine fellows were, as well as their officers, the circumstance had an immediate effect in depressing their spirits; and, worn out by exertion and fatigue, they all began to leave their quarters and gather round me. One of the officers, in the name of his shipmates, said—"Captain Crow you have done every thing that a man could do to defend the ship, and we are no longer in a state to continue the action—our rigging is much cut up, and our hull so battered that she makes a deal of water." Before I could recover breath to reply, Mr. Scott, the chief mate, added, "—and sir! we have struck the colours!" which

CHAPTER VII

words were more afflicting to me than the bodily pain I endured, and raising myself on the deck, I earnestly besought them again to hoist the colours, to return to their quarters, and to give the enemy three or four more broadsides to conclude with. My hope was that as "a chance shot will kill the devil," we might carry away some of their masts, or so injure them as to turn the scales of battle in our favour; but my entreaties were in vain: the poor fellows, conceiving all further attempts against two vessels, each of which was now plainly seen to be superior in force to our own, would be madness, were not to be induced to rally. Our opponents, in the meantime, although a lantern was hoisted at the peak to signify that we had struck, still continued to fire upon us; nor did they desist, until the lantern, the object of which they had mistaken, was cut down. I was then obliged to submit to the painful necessity of a surrender; and was carried from the deck and laid on a mattrass in the cabin, in a state of mental and bodily suffering which I shall not attempt to describe; while the crew hastened to collect their clothes, expecting to be immediately taken on board of the enemy's vessels as prisoners of war.

When the boats came alongside these poor fellows were standing at the gangway ready to surrender. But what was our astonishment, and I may add our dismay, when we found that those who boarded us were our own countrymen, and that we had been all the while fighting two English men-of-war! One was the Dart sloop of war, carrying thirty guns, thirty-two-pounders; the other the Wolverine, carrying eighteen guns, also thirty-two-pounders. This astounding intelligence, added to the disappointment and bodily pain I before suffered, so powerfully affected my mind, that I was for a time insensible to every thing except to the idea that a serious and irremediable misfortune had befallen me; and, in my anguish and vexation I struck my head several times so violently against the cabin floor that the blood started from my mouth and nostrils. Had I not been restrained by friendly hands I know not to what extremity my frenzy might have borne me; as it was, the blows were such that I have never since perfectly recovered from their effects. The thought flashed across me that my employer and the world would consider me highly culpable and rash, though I acted according to the best of my judgment for the preservation of the ship. I lamented moreover the loss of life which had taken place, and the situation of the wounded, nor was I without apprehension that the commanders of the sloops of war might construe my conduct into wilful obstinacy. These painful feelings were in some degree relieved by a flow of tears; but my sufferings were yet acute, when I was visited by two lieutenants, who, in the most polite and feeling manner, used every endeavour to console me with respect to the unfortunate action. One of them, in particular, whose name was, I think, Mr. Richardson (of the Dart) was extremely kind and considerate— observing that no blame whatever could be attributed to me, and that had they both been French vessels, as I supposed them to be, we should certainly have beaten them off. With respect to themselves, he informed me they had taken us for a large French privateer of thirty-six guns that had long annoyed our trade in that quarter, and for which they had been on the look-out for some time. They were certainly not without some reason for attacking us, although it was to be lamented they were so precipitate: and, on the other hand, when it is considered that I had sustained two actions on former voyages with French vessels, in the same latitude, and nearly in the same longitude, and that the French were in the habit of hailing in English as a decoy, no one will hold me culpable for refusing to bring-to to vessels that presented themselves at a time and place, and in a manner, that warranted the conclusion that they were enemies. The reason ascribed for the ship having backed her topsails and dropped astern, during the action, was that she had had two of her guns dismounted—a proof of the severity of the conflict. Indeed I have reason to believe the Dart was as severely mauled as ourselves. It was fortunate neither of them attempted to board, otherwise God knows what havock would have been made amongst them by the explosion jars, already mentioned, the effects of which our armourer was prepared to try, had any of them neared us sufficiently to enable him to throw them on board.

When the blacks came to know that I was wounded, and that we had been fighting our friends and not our foes, they rushed up in groups from below and gathered round me in the cabin. Some of them took hold of my hands, others of my feet, and on their knees expressed, in their way, their sorrow for the unfortunate affair, and offered, me their rude, but sincere condolence.

Daylight now appeared, and my officers had an opportunity of ascertaining the damage we had sustained in our hull and rigging. Our main-mast was nearly gone, and our bowsprit was in the same state. Three of our guns were dismounted and unfit for service. Our sails and rigging were nearly cut to pieces, and such had been the sharpness of the contest that the lower fore-studding-sail, on the larboard side, was

CHAPTER VII

burned to tinder. Besides a number of shot holes in the ship's upper works, several large shot had taken effect in her bottom, under water, and having penetrated through the outside plank and lodged against the timbers, the vessel made a considerable quantity of water.

Soon after we were visited by the lieutenants, the doctors of both vessels came on board to dress the wounded, whose cries were truly distressing. Some officers and men were also sent to render us every possible assistance in putting the ship in order. I was given to understand that Captain Spear of the Dart, and Captain Collier of the Wolverine, were astonished to find that a Liverpool Guineaman could sustain a conflict for so long a time with so superior a force. I cannot but think, however, as I have already intimated, that they ought to have been less hasty in attacking us. We were running down, with studding-sails set, in the latitude of Tobago; while they were standing upon a wind and off an enemy's coast—crossing in fact the very ground where Frenchmen might hope to intercept English vessels bound to the colonies. All these circumstances taken into account, no one, I should hope, who has a knowledge of nautical affairs, will accuse me of overstepping the bounds of my duty in defending my ship to the best of my ability.

We had reason to be thankful that so few of our people were killed and wounded, during an action of seven hours duration with two British men-of-war. This was in a great measure owing to the good order and discipline that prevailed amongst the crew of the Mary, whose steadiness and activity were beyond all praise. Not a man of them got a single glass of spirits from the afternoon previous to the action until it was all over; nor did a murmur escape any one of them on that account. Amongst them was one named Jem Berry, the smartest and most intrepid seamen I ever, I think, met with. He was as active aloft as a monkey in a tree; and I have often seen him run out on a studding-sail boom to reeve a tack. One day as he was standing at the end of the fore-yard-arm I sung out to him, "Yoa, Berry! what are you about there?" He answered, "Only waiting for a slant to lead in, sir!" and, watching for a lull in the sea, when the ship became more steady, he accordingly ran in like a cat upon the yard, without the security of any rope or holdfast whatever! So daring a feat prevented me from finding fault with his reply, the familiarity of which was contrary to the rules of discipline which I had ever made it a point to maintain.

The wounded being dressed, and our masts, sails, and rigging put in

order, we bade farewell to our countrymen of the two men-of-war—
the captain of one of which, very considerately, presented me with the
following Certificate, without which some degree of doubt might have
arisen in the minds of my friends relative to the facts of the unfortunate
engagement:—

> "*His Majesty's Sloop Dart, at Sea,*
> "*Dec. 1st, 1806.*
>
> "I do hereby certify that Hugh Crow, commanding the ship
> Mary, of Liverpool, and last bound from the coast of Africa
> with slaves, defended his ship in a running action under the
> fire of his Majesty's Sloop, under my command, and also
> his Majesty's Sloop Wolverine, both carrying thirty-two-
> pounders, from about ten P.M. till near daylight the next
> morning, in a most gallant manner (supposing us French
> cruizers from Cayenne), and did not give up till his rigging
> and sails were nearly cut to pieces, and several of his people[10]
> wounded. Latitude 11° 27' N.; longitude 53° W.
> (Signed) "JOSEPH SPEAR, Commander."

We made the land of Jamaica in a few days. On passing Port Royal
we found, that in consequence of some disaffection or breach of discipline
on board of one of the sloops of war then in the harbour, several poor
fellows had suffered execution. We beheld no fewer than ten or twelve of
the bodies of these unfortunate creatures hanging in gibbets erected on
the low lands, called "The Keys," some of them in chains, others in iron
cages; a sight, which, under the circumstances, excited more of pity for
their fate than of abhorrence for their offence, which few persons believed
was deserving of so awful a punishment. Our blacks, amounting to nearly
four hundred, were, at the time we passed, nearly all on deck. They became
dreadfully alarmed, lest they should be sacrificed in the same manner;
and we had much difficulty in preventing many of them from jumping
overboard, and in allaying their apprehensions.

On our arrival the wounded whites were carefully conveyed to the
hospital, and every attention was also paid to the wounded blacks.
Admiral Dacres, the then commander in chief, very kindly sent on board
a protection from impressment for all the crew; and my old Jamaica
friends hastened on board to bid me welcome. Notwithstanding all we

CHAPTER VII

had suffered our cargo was fine and healthy, and my friend Mr. Thomas Aspinall soon disposed of the whole to great advantage.

I embraced an early opportunity of writing to my employers a detail of the particulars of our voyage, not forgetting our encounter with the sloops of war. It is remarkable that shortly before our arrival at Kingston, a ship arrived there belonging to Liverpool, called the Hannah. This vessel while running down off Antigua, in broad day, was hailed in English by a fine smart-looking brig shewing English colours, and ordered to lie to. The order was complied with, no doubt being entertained but that the brig was an English cruizer, and the Hannah was immediately boarded and carried sword in hand before the officers and crew had time to recover themselves on finding they had come to at the mandate of a Frenchman. So much for placing dependance upon the language in which a strange vessel may choose to hail. The Hannah, was fortunately recaptured, and taken, with her valuable cargo to Kingston.

CHAPTER VIII

On the first Sunday after our arrival at Kingston, a circumstance occurred on board the Mary, which was the more gratifying to me as it was entirely unexpected. While I was lying in my cot, about nine o'clock in the morning, Mr. Scott, my chief mate, hurried into the cabin and said, "Sir! a great number of black men and women have come on board, all dressed in their best, and they are very anxious to see you : will you allow them to come down?" "By all means," said I, springing up, and hastily putting on my clothes to receive them—and in a moment they all rushed into the cabin, and crowding round me with gestures of respect, and with tears in their eyes, exclaiming—"God bless massa! how poor massa do? Long live massa, for 'im da fight ebery voyage"—and similar expressions of good will and welcome. I soon recognized these kind creatures as having been with me in one or other of the actions in which I had been engaged on former voyages, and though my attention to them when on board was no more than I had always considered proper and humane, I was deeply affected by this mark of their grateful remembrance. Poor Scott shed tears when he saw them clinging round me, and observed, "How proud, sir, you must be to receive this grateful tribute of regard! and how few captains can boast of a similar proof of their good treatment of the blacks under their charge." Indeed I could not refrain from shedding tears myself, when I reflected that the compliment came from poor creatures whom I had brought from their own homes on the coast of Africa. The women were neatly dressed in calicoes and muslins. Their hair was tastefully arranged, and they wore lone gold ear-rings. The men appeared in white shirts and trowsers, and flashy neckcloths, with their hair neatly plaited. The whole were at once clean and cheerful, and I was glad from my heart to see them. When they left the ship, which was not till they had repeatedly expressed their happiness to see me again, I distributed amongst them a sum of money, and they bade me good bye with hearts full of thankfulness and joy.

In a few days afterwards the governor of the colony, with his suite, did me the honour to pay a visit on board the Mary, a compliment seldom

CHAPTER VIII

known to be paid to the master of a merchant ship. I took the earliest opportunity of having the vessel surveyed by respectable masters, to ascertain what repairs she stood in need of before putting to sea. The mainmast and bowsprit were condemned, and the hull was found to have sustained serious damage. No suitable spars could be procured at Kingston, and application was made to the admiral and the commissioner of the dock yard, Port Royal, who, in a prompt and obliging manner, supplied us, not only with the requisite timber but with shot and other stores which we could not purchase in the island.

While we lay at Kingston I received a very welcome letter from my son, the contents of which, however, in one respect, gave me considerable un-easiness. I found that after all my advice his whole thoughts were bent upon going to sea. I took the opportunity of writing by my friend Capt. Luke Mann, of the Diana, on this and other subjects to the Honourable Deemster Crellin of the isle of Man, who had always taken a warm interest in our family. I requested him, as I had done on former occasions, to pay a sum of money to my mother, to be repaid him on my arrival at home, and earnestly urged him to use every argument with my son to dissuade him from his purpose of becoming a sailor. To the young man himself I wrote in the following terms, which were dictated by my experience in the turmoils, dangers and uncertainties of a sea-faring life, and the ardent desire of a father for the welfare of an only son:

> "*Ship Mary, Kingston,*
> "*Dec. 30th, 1806.*
>
> "My dear Edward—On my arrival here I found your pleasing and welcome letter. Believe me, my dear child, that I am much pleased with your style of writing, which is honourable to yourself and to Mr. Wadsworth your master. I am, however, very sorry to find that your young mind is so much bent on going to sea, and particularly on joining the navy, a service in which I can assure you, my dear Edward, I have not the good fortune to have either friends or interest. I therefore hope and trust that you will strive to turn your thoughts to a counting-house; for, in my opinion, a good upright merchant is equal to any profession in the world. When I get home I hope that you will have made up your mind in accordance with my wishes, so that I may have it

in my power to make interest to fix you in some respectable house either in Liverpool, or here in Jamaica, where I have so many kind friends. I hope you will continue to write frequently to Doctor Kelly, Deemster Crellin, and Mr. Phillips of Manchester; for a correspondence with these gentlemen you will find to be of great service in after life. I have to beg and request that you will avoid reading Lord Chesterfield's Letters, as I do not admire the sort of advice he gives to youth. Indeed a man ought, in my opinion, to be at least forty years of age before he ventures to read those letters; and be assured, my dear Edward, that my present admonition to you flows from the heart of an affectionate father. I trust you are now almost master of the French language, and of drawing and dancing, accomplishments which I know you have a taste for that is worthy of cultivation. I hope too that you continue to practise the use of the globes, and, with the rest of your studies, strive to obtain every possible information on general subjects, for without learning a man is a poor tool. If all be well I shall be at home towards the beginning of May, and when I see you shall have a deal of news to communicate about a very severe and most unfortunate action that we fought on the 1st instant with two English men-of-war whom we took to be Frenchmen. We had six men killed and several whites and blacks wounded. I was myself wounded twice but not dangerously: so you see I have suffered a good deal this voyage. However, after all, I am happy to tell you we have made a successful one. Adieu my dear Edward, and believe me to be, your ever affectionate father,   "Hugh Crow."

After getting in our mainmast and bowsprit and repairing the ship, we began to take in a cargo of sugar and coffee for England. While this was going on I received an additional testimony of the friendly disposition towards me of a number of individuals of the humbler classes in Jamaica, and of which I was not a little proud. This was an original song, of which the following is a copy, verbatim, and which is submitted to the reader as a specimen of the literary abilities and good humour of the blacks.

CHAPTER VIII

I.   Captain Crow da come again;
        But em alway fight and lose some mens,
        But we glad for see em now and den;
        Wit em hearty joful gay, wit em hearty joful gay.
        Wit em tink tink tink tink tink tink ara.
        Wit em tink tink tink tink tink tink ara.
        But we glad for see em now and den
        Wit em hearty joful gay, wit em hearty joful gay.

II.   But da em sorry and bery sick,
        For em da fight the two man-of-war ship;
        But we glad em gae dem tat for tit,
        Wit em hearty joful gay, wit em hearty joful gay.
        Wit em tink tink, &c.
        But we glad em gae dem tat for tit,
        Wit em hearty joful gay, wit em hearty joful gay.

III.   But did you ever see dem pills,[11]
        Dat dem send to cure em ill?
        But of dat dem got dem fill.
        Wit em hearty joful gay, wit em hearty joful gay.
        Wit em tink tink, &c.
        But of dat dem got dem fill,
        Wit em hearty joful gay, wit em hearty joful gay.

IV.   Then up to the hospital em da go, hay hay,
        For to see em wounded boys,
        And sat down and talk and pity and say.
        Wit em hearty joful gay, wit em hearty joful gay.
        Wit em tink tink, &c.
        And sat down and talk and pity and say,
        Wit em hearty joful gay, wit em hearty joful gay.

V.   The Captain Mann and em da go
        To Port Royal to Missey Man's crawl,[12]
        To get a beef take at Goodall's;[13]
        Den dem call for the bill, and pay for all.
        Wit em hearty joful gay, wit em hearty joful gay.
        Wit em tink tink, &c.
        Den dem call for the bill, and pay for all,
        Wit em hearty joful gay, wit em hearty joful gay.

VI.   For none like dem from Guinea come,
        For dem always joful never glum,
        And never gae dem boys fum fum,[14]
        Wit em hearty joful gay, wit em hearty joful gay.
        Wit em tink tink, &c.
        And never gae dem boys fum fum,
        Wit em hearty joful gay, wit em hearty joful gay.

VII.   But did you eber the governor see
        When em went on board of he.
        Den em say Sir Hugh you must be,

Figure 11: 'Song made by the people of Colour in Jamaica on CAPTN. HUGH CROW'.

> Wit you hearty joful gay, wit you hearty joful gay.
> Wit em tink tink, &c.
> Den em say Sir Hugh you must be,
> Wit you hearty joful gay, wit you hearty joful gay.

Meanwhile, I did not forget to visit daily my poor wounded whites in the hospital, several of whom, notwithstanding every care and attention on the part of the matron and the visiting surgeons, prematurely paid the debt of nature. It was a consolation to me to be informed that, even in the height of their sufferings they frequently mentioned my name, in terms of attachment and respect.

I may here remark, that on this and on former voyages I had frequent opportunities of observing the drollery and good humour of the negro character. I was one day met by a fine young black, who in a very polite manner thus accosted me : "Cappy Crow, how you do ?" "I do not know you, boy"— "Cappy Crow," he rejoined "me sabby you bery well!" "When and where," said I, "did you know me ?". He replied, "Me sabby you very

90

CHAPTER VIII

much when you live for you ship for big water—when you look ebery day wit crooked tick for find da pass;" meaning, he knew me when he was on board of my ship at sea, when I took daily observations with the quadrant to find out the way. After a little conversation I gave the poor fellow some money, and away he went delighted with the present, and the friendly notice I had taken of him.

I was one morning standing conversing with a Mr. Donaldson when we observed two young blacks going to fight. After they had sparred for some time, the taller of the two, who happened to be Mr. Donaldson's servant, having received a blow on the breast, ran towards us followed by his antagonist. Mr. D. on seeing this said to his man, "Cuffee, you are a big coward, and must have a bad heart:" to which Cuffee instantly replied, "No, massa! me heart bery good and wish for fight, but me foots no willy tan, you see, and so run away with it!"

During my last visit to Bonny I had purchased a monkey of the largest size, which was a source of amusement, but more frequently of annoyance, on board of the Mary. This fellow attached himself particularly to me, and as he constantly kept at my side, considering me, no doubt, his protector in his new mode of life, we became in a short time pretty well acquainted. He was uncommonly expert in imitating any thing he saw done, particularly if it were mischievous. Although I was sometimes obliged to check his propensity to evildoing, we for some weeks continued to maintain a mutual good understanding as shipmates. But the best of friends, alas! will sometimes quarrel, and so it was with us. One day while we were in the middle passage, we were overtaken by a squall, and while I was busy ordering sail to be taken in, my gentleman snatched the speaking trumpet from my mouth, with intent, no doubt, to assist me by making his own sort of noise upon it. Jealous of my prerogative I insisted upon a restoration of my instrument of office, the trumpet: this he resisted, and a scuffle ensued, which ended in my being obliged to knock him down with the end of a rope. Before I had time to look about me the fellow sprang at my neck, and after chattering and making faces of great consequence, he bit me several times. This was beyond endurance: he received a drubbing, which made him so outrageous that we were obliged to chain him. It appears he never forgave me for this infliction, for one morning very early, while I was lying asleep, he by some means got loose, and thirsting for revenge, ran down to the cabin, where mounting the table near my cot, he made no ceremony in pulling off the whole of the clothes that covered me, and that with such alacrity, that I had no time to stand upon the defensive. The fellow then sprung to the beaufet and began, as fast as he could, to pitch the wine glasses, and tumblers, and whatever else he could lay hold of, out through the cabin windows. The steward, at length, luckily came in, and we secured him. Owing to these and similar pranks, I determined to part with him, and a few days after we arrived at Kingston, I had him advertised in the newspapers, by the name of Fine Bone, from Bonny, on the coast of Africa, to be sold, for high crimes and misdemeanors. Having equipped him in a jacket and trowsers made for the occasion by a fashionable tailor, and a cap of the newest cock, he was on the day appointed sent on shore to a vendue store, where several hundreds of persons were waiting, brimful of curiosity, to see what kind of a being he was. He was put up in due form, and after a good deal of merriment among the bidders, and particularly among the Jew gentlemen present, whom he seemed to scrutinize with very knowing looks, he went off for £5 6s. 8d. I must not say, in auctioneering phrase, that he was "knocked down" for that sum, for he would have been a bold man who would have knocked him down, unless, indeed, in such a manner as to give him his quietus. For myself, I did not venture to go on shore on the day of sale, for if he had seen me in the street he would certainly have run after me, and claimed the privilege of an old acquaintance in a manner more earnest than welcome. Next morning the wags in the town reported that they had seen him, during the night, at Weststreet assisting the pressgang; and others gave out that he had run off with two half firkins of butter from a provision store, and would certainly be tried and banished the colony for so grave an offence.

After completing our cargo we got the vessel well manned and prepared for sea. We mustered in all sixty individuals, amongst whom were seven gentlemen passengers, two of whom were lieutenants in the navy—Mr. Tomkinson and Mr. Russell— since made captains. We sailed in March, 1807, with a fleet of twelve running ships, most of which were well manned and armed. My friend Captain Mann, of the Diana, acted, by appointment, as commodore, and led on our little fleet in a style that would have done honour to regular vessels of war. We got through Crooked Island passage on the sixth day after we sailed; and soon after (as is frequent in convoys of merchantmen) some jealousy arose amongst the captains, and they began to differ in opinion as to what precise course they should steer. Captain Mann, Captain C——, and myself, therefore

CHAPTER VIII

parted company, and had a pleasant run of it together to Liverpool, where we arrived on the 2nd of May, after a passage of five weeks. I was received by Mr. Aspinall with his usual kindness and hospitality.

We, however, got home "the day after the fair," for the African slave trade was abolished on the day preceding our arrival. The abolition was a severe blow for England, and particularly as it affected the interests of the *white* slaves who found employment in the trade. It has always been my decided opinion that the traffic in negroes is permitted by that Providence that rules over all, as a necessary evil, and that it ought not to have been done away with to humour the folly or the fancy of a set of people who knew little or nothing about the subject. One thing is clear: instead of saving any of the poor Africans from slavery, these pretended philanthropists, have, through the abolition, been the (I admit *indirect*) cause of the death of thousands: for they have caused the trade to be transferred to other nations, who, in defiance of all that our cruisers can do to prevent them, carry it on with a cruelty to the slaves, and a disregard of their comfort and even of their lives, to which Englishmen could never bring themselves to resort.

As we could not again clear out the Mary for an African voyage, I was, on my landing, solicited by Mr. Henry Clarke to take command of his ship, the Kitty's Amelia, which had been cleared out previous to the passing of the abolition bill. I accordingly accepted of the offer, the ship being a fine vessel of 300 tons, carrying eighteen guns. Having got her newly repaired and coppered, we went into the river to take in our crew; but had no sooner come to anchor than we found, to our astonishment, that she had about six feet of water in the hold. We were therefore obliged to run in and discharge preparatory to getting her again into the gravingdock. Some days elapsed before we discovered that the leak was occasioned by two large auger holes having been left open, through the carelessness of the carpenters. The ship when first taken out of the graving-dock made a deal of water, but on getting into George's dock the holes became filled with mud and rubbish, and she became tight again: such was exactly the case when we returned to the dock. It was fortunate therefore that the mud burst through the holes while we were yet in the river, for had it not been dislodged until we were out at sea the probability is that we should have lost both the ship and our lives. As it was, both pumps were required to be kept constantly and rapidly at work to keep the water under—with so much force did it rush in by these comparatively small apertures.

CHAPTER IX

HAVING written to my insurance brokers in London to know at what premium they would insure my commissions per Kitty's Amelia, I received the following gratifying answer:

"London, June 16th, 1807.

"Captain Crow,

" Dear sir—In reply to your favour, which was received in due course this morning, we have to advise you we can insure your commissions per Kitty's Amelia, from Liverpool to Africa, at the very low price of fifteen guineas per cent., and take this opportunity of assuring you we have never heard greater praise bestowed on any commander than the underwriters in general have expressed in consequence of your very gallant behaviour, which will always procure their decided preference to whatever vessel you may sail in. With much esteem, believe us, dear sir, your most assured humble servants,

"KERWEN, WOODMAN & Co."

This letter, which I valued more than the presents of plate I had received on a former occasion, was the means of procuring that part of the insurance of the ship and cargo which was done in Liverpool, at the same moderate rate—which was, in fact, five per cent lower than that demanded for any other vessel.

The ship having undergone the necessary repairs I took on board a fine crew of between fifty and sixty men, and sailed on the 27th of July, 1807. We had been out but eight or ten days when we had the misfortune to fall in with H. M. frigate the Princess Charlotte, commanded by Captain Tobin, who, although we had a protection, impressed four of our ablest seamen. I felt on the occasion as if so many people had fallen overboard whom I had not the power to assist, and my abhorrence of the impress service became,

CHAPTER IX

if possible, more firmly rooted. We had three commissions, but though during the voyage we chased and boarded several vessels we had not the good fortune to make any prizes. After a passage of about seven weeks, we arrived safely at Bonny.

It had been reported to the chiefs and the natives, by the captains who preceded me, that I commanded the last ship that would sail to Bonny for negroes. My friend King Holiday consequently repaired on board as soon as we arrived, to inquire if the intelligence were true. We had, as might be expected, a long palaver on the subject, in the course of which the king expressed himself, as nearly as I can remember, in the following terms:

"Crow!" he remarked, "you and me sabby each other long time, and me know you tell me true mouth (speak truth); for all captains come to river tell me you king and you big mans stop we trade, and 'spose dat true, what we do? for you sabby me have too much wife, it be we country fash, and have too much child, and some may turn big rogue man, all same time we see some bad white man for some you ship, and we hear too much white man grow big rogue for you country. But God make you sabby book and make big ship—den you sen you bad people much far for other country, and we hear you hang much people, and too much man go dead for you warm (war). But God make we black" (here the poor fellow shed tears) "and we no sabby book, and we no havy head for make ship for sen we bad mans for more country, and we law is, 'spose some of we child go bad and we no can sell 'em, we father must kill dem own child; and 'spose trade be done we force kill too much child same way. But we tink trade no stop, for all we Jew-Jew-man" (the priests) "tell we so, for dem say you country no can niber pass God A'mighty." The last words he repeated several times; and the reader, it is presumed, will find his remarks not altogether destitute of sense and shrewdness.

About this time King Holiday's wife was, to his great affliction, taken ill of the small-pox. Those siezed with this dreadful disorder it was customary at Bonny to remove out of the town to some solitary place amongst the bushes, where they were attended by an elderly person; but owing to the want of proper shelter and attention, or the virulence of the disease, very few of the patients recovered. It may here be remarked that vaccine inoculation being entirely unknown in those countries, the small-pox, which is dreaded as a plague, frequently depopulates whole towns. Captain Adams, in his Sketches of the Western Coast of Africa, remarks, that in Dahomy so fatal at one time was this complaint that "when the common people wished to impress on the minds of their hearers the truth of their assertions they wished the small-pox might *strike* them if what they were relating was not true." The king of Dahomy at length put a stop to this practice by proclaiming that to this adjuration alone might be attributed the frequent occurrence of the malady. Holiday's wife, who was a fine looking woman, being of one of the first families in the place, a meeting was called of all the Jew-Jew-Men and the Chiefs, at their Palaver or Parliament-house, to hold a consultation respecting the case of the illustrious invalid. My friend King Pepple invited me to attend this meeting, which I could not but consider as a high compliment. I went on shore, and being ushered into the Palaver-house, I took my seat, as ordered, alongside of King Holiday, who appeared to be absorbed in grief. I did not expect that Pepple would attempt to debate the subject in English, but such was his intention, and the result was somewhat curious, particularly on so solemn an occasion. One of his ministers (whether Secretary of State for the Home or Foreign Department, or Lord Chancellor, I was not informed) was a clever man, named John Africa, had been several times in England, and spoke English with tolerable fluency. Such was the high opinion entertained by us ship-masters of John's political abilities and general acquirements that we used to address him by the cognomen of "Billy Pitt." Few, indeed, possessed more of the favour or confidence of his majesty than this man, and a peculiar honour was designed him on the present occasion. The house was crowded, and after a solemn pause, Pepple, as the head of the legislative body, stood up in a majestic manner, and addressing himself to John Africa said in an elevated tone, "John! all big man tan for house : you must makey mouth just"—that is—" All the great men have assembled in the house: and you must speak to the purpose." When I heard these words, I could not for my life refrain from smiling, which he no sooner perceived than he burst out into an immoderate roar of laughter. This breach of respect to the house being in some degree caused by my smiling—out I ran, without my hat, followed by Pepple and several of the great men—leaving the meeting in a state of wonder and confusion. I ventured to expostulate with the king on his endeavouring to open the discussion in English, and to give vent to his merriment at a time when his colleague, poor Holiday, was plunged in the profoundest grief; but he only laughed the more, and pleaded in excuse for his conduct that he wanted to surpass all the kings of his country in speaking good English. He at length appeared to regret this untimely

CHAPTER IX

sally, and said, "Crow, you and I must never meet for big palaver no more." Poor Holiday's wife died under some bush on the same night, to the great grief of her husband, and the regret of every one in the town.

Before my arrival, on this voyage, the great men of Bonny had heard from the other captains of the unfortunate action between the Mary and the two sloops of war, and John Africa, who was also the government interpreter, was charged with the duty of communicating to me the congratulations of the cotemporary kings on my return to their country. This commission he performed in nearly the following words:

"Crow! the kings and all big man hear you fight too much in you fine ship las voge, all same we sabby you fight for tother voges, and dem sen me for tell a you dem tink you alway prove yourself man, and two king and all big mans say you must come to dem house all times you go shore." This message was, I assure the reader, very gratifying to my feelings, and I made my acknowledgments in such a manner as I thought would best confirm the princely favour which it conveyed.

I one day on a visit to King Pepple found him in company with a chief named Calabar Foobra, a man who pretended to be a great warrior. He stated that having made war with his chief he was obliged to fly his country, and had come to Bonny for protection. When I had taken my seat, Pepple requested me to relate before this persecuted stranger what I knew about our great wars in Europe. I accordingly told him of the tens of thousands who in our wars were killed in one day on the field of battle, and of the vast numbers who were wounded. Pepple and his guest expressed some surprise, and after their inquiries were satisfied the king shrewdly remarked, " What is the matter, Crow, that you big man for you gran Palaver-house make all dat noise for we country and we trade ? We no kill too much man all same you, and 'spose we black, and no sabby book, God A'mighty make we so, and we b'lieve God make we all and make white man sabby book; but you country want for pass all country, and now dem stop we trade, and want for pass God A'mighty, but all you big man and all you country neber can pass God A'mighty." I endeavoured to make some reply to this charge when Calabar said, " Crow you please hold you mouth a lilley. We big warm[15] passey you big warm two time; for dat time me fight for me country too much man go dead."

I inquired, "How many men did you kill?" He replied, "Three men go dead, and too much man lose him foot and him fingers." Pepple here fell on a sofa in a roar of laughter that completely silenced the expatriated warrior, who looked somewhat disconcerted. The king thus addressed him, "You be poor fool man, for Crow tell you too much big thousand go dead for he country warm, and you tell him *three* man go dead for you fight, and som man lose he foot and he finger. What wo wo palaver[16] you make!" Poor Foobra was quite crestfallen at this jeer, and was glad to dismiss the subject.

As ours was the last ship that had arrived, and there were ten or twelve vessels that had a priority in receiving their cargoes, I had a good deal of time to spare, and frequently went in the pinnace, which was manned by nine fine young blacks, with a gun in my hand, in search of game in the neighbourhood of the town. I happened one evening to be near a place called Pitterside, about three miles from the ship, and had strolled with my crew some distance along a fine sandy beach under the shade of a delightful grove, when we saw a woman with a bundle running towards us from the wood in great terror and trepidation. In her hurry and confusion she fell down before she reached us, and at the same moment we beheld four or five savage-looking Creek-men in active pursuit of her, and all armed with large knives. Our first impulse was to run up to the woman, and my black boys with a loud voice requested me to level my musket at the men, otherwise they would kill her. When the savages observed our threatening attitude, disappointed of their object, they stood still within a few yards of us, grinning fiercely, and showing their teeth in a most frightful and menacing manner. My boys had a short parley with them, and but for the gun, which they told them I should certainly fire if they offered violence, they would in all probability have taken the lives of some of us as well as that of the woman. They at length retired, and never was a poor creature more grateful than the affrighted female for the preservation of her life. She had, it appeared, crossed the usual boundaries in search of fire wood, and such was the law of the country, that had my black boys been unaccompanied they could not with safety have interfered to save her life. These Creek-men are a race of cannibals. When they attain the age of seven or eight years their teeth are sharpened with a file, and they do not hesitate to acknowledge that they devour each other when occasion offers. They live almost constantly in their canoes, in creeks and corners, and procure a precarious subsistence by marauding and plundering. After seeing the woman safely home we returned to Bonny. My pull-away boys related what had occurred, and the kings and others—particularly the wives of the chiefs were very earnest in their thanks to me for interposing

CHAPTER IX

to save the poor black woman. So lawless are the Creek-men, and so little can they be restrained in their predatory and often murderous excursions, that it is usual in Bonny to conciliate them by frequent presents. My friends had often warned me not to wander near their haunts, and after the occurrence just noticed I took care not to approach their dwellings without being attended by my young boat's crew all well armed.

While waiting for my cargo I requested my friend King Pepple to procure for me some dozens of sprouted cocoa-nuts to be planted on a beautiful little island about nine miles below Bonny, called the North Breaker Head. This place when first I knew Bonny, in 1791, appeared above water about the size of a long boat, and neither bush nor shrub was to be seen upon it. It continued, however, gradually to emerge from the sea, so as by the time I allude to to have become a very delightful spot of between two and three miles in circumference. Nearly in the centre of it there was a pond of brackish water, in which there was abundance of oysters. About one-third of the island was covered with shrubs and young trees twelve or fourteen feet in height, which were at times crowded by flocks of birds from the main land. Turtle frequented the shore, in their season, to deposit their eggs in the sand; and as fresh water was found at five or six feet from the surface the island was on the whole a delightful place of resort for the masters of vessels at Bonny. Provided with fishing nets and guns we there enjoyed many a pleasant day's excursion.

Having received the cocoa-nuts, the sprouts of which were several inches in length, I proceeded in company with my friend Captain Baldwin to the little island, and there planted them in such a position that when grown they might serve for a land-mark to vessels going into Bonny. Thus employed we passed a most agreeable day, and our black boys were delighted with the honour, as they deemed it, of assisting to plant the cocoa-nuts, declaring in their way that "No man never go dead that live here this day"—that is, that the persons who had planted the trees would live in the grateful remembrance of ages yet to come.[17]

After a lapse of some weeks trade began to revive; but unfortunately for us in the hurry and bustle of fitting out the vessel at Liverpool that she might be ready for sea before the passing of the bill abolishing the slave trade, a quantity of goods that had been returned on her former voyage (when the ship was sickly) had been carelessly repacked without drying or airing in damp water casks; and these were no sooner opened than a malignant fever and dysentery broke out amongst the crew. The first who died was a fine promising young man, Mr. Ray, our second mate. The sickness continued to rage amongst both whites and blacks. The goods being found to be almost rotten we were obliged to give them away or throw them overboard. The loss of these articles of trade, together with the sickly state of the crew, tended to retard the purchase of our cargo, and my mind became in consequence much harrassed and depressed. To add to our troubles the weather was extremely unpropitious. We had at intervals some of the most awful thunder and lightning, attended by heavy rains, I ever witnessed; and one night, in particular, such was the concussion produced by the explosion of the electric fluid that the ship actually shook from stem to stern like a basket.

The ill health which at this time prevailed in the ship was in no degree attributable to any want of attention to the comfort of all who were on board, with regard either to food or cleanliness. And here it may not be uninteresting to the reader to learn with what kind of provisions the negroes were supplied. We frequently bought from the natives considerable quantities of dried shrimps to make broth; and a very excellent dish they made when mixed with flour and palm oil, and seasoned with pepper and salt. Both whites and blacks were fond of this mess. In addition to yams we gave them, for a change, fine shilled beans and rice cooked together, and this was served up to each individual with a plentiful proportion of the soup. On other days their soup was mixed with peeled yams cut up thin and boiled with a proportion of pounded biscuit. For the sick we provided strong soups and middle messes, prepared from mutton, goats'-flesh, fowls, &c. to which were added sago and lilipees, the whole mixed with port wine and sugar. I am thus particular in describing the ingredients which composed the food of the blacks, to show that no attention to their health was spared in this respect. Their personal comfort was also carefully studied. On their coming on deck about eight o'clock in the morning, water was provided to wash their hands and faces, a mixture of lime juice to cleanse their mouths, towels to wipe with, and chew sticks[18] to clean their teeth. A dram of brandy bitters was given to each of the men, and, clean spoons being served out, they breakfasted about nine o'clock. About eleven, if the day were fine, they washed their bodies all over, and after wiping themselves dry were allowed to use palm oil, their favourite cosmetic. Pipes and tobacco were then supplied to the men, and beads and other articles were distributed amongst the women to amuse them, after which they were permitted to dance and run about on deck

CHAPTER IX

to keep them in good spirits. A middle mess of bread and cocoa-nuts was given them about mid-day. The third meal was served out about three o'clock, and after every thing was cleaned out and arranged below, for their accommodation, they were generally sent down about four or five in the evening. Indeed I took great pains to promote the health and comfort of all on board by proper diet, regularity, exercise, and cleanliness; for I considered that on keeping the ship clean and orderly, which was always my hobby, the success of our voyage mainly depended.

The individual who, at this time, acted as my chief mate, and who, in consequence of the African trade being done away with before I got home to Liverpool, had been represented as captain of the ship on her clearing out, began to conduct himself in a very improper manner, although every indulgence was granted him which a man in his situation could desire. He took every opportunity of making me and all on board as unhappy as he could, and, at one time, he had instigated the crew to an almost open state of mutiny, by constantly plying them with spirits. For the safety of the ship, and that the object of the voyage might not be frustrated, I was, reluctantly, obliged to call a meeting of the captains then at Bonny, to obtain their opinions, and, if necessary (as authorized by my instructions), to put him upon his trial. The result was that an investigation took place, during which he had every facility allowed him for a defence, and the unanimous opinion was that he should be dismissed from his situation. Indeed the unfortunate man himself acknowledged the propriety of the decision. It was fortunate that I was in possession of documents from my owners, authorizing me, should he not conduct himself in a proper manner, to refer the case to the decision of masters. The man was almost constantly in a state of intoxication, and my remonstrances, though conveyed with the utmost patience and good-will, exasperated him to such a degree that I often entertained apprehensions that he would either be the cause of my death, or, in his folly and intemperance, blow up the ship. After his dismissal I still—to lighten his mortification, and knowing him to be of a respectable family in Liverpool, and not deficient of abilities—permitted him to remain in the cabin as before, but not to assume any command in the ship. In a few days every thing became orderly and pleasant on board, and we completed our purchase of as fine a cargo of blacks as had ever been taken from Africa.

I at length sailed for the last time from Bonny, where I had, on successive voyages, met with so much kindness and hospitality. In order, if possible, to recruit both whites and blacks we came to an anchor close to my favourite little foundling island the North Breaker Head, where I had planted the cocoa-nuts only a few months before. To my surprise and gratification they had already grown about three feet in height, and were in a thriving condition. At this delightful place we lay about a week fumigating and airing the ship, and doing every thing to reduce the sickness that still prevailed on board. Our efforts were however of little avail: the disease baffled the skill of both our doctors, and I was deeply afflicted to see both whites and blacks dying daily around me.

Having done every thing in our power for the poor patients we sailed from the island, in anxious expectation that the sea air would produce a general convalescence. But, alas! "disasters seldom come alone." In a few days after our departure we experienced a continuation of the most singular and unwholesome weather I had ever witnessed in those latitudes. During the day we had nothing but calms with an atmosphere uncommonly sultry and oppressive; and throughout the night we were visited by such awful storms of thunder and lightning that the ship shook and rocked like a cradle. Torrents of rain also deluged the deck, and during their continuance prevented us from paying that attention which we wished to the sick. The deaths, in consequence, became more alarmingly frequent. The ship was every day several hours becalmed, and lay like a log on the water, her decks, rigging and and sails soaked and drenched by successive down-falls of heavy rain; while the burning heat of the sun, as his rays flashed out at intervals, and the noxious smell of the sulphur from the lightning, made our situation truly horrible. The heat was at this time more intense and oppressive that it is possible for those who have not experienced the like to conceive. At length it came on to blow, but from an unfavourable point, and sixteen tedious days elapsed before we reached the Portuguese island of St. Thomas, though with a fair wind we might have accomplished the voyage in two or three days. I resolved to spend some time here to recruit. We procured refreshments, and as the weather continued fine, the sickness in a few days began to abate. My spirits, which had long been depressed, again rallied, and I could not but remark how soon the nerves recover their tone when the mind is relieved, even partially, from the anxiety that affected them.

The island of St. Thomas is of considerable extent, and, as I have before remarked, produces provisions in abundance. The hills are high and wooded to their tops, and the low country is verdant and pleasing.

CHAPTER IX

Amongst its productions are the beans called calavancies, plantains, casavi root, and the usual vegetable productions of tropical countries. The town is called Chaves, and is situate on a bay in which the vessels usually anchor.

Having heard of the remains of a bishop's palace that lay within a few miles of the town, my curiosity was excited to see it. It happened that Captain Tool, of the brig Ruby of Liverpool was then in the bay, and we agreed to visit the ruins together. Captain T. was a catholic, and being a tolerably good scholar, was a suitable companion for such an excursion. When we reached the palace, we found it to be, together with the surrounding building, in a state of dilapidation, but the lands attached to it were laid out and planted in a neat and judicious manner. I had here an opportunity, for the first time, of forming some idea of that horrible tribunal the Inquisition. After having passed through several rooms, and having surveyed these gloomy abodes of misery, we at last discovered a small apartment in which it appeared, the most dreadful tortures had been inflicted on the wretched beings who had fallen into the hands of the inquisitors. The sufferer was, it seems, secured by the neck, in a stock, directly over which was fixed an instrument which let fall a succession of single drops of water upon the shaven crown of his head. The repeated action of the water, thus continually dropping, would produce intolerable agony; in fact, it would in time work its way into the brain. Under this terrible infliction the unfortunate victim continued until death put an end to his sufferings.[19] By what I could learn, scarcely a bishop had for many years been able to withstand the fatality of the climate, so that the Portuguese government had not for a long time sent any such clerical dignitary to the island.

The sick continued gradually to recover, and we again prepared to put to sea. On my taking leave of the governor, with whom I had contracted an intimacy, he made me several presents, amongst which were some monkeys, of which I shall have occasion to speak hereafter. We sailed in company with the Ruby, but had hardly left the island, which is subject to tornadoes, when it came on to blow a severe squall, in which the brig carried away some of her spars, and amongst the rest her main-yard. I was happy to have it in my power to supply my brother chip with a spare spar to replace it, but as some delay was necessarily occasioned by the accident we were obliged to leave the brig, and proceed singly on our voyage. In a few days the sickness began to break out afresh, and to my infinite regret we daily lost both whites and blacks. Amongst the number was the chief mate. I cannot describe the anxiety of mind which I endured under these trying circumstances, and which was aggravated by the apprehension that should anything happen to me there was no one on board who was capable of conducting the ship to port.

One afternoon when we were ten or twelve hundred miles from any land, and were sailing at the rate of seven or eight knots, the alarm was given that the ship was on fire in the afterhold. I was in the cabin at the time, and springing upon deck the first persons I saw were two young men with their flannel shirts blazing on their backs: at the same time I perceived a dense cloud of smoke issuing from below, and looking round me I found the people in the act of cutting away the stem and quarter boats that they might abandon the vessel. At this critical juncture I had the presence of mind to exclaim in an animating tone, "Is it possible, my lads! that you can desert me at a moment when it is your bounden duty, as men, to assist me ?" And observing them hesitate, I added, "Follow me, my brave fellows! and we shall soon save the ship." These few words had the desired effect, for they immediately rallied, and came forward to assist me. To show them a proper example I was the first man to venture below, for I thought of the poor blacks entrusted to my care, and who could not be saved in the boats, and I was determined rather than desert them to extinguish the fire, or to perish in the attempt. When we got below we found the fire blazing with great fury on the starboard side, and as it was known to the crew that there were forty-five barrels of gunpowder in the magazine,[20] within about three feet only of the fire, it required every possible encouragement on my part to lead them on to endeavour to extinguish the rapidly increasing flames. When I first saw the extent of the conflagration, and thought of its proximity to the powder, a thrill of despair ran through my whole frame; but by a strong mental effort I suppressed my disheartening feelings, and only thought of active exertion unconnected with the thought of imminent danger. We paused for a moment, struggling, as it were, to determine how to proceed. Very fortunately for us our spare sails were stowed close at hand. These were dragged out, and by extraordinary activity we succeeded in throwing them over the flames, which they so far checked, that we gained time to obtain a good supply of water down the hatchway, and in the course of ten or fifteen minutes, by the favour of the Almighty, we extinguished the flames! Had I hesitated only a few minutes on deck, or had I not spoken encouragingly to the people, no exertions whatever could have saved the

CHAPTER IX

ship from being blown up, and as the catastrophe would most probably have taken place before the hands could have left the side in the boats, perhaps not a soul would have survived to tell the tale. I hope, therefore, I shall be excused in assuming to myself more credit (if indeed credit be due) for the presence of mind by which I was actuated on this occasion than for any thing I ever did in the course of my life. The accident I found was occasioned by the ignorance and carelessness of the two young men, whose clothes I had seen burning on their backs: through the want of regular officers they had been intrusted to draw off some rum from a store cask, and who not knowing the danger to which they exposed themselves and the ship, had taken down a lighted candle, a spark from which had ignited the spirit.

I shall never forget the scene that followed the suppression of the flames, When I got on deck, the blacks both men and women clung round me in tears—some taking hold of my hands, others of my feet, and all with much earnestness and feeling, thanking Providence for our narrow escape, an expression of gratitude in which, I assure the reader, I heartily joined them.

On this passage I witnessed a remarkable instance of animal sagacity and affection. As I before mentioned we had several monkeys on board. They were of different species and sizes, and amongst them was a beautiful little creature, the body of which was about ten inches or a foot in length, and about the circumference of a common drinking glass. It was of a glossy black, excepting its nose and the end of its tail, which were as white as snow. This interesting little animal, which when I received it from the governor of the island of St. Thomas diverted me by its innocent gambols, became afflicted by the malady which yet, unfortunately, prevailed in the ship. It had always been a favourite with the other monkeys, who seemed to regard it as the last born, and the pet of the family; and they granted it many indulgences which they seldom conceded one to another. It was very tractable and gentle in its temper, and never, as spoiled children generally do, took undue advantage of this partiality towards it by becoming peevish and headstrong. From the moment it was taken ill their attention and care of it were redoubled, and it was truly affecting and interesting to see with what anxiety and tenderness they tended and nursed the little creature. A struggle frequently ensued amongst them for priority in these offices of affection, and some would steal one thing and some another, which they would carry to it untasted, however tempting it might be to their own palates. Then they would take it gently up in their fore paws, hug it to their breasts, and cry over it as a fond mother would over her suffering child. The little creature seemed sensible of their assiduities, but it was wofully overpowered by sickness. It would sometimes come to me and look me pitifully in the face, and moan and cry like an infant, as if it besought me to give it relief; and we did every thing we could think of to restore it to health, but in spite of the united attentions of its kindred tribe and ourselves the interesting little creature did not long survive. The sickness that afflicted many of the whites and blacks on board began to abate as we approached the West Indies, but though our destination was to Trinidad to receive orders, my instructions empowered me to use my own discretion, and I thought it prudent, as the convalescence was not yet general, to run on with all speed for my old favourite port, Kingston, Jamaica. We arrived there after a toilsome passage from St. Thomas of about eight weeks. Never, in the course of my life, did I suffer so much through fatigue and anxiety of mind as on this voyage, during which we lost no fewer than thirty whites and fifty blacks: amongst the former were our two doctors, who died immediately after our arrival at Kingston. The thoughts of the sickness (which originated from the damaged goods, as before stated) and the frequent deaths weighed heavily upon my spirits, and I have many a night lain down to rest so oppressed with grief and fatigue that I declare I had no wish ever again to see the light of day.

On our arrival at Kingston I found, to my surprise, about sixteen sail of African ships, some of which had been there five or six months, with the greater part of their cargoes unsold, and most of them losing daily both whites and blacks. This was a melancholy prospect for me, but my old friends did not lose sight of me, and the first thing I saw on landing was an advertisement in both the Kingston newspapers stating that Captain Crow had arrived with the finest cargo of negroes ever brought to Kingston. This I must confess was saying rather too much : the puff, however, had all the effect desired, for on the fifth day after we began to sell not a single negro was left on board, and we moreover obtained much higher prices than any of the other ships. Thus, after all our disasters, we made a very advantageous voyage.

Much as we had suffered from sickness in the Kitty's Amelia, it appeared that many other ships had lost twice the number of blacks that we did. Indeed the hurried manner in which we were obliged to wind up the African trade was almost the ruin of several merchants. Most of the Guinea ships at the close of the trade were sent out without proper cleansing and fitting up; whereas on former voyages they were perhaps the cleanest vessels in England. Sickness was the melancholy consequence, and the number of vessels which then arrived almost simultaneously at the islands, so glutted the market that there were few of them that did not sink money.

The consequences of the abolition of the African trade appeared to me, then, and appear now to be, pernicious not only to individuals but to England at large. Besides other advantages it was a nursery for our seamen as well as a benefit to our West India colonies. How, indeed, could England rear and maintain those men who are to defend the state, were it not for her colonies. But for the employment which they afford we should be as destitute of defence as the Africans themselves. If the pretenders to humanity have a mind to do good, let them first begin at home: let them look to Ireland, which is in a most deplorable state of slavery and disaffection —for which no politician has yet discovered an adequate remedy.

It may be added that when the African trade was abolished, many fine young men being thrown out of employment entered into the American service, and there is no doubt were afterwards employed to fight against the country that gave them birth, their prospects at home being entirely blighted.

It was on a Sunday morning when I landed at Kingston, and I found a number of my old shipmates (blacks) all neatly dressed waiting on the wharf to receive me : some of them took hold of my hands, and the general expressions of welcome and good will were "God bless massa! How massa do dis voyage? we hope massa no fight 'gen dis time." While they thus congratulated me on my arrival, a wag, one of their own party jeeringly exclaimed— "Who be dis Captain Crow you all sabby so much?"—and my black friends replied, "What dat you say, you black negro?—Ebery dog in Kingston sabby Captain Crow, and you bad fellow for no sabby him,"—with which they fell a beating him with so little ceremony, that I was obliged in good nature to interfere. I rather suspect this was a joke contrived among them when they saw me coming on shore, for the blacks have craft and sport sufficient for a frolic of the kind. Be this as it may I was not a little gratified by their friendly visit.

My friend, Captain Brassey, happened to be then at Kingston with a schooner (the St. George) belonging to our owner in Liverpool, and as I had loaded the Kitty's Amelia, I thought it prudent to give him the larger vessel that he might sail with the first convoy, while I remained some time in the island to collect debts due to my employers.

While I remained there with the schooner some wags from among my black acquaintances used to come down to the wharf of a night to enjoy a joke at my expense. After hailing the King George, they would inquire if Captain Crow were on board, and when I made my appearance they would sing out, "Captain Crow, you have bery fine ship now—one-pole-and-half ship"—in good-natured derision of the smallness and rig of the schooner compared with the ship, and when they had played off their raillery they would turn upon their heels, and leave me to digest it as I might. Indeed the attentions and greetings of my black friends were frequently rather annoying. Sometimes I could hardly turn but I would be met by groups of these kind creatures, who would pull off their hats and shake hands with me all round—an operation which, when it had to be performed perhaps a hundred times in an hour, I often purchased a respite from by dispensing amongst them a little money to drink my health.

Owing to the fatigue and anxiety I had undergone, it was not long before I caught a fever, in which I continued for some time dangerously ill. Indeed but for the extreme attention of my friends, and in particular of Doctor Chamberlain, I should probably have sunk under it. Through the goodness of Providence, however, I soon recovered my wonted health.

About this time I despatched several letters to my friends in England, and amongst them was the following to my son:

> "Kingston, Jamaica, Jan. 2, 1808.
>
> "My dear Edward—On my arrival here I found your welcome and pleasing letter, and notwithstanding the great distance between us, be assured that nothing is dearer to me than yourself and my native little island, and I flatter myself nothing can give you greater pleasure than the news of my safe arrival. I am sorry to tell you that I have suffered a great deal this voyage. Indeed I cannot describe the anxiety of mind and fatigue I have gone through owing to a severe sickness that broke out among the whites and blacks and carried off a great many of both.
>
> "It pains me to find, that after all my writing to and

CHAPTER IX

reasoning with you, you are still determined on going to sea: and as you will neither listen to remonstrance nor persuasion you must not blame me hereafter should you find your expectations of happiness in that line of life not to be realised. I shall write to my friend Dr. Kelly to make interest to place you under some good captain in the navy. You must therefore lose no time in applying yourself diligently to the acquirement of navigation, that you may be qualified for the profession which your mind is so much bent on. If all go well you may expect to see me towards the middle of August, and although I have given my consent to your going to sea, I hope you will yet reflect seriously on the subject, and strive to turn your thoughts on a counting-house, or some other profession. This advice is from one who regards you with the utmost affection. Give my respects to Mr. and Mrs. Wadsworth, and until I meet you, may God bless you! Yours ever,

"HUGH CROW."

This letter, I lament to say, did not dissuade my son from going to sea, and the result (as the sequel will show) was, to my grief and mortification, more distressing than I could have apprehended.

During a stay in Kingston of between five and six months I had the good fortune to get all my employers' business settled to my satisfaction, after which I returned home passenger in a fine ship called the Phœnix, commanded by my particular friend Captain Matthew Leary. Our fleet consisted of about a hundred sail, under convoy of H. M. ship Veteran of sixty-four guns, and after a most agreeable passage we arrived at Liverpool on the 17th of August, 1808. I was welcomed by my owners with their accustomed kindness and hospitality. I was, however, somewhat disappointed in not receiving from the parties concerned, according to promise, a sum of money for my sailors for their conduct in the unfortunate affair of the Mary, on a former voyage: for I had been assured that both the money and a piece of plate for myself would be presented on my return. Perhaps the following remark by Dr. Johnson, in his life of Sir Francis Drake, may cast some light on the cause of our disappointment: he says—

"A man by nature superior to mean artifices, and bred from his earliest days to the labours and hardships of a sea life, is very little acquainted with policy and intrigue; very little versed in the methods of application to the powerful and great, and unable to obviate the practices of those whom his merit has made his enemies."

Soon after my arrival I took the opportunity of sending to Admiral Russel, then at Yarmouth, a fine turtle, with a few lines. He was then Commander-in-chief of the fleet in the North Sea. In his very flattering reply, in which he was pleased to stile me "the brave and honest," he says, after many thanks for the present, "I had written to our friend and brother-in-law, Dr. Kelly, to put off your kind intention until next year, but your movements are, what a seaman's movements ought to be, *rapid*, for the next morning pop comes your letter of a line and a half, and before I got to the end of it I was boarded by the turtle."

I also wrote to my friend and countryman Doctor Kelly, and received a very gratifying answer. After stating that he had received a letter from his brother-in-law, and acknowledging the receipt of a present of shells, pepper, &c. sent by me to Mrs. Kelly, he thus proceeds:

"Admiral Russel desires me (in these words) to 'tell the warlike Crow to send him his son that he may train him up to emulate his father.' You see therefore that no time is to be lost, but that you should immediately get him his midshipman's uniform, &c. and what linen he may require." He concludes by kindly offering to do every thing to expedite my son's journey to the admiral's ship at Yarmouth, promising to forward him from London, and to write to the admiral's chaplain (a country-man of ours) in his behalf. Indeed had I not assured myself of the friendship of this valued correspondent I should never have consented to my son going to sea. The doctor was a gentleman of polished manners and superior abilities, by which he rose to high preferment in the church, and obtained very considerable interest with persons in office.

It was not however my son's destiny to join the admiral's ship. My friend Captain Mends (now Sir Robert) was about this time regulating captain in Liverpool, and being appointed to the command of the Arethusa frigate, he wished my son to go with him. This was agreed upon, and Mrs. Mends had the kindness to take him with her in a carriage to join the frigate at Sheerness. The very handsome appearance, and amiable

CHAPTER IX

manners of my son, who was then about fifteen years of age, prepossessed all who saw him in his favour; but the hopes which I naturally entertained of his success in life, were, alas! destined to be prematurely blighted. After fixing him, as I trusted, permanently, I bore up for my native land, the isle of Man, thinking to moor there in peace and security for life.

Amongst others of my correspondents was M. Atkinson, Esq. of Currhill, Newcastle, whom I had before met abroad. In a letter from him of 6th Feb. 1810, he says, "I most heartily congratulate you on your having at last let go your anchor in your native land, after so many dangers, and you have my sincere good wishes for a long continuance of domestic happiness. If you should happen to be in this part of the country I hope you will not pass me. I can show you that I have got a comfortable house, a good wife, and two fine boys, and assure you a hearty welcome, and more so if you will bring Mrs. Crow along with you. I shall have much pleasure in being of service to your son if it should ever be in my power. I knew Captain Mends very well, but it is now long since I have seen him. I saw in the newspapers an account of your most unfortunate engagement on the middle passage. There would have been some satisfaction in engaging an enemy so long, but to have all the disagreeable part with friends is melancholy indeed. You were certainly in an enemy's country."

My son's career was short and unfortunate. He had only been about ten months on board the Arethusa frigate when he was taken prisoner in one of the ship's boats while in the act of cutting out some vessels from a small harbour belonging to the French, in the bay of Biscay. He was marched with his fellow prisoners over the Pyrenees to that nest of wickedness and debauchery, Verdun. Many hopeful and respectable young men, and my unfortunate son amongst the number, during their detention on parole, at that place, became contaminated with loose and immoral principles, which paved the way for their ruin. My son, who was a young man of determined courage, succeeded in effecting his escape by himself from Verdun, in a very extraordinary and daring manner, after having been confined there about eighteen months. But alas! the French prison and its temptations had been his total ruin, and better, perhaps, it would have been for my lacerated feelings had he there died. After his arrival at home I wrote to Captain Mends, and received the following kind reply:

"Arethusa, Corunna, September 28th, 1810.

Dear sir—I have received your letter of the 27th August, and very sincerely congratulate you on the safe arrival of your son. I make no doubt he now speaks French very well, which he will find extremely useful, more so perhaps than the little over-plus money which he has spent.

I expect to be in England in the middle of November, and shall willingly receive him again into the ship. I am very truly, dear sir, &c.

"R. MENDS."

This friendly disposition towards my son was, however, unavailing, for on his way to join the frigate he unfortunately fell in with some bad company, and yielding to their insidious persuasions, so far forgot himself as to enlist in the 9th Light Dragoons. The distress of mind which I endured on receiving this intelligence it is impossible for me to describe. It had nearly caused my death, and never till then did I know what the heart of a parent could feel for an erring child. Through the benevolent interference of Captain Mends and others his discharge was procured, but he did not live long to profit by their kindness: for he died in a few days after in Lisbon, by all accounts, of a broken heart. This event occurred in the year 1812, and thus were my fondest hopes for ever blasted. I am persuaded I shall carry my sorrow for that ill-fated youth to the grave, and these lines, which so vividly call to mind all he was and might have been, I write with many tears.

Previous to hearing of my unfortunate son's death I wrote to Captain Tomkinson, R. N. on the subject of his promotion, and received a most friendly reply. The following are the principal contents:

"H. M. S. Mosquito, off the Texel,
"27th May, 1812.

" My dear Crow—It was with the greatest pleasure I received your very kind letter of the 17th January last. It would have reached me sooner had I not been changing ships, but be assured no letter was ever more welcome. For I will candidly tell you that I had a very bad opinion of the captains in your trade, until I had an opportunity of forming a better judgment from being with you, which

CHAPTER IX

fully convinced me that there were more un truths said of Guineaman than any other class of people, and though there were undoubtedly bad people in it, yourself and Captain Mann were examples that have fully assured me there were also as upright men in it as in any other profession in the world."

After stating that he had been in several engagements, had been promoted to the rank of captain in consequence, and had then command of the Mosquito, a fine vessel, he says,

"I have not heard of Admiral Russel since we parted. I think you told me you intended sending your son into the navy. Have you done so? If you have I shall feel at all times much pleasure in rendering him any service in my power on knowing where he is. I am much concerned at your loss of men on your last voyage, but it is a thing to be expected in such vile climates, assisted by the little care sailors in general take of themselves.[21] I am glad, however, the voyage turned out well. I wrote you from the Cape of Good Hope, but it appears you did not receive my letter. It is not unlikely that when on half-pay, as I have a young cousin married to a Mr. C——, who has a house at Edge-hill, but I shall visit Liverpool. If so, and I can spare time, I certainly will come over to your island for the purpose of shaking you by the hand.

"I approve very much of your having purchased an estate. Were I you I would have nearly all the money I possessed invested in the same way; for the times are really so bad that it is scarcely possible to tell whom to trust, and the land cannot run away.

" I wish you every happiness, and beg you to believe me always to be your sincere friend and faithful servant,
"JAMES TOMKINSON."

It gave me great satisfaction to find that so respectable an officer as Mr. Tomkinson admitted we masters in the African trade were not such wretches as commonly represented, but that men of integrity and humanity were to be found on board of Guinea-men, as well as in other lines of life.

About this time I also wrote to many of my friends, and amongst others to my worthy friend Mr. Thomas Aspinall, without, however, noticing the painful subject of my son's death, intelligence of which it appears had reached him from another quarter. He replied in the following kind letter of condolence.

"Rodney-street, Liverpool,
"September 28th, 1812.

"Dear sir—I received your letter dated in August, some time ago, and should, I assure you, have replied to it earlier, but I have been confined now for nearly six months, with one of the severest attacks I have experienced since I came to England. Sincerely sorry was I to hear the accounts of your son's misconduct after all that you had done for him, in getting him fixed in such a situation, that had he behaved, as many young men who entered the naval service under far favourable auspices, he might have, in time, been not only a comfort and blessing to you, but an ornament to his country. But Crow, we must all submit to the will and decrees of Providence. Bad company I have no doubt was the ruin of the young man, as it is the ruin of thousands besides.

"I suppose it must have come to your ears since you wrote to me (as it has to mine) that your son died some time ago at Lisbon. This would no doubt be an additional affliction to you, and on which I sincerely condole with you, as he was an only child, on whom you had doubtless rested your hopes. Your consolation must be, that God orders all things for the best, and you had done every thing that a kind and indulgent father could do, in putting him in the way to do well for himself. Captain Leavy has just returned from Jamaica in the Neptune, a full ship, and sails again for Kingston next month; Higson, who loaded him, was very well as late as the 9th of August, the date of his last letter to me. My brother Will's family are still in the country. Mrs. Aspinall is very unwell through confinement in attending me; she desires to be remembered to you. I remain always, dear sir, your friend and well-wisher,

"THOMAS ASPINALL."

CHAPTER IX

The excellent person who wrote this kind letter, was much respected in Kingston as a merchant and a magistrate. I had long been acquainted with him there, and when he retired from business, I had the pleasure of accompanying him home to England with his family in the Phœnix, Capt. Leavy, and by a further acquaintance, more firmly cemented the friendship that existed between us.

I wrote also to my friend Capt. Warrand, R.N. and his reply, in addition to the kindest condolence on the death of my son, contains an account of the writer's engagement with a French lugger, in the off-hand style of a true sailor, which may be acceptable to the reader. It is as follows :

"H. M. S. Sea Lark, Hamoaze,
"29th August, 1812.

"My dear sir—Your very acceptable letter of the 11th instant is now before me, and I am glad to learn from you that the seed came safely to hand. Many thanks for the good wishes of yourself and all known to me in the isle of Man.

"We certainly had a hard fight; thanks be to God we got so well over it. As you express a wish to know the particulars, which you have not seen in the papers, I will give you the heads :

"When in Stokes's Bay, on the 21st ultimo, a signal was made for an enemy's cruizer in the south-east. We weighed at seven A.M. and chased in that direction. At ten o'clock we saw a lugger, from our mast-head, firing upon two large merchant ships. As soon as he made us out to be a vessel of war he ceased firing, altered his course, and crowded every stitch of sail to avoid us, running about south by east. The wind being west by south we gained on him fast, and I plainly recognized him to be a lugger I had often seen at anchor under the isle of Bass. At two o'clock we gained so considerably upon him that he shifted his lugs, hauled up his ports, showing nine guns on a side, and cleared for action. I was not to be diverted by this manœuvre, and never altered my course until I had him dead to leeward. I then squared for him, so that a few minutes before three I found it necessary to shorten sail. As we neared him, he gave three cheers, hoisted his colours, and poured into us a tremendous broadside with his guns and muskets. The man at our helm was wounded. The helm went hard aport. We quickly shifted it, and run him smack on board abaft the fore-chains, carrying away all his bulwark. The moment we were alongside, we began in our turn to touch him up, which we did really so handsomely, that at half-past-four, having nearly cleared his decks, we boarded him and got possession.

"We have lost seven brave fellows, and among the number, poor Joe, my coxswain. We had twenty-five wounded. Your humble servant lost two of his left-hand fingers. We killed fourteen of the French in the first onset. Four more were killed in boarding, and sixteen wounded. The lugger had, when we commenced action, eighty-five people on board. We had forty-seven men, three boys, and a French pilot. She was a new vessel, only a few months old, with eighteen guns and provisions for a month. So much for our action. "I saw Captain Brown[22] the other day. I knew he had written to you. I sincerely condole with you for the loss of your son, and am certain you will bear it as a man ought. My wife begs to be remembered to you. I wish they would let me have a turn to Ramsey, so that I might show you my craft. If I can be of any service to you here, command me. Let us hear from you often, and believe me to be, yours sincerely,

"THOMAS WARRAND."

In the month of June of the same year I had the honour to be proposed and appointed a member of the House of Keys, in the isle of Man. I however declined the distinguished appointment with suitable acknowledgments, for, after all my trials and hardships, it was my wish to spend the remainder of my life in retirement.

After the melancholy death of my son, I continued to lay off and on, and to wander about seeking to divert my mind from the painful remembrance of that heart-breaking event. One day, while I was on one of these excursions, I fell in with eight poor sailors, who had just been landed in a famishing state from a vessel bound from Bristol to

CHAPTER IX

Greenock. They had been prisoners in France, and wished to return to their native country, but the vessel in which they sailed had fallen short of provisions. I thought it my duty to render them every possible assistance. I represented their case to some friends, and we finally procured a vessel for them, in which, after being refreshed, they sailed for Greenock full of expressions of thankfulness. The gratification of having done our duty to these our fellow creatures in distress was sufficient reward; but these poor fellows carried their gratitude home with them, and published in Scotland a very grateful acknowledgment of the kindness they had met with in my little native island.

Several of these men bad been six or eight years in France, yet nothing was done to procure their exchange, and that of their numerous fellow prisoners, by Mr. Wilberforce and his party. Many hundreds of these white slaves, who were taken fighting to support such great men in luxury and security, consequently perished in misery and want; but this excited little concern in the breasts of our modern reformers, who busied themselves in matters of questionable utility not so near to home.

As I have in the course of my narrative made frequent allusions to the unfortunate slaves; lest my remarks be misconstrued, I owe it to myself, here to disclaim being a friend to slavery. God forbid that I should favour a system through which my fellow creatures should suffer any species of oppression, hardship, or injustice! I consider that the abolitionists have not understood the subject, and that their measures have done nothing towards the real abatement of slave-dealing in Africa. They have in fact as I have before remarked, transferred the whole of the trade into the hands of other nations, who carry it on with extreme cruelty. In the course of my remarks, I have viewed the abstraction of slaves from Africa to our colonies as a necessary evil, under existing circumstances. I may be mistaken on this point; but I am convinced, nevertheless, from what I have observed, that the negro slaves of the West Indies are generally happier there than when they lived as slaves in their own country, subject to the cruelties and caprice of the inland chiefs, and living in a savage state; and, for my own part, were slavery to be my lot, I would rather be a black slave in the West Indies, than a white one at home; for there is no comparison between the comforts of the one and those of the other. Think for instance of the poor fishermen, during the winter season—some of the greatest slaves in existence. Think of the miserable beings employed in our coal-pits, and in our iron, lead and copper mines—toiling under ground in unwholesome air, which is constantly liable to fatal explosions! Think of all the men, women, and children, confined by hundreds, in heated factories, their health rapidly wasting, and their earnings scarce sufficient to keep soul and body together! Think of other slavish employments—often under masters quite as arbitrary and unfeeling as the planters! Think of the thousands who are rotting in jails for petty offences, to which many of them are driven by want and starvation! Think of the thousands that have been imprisoned—ruined—for killing a paltry hare or a partridge! Think of the wretched Irish peasantry! Think of the crowded workhouses—and do not forget to think of poor Jack, who after devoting himself to a life of toil and danger in a vocation to which his country owes much of her prosperity, is dragged by the hair of his head to shed the blood of his fellow creatures at the hazard of his own life; or, perhaps, to wear out an embittered existence in foreign stations, far from those who are nearest and dearest to his affections! Let the reader contrast these things with the general comfortable condition of the negroes in the West Indies, and he will have no difficulty in pronouncing to which side (the black slave or the white) the balance of happiness preponderates.

It is clear, that from the various natures, dispositions, talents and energies of men, there must exist in every society a mixture of rich and poor, and that slavish occupations will necessarily fall to the lot of those who are incapable or undeserving of higher employments. This is a dispensation of that wise Providence that rules over all; and I will in conclusion venture to affirm, while I deplore the fact, that the genuine friends of humanity who are not hoodwinked by prejudice or ignorance, or blinded by selfinterest, will find, that slavery in its essence exists at home as well as abroad.

[IN the following concluding chapters the Editors have availed themselves of some authentic information, obtained from various sources, and particularly from individuals who have been engaged in trading to the coast of Guinea, to amplify some particulars relative to the habits and customs of the natives, upon which the author had but slightly dwelt, as he probably considered them to be more generally known than they are. They have also supplied some remarks to complete the chain of narrative, where it appeared to be slightly broken or abrupt. These additions extend only to facts on which the curiosity of the reader may naturally be excited, and are such as the deceased would probably have supplied, in nearly the same words, had be been questioned by those friends whom he frequently

CHAPTER IX

entertained by his narratives of what he had seen or under-gone. They have, as they anticipated, found his account corroborated by the best published authorities, as well as by private individuals, in such facts as had fallen under their common observation, yet having mixed up, though slightly, with his own remarks those of others, in the following pages, they have not, lest his identity throughout should be implied, placed him in the character of narrator, excepting in those passages which are exclusively his own. It may be added, that our author was often more copious and satisfactory in his remarks, when animated by the fellowship of his associates, than he appears in his manuscripts; and it is to be regretted, that he omitted to note down many of his valuable observations on the negro character and the country.

It is but candid in the Editors here to admit, that they have found themselves unequal to the task of conveying many of the incidents and anecdotes in the preceding pages (and which were but rudely sketched by the author) in the blunt, original, and diverting manner, for which he was considered remarkable; and they have not therefore ventured to introduce several others which are fresh in their recollection, and with which he was wont to entertain his friends.]

CHAPTER X

THERE is perhaps no portion of the civilized world so little known in proportion to its magnitude as the great continent of Africa. With Egypt, and the line of coast bordering on the Mediterranean, we have, from their proximity and state of civilization, obtained considerable acquaintance, as well as of some few settlements on the more southern shores; but of western and central Africa generally, comprising a vast extent of territory, little is known beyond what is derived from the general remarks and conjectures of travellers or voyagers, whose observations and inquiries were, owing to the difficulties they encountered in their progress, necessarily limited and indefinite. Even the termination of the Niger, that noble stream, a large extent of whose course has been traversed by European travellers, and which it has long been anxiously anticipated would, when explored, open a passage for the introduction of commerce and civilization to the heart of ancient Nigritia, remains to be yet definitively ascertained,—although a recent writer[23] (reasoning from the observations of several travellers and the reports received by them, from the natives) urges, with considerable plausibility, that its embouchures are to be found in the several large rivers that discharge themselves into the Bights of Benin and Biafra. To the interior of the western coast few Europeans have penetrated, except by the toilsome and often fatal course of some of the grand rivers; and it may be added that many of the ports of the native kings resorted to by Europeans have been but imperfectly described, those who visit them being generally content to hasten the barter of their commodities with the natives, and to quit a shore which they had only visited for the purpose of immediate gain.

The remarkable deficiency of information on Africa is not, however, to be attributed to any apathy or indifference on the part of European nations; for, the spirit of discovery, which had been dormant during the middle ages, was revived with great enthusiasm in the fifteenth century. The Portuguese were the first to take the lead in despatching expeditions and planting settlements; and they eventually penetrated further than

CHAPTER X

any other moderns (as Robertson informs us) except Park and Browne. The English, French, and Dutch, followed their example; but unhappily numerous obstacles have hitherto checked the progress of discovery, and defeated the object of opening an intercourse with the interior, which might lead to the entire civilization of the country, and elicit its resources by the introduction of commerce. The deserts, "those wild expanses of sand and sky," on the north, the pathless forests on the west, the toilsome navigation of the rivers, where proper supplies cannot always be procured, the barbarous and dangerous tribes, which, interspersed amongst the milder brethren, frequently intercept the course of the traveller, and do him personal violence, or deprive him of the means of proceeding—the want of roads through mountainous and thinly-peopled regions—and above all the fatal effects of the climate upon European constitutions—have confined our settlements to a few spots on the western coast, and have rendered the prosecution of further discoveries an enterprise of much difficulty and danger, if not indeed of desperation.

It were to be lamented, however, if, even with all these acknowledged disadvantages, the intercourse between Europe and Africa should be discouraged. On the contrary, there are warrantable grounds for its extension, and particularly since the abolition amongst our own countrymen of the slave trade. It is undeniable that the productions of Africa are such as would become of primary importance in commerce, if abundantly introduced amongst us, and were the attention of her chiefs drawn to the exclusive cultivation of the soil, civilization and wealth would flow in upon them, while the clearing of the woods, and the operations of husbandry would, in all probability, conduce to purify the air in the unwholesome but fertile countries of the west, and thus remove the chief obstacle to the establishment of European settlements, or colonies in eligible situations. With the extension of commerce would be introduced the arts of polished life—slavery would disappear, and the African states, redeemed from ignorance and superstition, would be enabled to assume their station amongst the civilized nations of the world. To achieve such an object were worthy of the highest efforts of humanity. It would be the redemption not of a single kingdom, but of a whole continent; and it is therefore presumed that any information thrown into the stock already before the public that may tend, though in a slight degree, to bring about a consummation so devoutly to be wished, will be acceptable to the philanthropist, while it may gratify the curiosity of the naturalist, and, at the same time, be of some advantage to those who may direct their mercantile pursuits to that part of the coast of which our author treats.

Vessels bound from England to Benin, Bonny, or Old Calabar, usually make the Canary Islands in the first instance, proceed thence between the Cape de Verde Islands and the main, and, as appears to have been the usual tract of our author, make the land of Cape Palmas, in latitude 4° 4' N.; longitude 7° 26' W. Several voyagers, and particularly Captain Tuckey, who commanded the late unfortunate expedition to explore the Zaire or Congo, caution vessels against the eastward current which sets along the coast of Morocco into the Straits of Gibraltar, and through which, we learn from various accounts, many vessels have been stranded northward of Cape Badajor, and the crews carried into captivity. In January and February, ships are often taken between the Cape de Verde and Benin by the wind called the Hermitan, which blows from the north-east quarter, generally for some days together, and sometimes for a fortnight. As this wind passes over the great desert of Saharra, the atmosphere, during its continuance, is more or less darkened, as if by a haze, by floating particles of impalpable earth or clay, which embrown the decks and sails of vessels, even at a great distance from the shore.

Cape Palmas should be left well to the northward by vessels bound to the leeward coast, as a strong current frequently sets in that direction, and may otherwise retard them in getting round the point. The next high land is that of Drewin. Running eastward, the first town of any importance is Lahoo, which contains about one hundred and twenty houses. The inhabitants have long been known to deal extensively in ivory. This place was visited by Captain Adams, of Liverpool, who gives an interesting picture of its situation and appearance.

Having made known his intention to land, the natives, who seemed much gratified, despatched a canoe to bring him ashore. "I was taken," says he, "to the house of the chief, who treated me with much attention, kindness, and hospitality; but the beautiful tropical picture, which the river at this time presented, would have amply repaid me my trouble, if I had no other cause for being pleased with my journey. This little river, after bending its course from the north to the back of the town, runs to the eastward, a few hundred yards, parallel to the sea shore, and then joins the sea. Its mouth is narrow and choked with hard sand, on which the sea breaks with great violence, so as to render it very dangerous either for boats or canoes to approach its entrance. It was now the dry season; its stream

CHAPTER X

was almost pellucid, and its surface so tranquil that the graceful palms which adorn its banks were reflected from its surface as from a mirror; and a few canoes, in which people were employed fishing, gave animation to the scene. The town formed the foreground, and a cluster of large Ceiba and other trees the screen to this interesting tropical picture. A boundless expanse of ocean placed within a few hundred yards of it, on which I had toiled many years, and a foaming surf rolling in upon the shore, formed a striking contrast to the tranquillity and beauty of the landscape spread out before me, which gave it charms that in my eyes it might not otherwise have had. Men, women, and children accompanied me when I went to view the entrance of the river, and I was much surprised to see many of the females, approaching the adult age, in a state of nudity, as compared with those of their own sex and age living on the Gold Coast, and without seeming at all conscious of the indecency of their appearance."

Proceeding eastward, the chief ports are the Great and Little Bassam, Assinee and Appollonia, from all of which gold and ivory are obtained. The plains of Bambouk, which lie on the north-west of the mountains, in which the Senegal, the Gambia, and the Niger take their rise, are said to furnish the greater quantity of the gold sold on the western coast, and it is also found in the sands of the several rivers and brooks, particularly after heavy rains.

In all the ports on this coast there is now observable amongst the inhabitants a degree of comparative civilization, which it is gratifying to contemplate; and it is to be hoped, that the Africans will every year become further removed from the state of degradation in which they are described by Loyer, who visited Issini (or Assinee) in 1701, and describes them in the following remarkable and somewhat flippant terms: "We meet with kingdoms whose monarchs are peasants, towns that are built of nothing but reeds, sailing vessels formed out of a single tree: where we meet with nations who live without care, speak without rule, transact business without writing, and walk without clothes, people who live partly in the water like fish, and partly in the holes of the earth like worms, which they resemble in nakedness and insensibility."

Passing cape Three Points, the voyager comes to Dixcove, a British fort where the precious metal is also procurable, and of a fine quality. The cove or inlet is navigable for only small vessels. Cape Coast Castle, Amamaboo, Tantum, Winnebah, and Accra, are British forts on the Gold Coast, beyond which, on the east coast, little gold is to be found. The Fantees and Ashantees may be considered as one nation, the former occupying the coast, and the latter the interior. "The women here," says Adams," as well as in most parts of Africa, sow, reap, grind corn, carry wood and water, and perform all the drudgery of housekeeping, while the husbands are, perhaps, gossiping, drinking, or sleeping." No kingdom of western Africa seems to have attained a higher degree of power and civilization than that of Ashantee. The district of Accra contains Aquapim, which is subject to the king of Aquamboe, a powerful prince. Further east is the river Volta, on an island in which Dr. Isert, an indefatigable Dane, attempted to establish a colony; but being opposed by the natives, he removed to the mountains of Aquapim, sixty miles above Accra, and at the same distance west of the Volta, which is navigable to the latitude of the colony. In his letters to his father in 1788, he declares that the natives of Aquapim live in a state of social harmony, which inspired him with the idea of paradisaical happiness, and that the soil yielded the most luxuriant crops with very little labour. This colony and another branching from it continue to prosper. Passing cape St. Paul's, the shores of the kingdom of Dahomy, of which Grewhe is the principal seaport, extend for a considerable way to the eastward. The town of Ardrah, one of the most considerable on the western coast, is situated inland on a lake, and is computed to contain 10,000 inhabitants. The neighbouring country is well cultivated, producing all the necessaries of life in abundance, and many of the valuable plants common to the West Indies, including sugar cane, cotton, indigo, and fruit trees. There and at Eyeo and Jaboo the dye of the indigo is successfully used by the natives. At Ardrah (says Adams) the manufactures of Europe and India are exhibited for sale in the market, and also cloth from Eyeo and Jaboo, spun cotton, kid skins, &c. of native production. The cloth of Eyeo, as well as its articles of iron, he represents as of a quality superior to that of any of the neighbouring states, and he considers the natives a fine race of people. The most considerable town is Lagos, which contains about 5000 inhabitants. It is situated on a river of the same name. The Bight of Benin thence sweeps round to the southward. The Cradoo Lake near its junction with the sea communicates with the Lagos river, which is of no great size, and southward by a creek with the river Formosa. The land between the two rivers is, according to French authorities, intersected by outlets forming numerous islands.

The Formosa is one of the largest rivers that enter the ocean in the Bights of Benin and Biafra, and is considered by M'Queen (whose reasonings, as before stated, are the result of the perusal of several

CHAPTER X

authors) to be one of the embouchures of the Niger. It is not however, according to Adams, above two miles broad at its mouth, with (as is not unfrequent in African rivers) two bars of mud, on which there is a depth of only twelve or thirteen feet of water at spring tides. "This river," says Robertson, "sprouts into innumerable branches, some of which may very well deserve the name of rivers." "To Agatton," he adds, "above 200 miles up, vessels may sail by hundreds of its branches, besides creeks, some of which are very wide. The Portuguese, who had settlements in the interior, state that these intersecting waters communicate with the river Lagos, the Volta, New Calabar, Bonny, and several other rivers. The Formosa runs through a fertile and beautiful country, hence the name, and it is said to bring down innumerable floating islands of considerable extent on its waves. The kingdom of Benin chiefly occupies the northwest of this river; and the capital, which contains about 50,000 inhabitants, lies on a creek branching from it. This country for a considerable distance from the sea is swampy and thickly wooded, and the first dry land is near the town of Gatto on the Benin river, which may be about thirty-five miles from the entrance of the creek. Benin trades in slaves and ivory. The number of blacks exported was at one time very considerable, but the unhealthiness of the climate reduced the trade with the English. The country inland to the northward, between Formosa and Ardrah, rises in a fine gentle ascent, commanding delightful prospects, and is said to be more healthy than the coast. The soil is fertile, and cotton, indigo, and other valuable productions, may be had in abundance.

The streets of Benin are long and broad, so that it covers a considerable extent of ground. The kingdom extends twenty days' journey from north to south, and it claims sovereignty over Bonny and New Calabar. The trade is considerable, and is annually increasing. Many of the people on the shores and creeks are employed in the dry season in making salt, particularly in what is called the Brasspan country, which takes its name from the utensils supplied from Europe for the manufacturing of this article by evaporation from sea-water. The salt and other articles are carried into the interior in large canoes built about Bonny; and Robertson mentions Boussa, on the Niger, as a great mart for this trade, and the place where the people from the seaward meet with the caravans from Barbary to exchange their merchandize.

A remarkable instance of the simplicity of character and good faith of the native African traders is recorded in the description of the gold trade of Timbuctoo and Melli by an Italian named Cadamosto; and which, as it relates to the article of salt, although in the year 1507, may be here briefly introduced to illustrate our author's generally favourable opinion of the African character. He remarks, that at Tegazza, six days' journey inland, there is a quarry of rock salt, quantities of which are every year carried both by camels and men to Timbuctoo, and thence to Melli, a kingdom of negroes, whence it is in great demand not only as a luxury but as a medium to counteract the effects of the excessive heat of the blood. They carry it to a great water, which our author concludes to be a river, because if it were the sea there would be no need of salt. "Having reached this water, they observe the following method: all those who have the salt make piles of it in a row, each marking his own, and having made the said piles, they all turn back; then comes another generation of negroes, who do not wish to let themselves be seen or spoken to. They come with large barks that appear to issue from certain islands and land, and having seen the salt, place a quantity of gold opposite to each pile, and then return, leaving the gold and salt; and when they are gone, the salt negroes come, and, if the quantity of gold please them, take the gold and leave the salt: in this manner they make their trade without seeing each other, by a long and ancient custom : and though it appears a hard thing to believe, I certify having had this information from many merchants, Arabs, and Azanaghi, and likewise from persons worthy of credit."

The medium of exchange at Benin is salt. The land in the neighbourhood is fertile, but, like most of this line of coast, little cultivated, and from its marshy nature unwholesome to Europeans. Warré, the capital of a kingdom on the Formosa, south of Benin, is situated on a beautiful small island, a little elevated above the surrounding low country. A considerable trade is here carried on with Bonny and New Calabar, the branches of rivers, or creeks, which intersect the country affording communications for canoes. The Portuguese here laudably attempted for many years, as at other places on the coast, to establish the Christian faith, but with little success. Captain Adams was surprised to find amongst them several emblems of the Catholic religion, consisting of crucifixes, mutilated figures of saints, &c. The building in which the missionaries officiated was still standing unmolested, but unused, and a wooden cross was observed at the crossing of two roads. It did not appear, however, that they had succeeded in making proselytes; King Otoo's subjects appeared to trouble themselves very little about religion of any kind. The king of Benin and his retinue are sumptuously clad in damask, taffety, &c. after their peculiar fashion, and the people are represented as neat and ornamental in their dresses. On occasions of festivity, the men wear a sort of robe of calico, the women's necks are adorned with coral, and their arms, and often their legs, encircled with rings of burnished brass or iron. On common occasions they merely wear their paan, or sash, which serves for drawers. During the annual inundations, which take place at Benin and the adjacent coast, the Formosa overflows its banks from Gatto to the sea, covering an extent of territory of forty miles in breadth. Between that river and cape Formosa are the mouths of the Forcados, another large river, and several other streams. Rounding the cape six considerables rivers are distinguishable between it and the estuary of the New Calabar and Bonny rivers.

The town of Bonny is situated on a small island formed by the junction of the river Bonny, or Bannee, and the Andovy, or St. Anthony's, by a branch or creek near their mouths, and may be said to be a portion of that low line of coast between the Bight of Benin and that of Biafra, and which, intersected by numerous rivers and lakes, runs almost east and west from cape Formosa to the mouth of the Old Calabar. The Bonny and the New Calabar rivers form, at one place, a common estuary of eleven miles in breadth. This estuary bounds the island on the west, and it is washed on the south by the Atlantic Ocean, which generally rolls in with great violence along the whole of the coast of Guinea, rendering the passage of the several bars of the rivers difficult and dangerous. The island of Bonny may be fourteen or fifteen miles long; another writer[24] makes it about twentyfive miles long, and twelve broad; but our author, who was a practical man, may be depended upon. The island is low, and full of swamps and marshes; the whole coast indeed is composed of alluvial, soil, which appears to be the deposit of ages from the large streams whose embouchures are found between Cradoo lake and the river Del Rey, eastward of Calabar. These rivers are about twenty in number, and their united breadth at their embouchures it is computed would exceed forty miles. Three of these alone would, according to M'Queen, make a breadth of water of twenty-seven miles; but admitting some exaggeration in one whose object it is to prove them to be embouchures of the Niger, they are extensive streams. The opinion, that the land is alluvial, is strengthened by the fact that, in some places, it is known to have gained upon the sea,[25] and that places near the mouth of the Bonny, which were observed to be stagnant pools some years ago, have become dry and arable. The circumstance of inundations, annually spreading over a great part of the low country, affords a further confirmation of this assumption, and the unwholesomeness of the air on those coasts is easily assignable to the exhalations from the marshy and humid soil, and the vegetable decomposition maintained by a tropical sun in a country so densely wooded that the verdure may be said to attain a rank luxuriance. The current out of the mouth of the Bonny and Calabar rivers is considerable, and some have asserted that they discharge as much water as the Congo.

The town of Bonny is about six or seven miles from the sea, and lies on the north-west of the island. Here the river is fine and spacious, being two miles broad, and of sufficient depth for vessels of a large tonnage. By vessels from Europe the shore may be kept on board all the way from cape Formosa to the embouchure of this river; between Foché Point on the west, and Rough Corner on the east, it is six or seven miles in width. The vessels usually anchor about half a mile from the shore, near the narrow water or creek, between the two rivers that insulate Bonny from the main land; and there they find good holding ground in about thirteen fathoms water.

The town, which lies on the right bank going up, is built, like most of the native towns on the west of Africa, without any regard to regularity or design. The streets run in zig-zag confusion mingled with trees; and being narrow, and without any sort of pavement or gravel, they become, in the rainy season, wet and miry to such a degree, that they are scarcely passable. The island, indeed, is sometimes partly flooded during the periodical inundations.

The houses, in accordance with the perplexing crooks and turns in the streets, are built, according to the wealth and humour of the parties who inhabit them, of all sizes and a plentiful variety of shapes, some being round, others rectangular, &c. These habitations, which may properly fall under the name of huts or wigwams, are about six or seven feet high. They are constructed, not even the king's houses excepted, by driving stakes into the ground, which constitute the frame-work. These are crossed with bamboo canes, which are afterwards roughly plastered with a kind of brown clay, which bakes in the heat to a considerable hardness. They are covered in with palm-tree leaves and bamboo, stitched and matted together, which form a good thatch, resembling that of our old-fashioned country cottages. The sizes of the houses are of course regulated by the respectability of the parties who own them; but this circumstance, in one

CHAPTER X

remarkable respect, here and in other towns on the Guinea coast, resolves itself chiefly into the number of houses which the owner can tenant with females; for polygamy being here practised, the more wives a man can reckon, the more he is esteemed; and as it is a municipal regulation that he shall provide a separate house for each on her marriage, those of the middle class have two or three distinctly domiciled; and a person of standing is frequently himself the owner of a little district peopled by his own numerous family. The furniture of these dwellings comports with their simplicity. A few calabashes, some earthen culinary utensils of home manufacture, a wooden mortar or two, and a few mats, together with their fetiches, or charms, (of which more here-after) constitute the general stock of the poorer classes, to which the better off add some homely articles introduced from Europe, to the uses of which they but slowly yield themselves, as they consider them (so confirmed are they in their own habits) as luxuries of a rather incommodious kind, although they are proud of possessing them. It may, however, be remarked, that here, as well as at New and Old Calabar, many improvements have taken place in the dwellings and manners of the inhabitants, amongst whom reading, writing, and many of the arts of civilized life have been partially introduced, and retained for the purposes of trade.

The inhabitants of Bonny, when our author last visited that port, amounted to about 3,000. They are chiefly a mixture of the Eboe, or Heebo, and the Brass tribes; the latter deriving their name from the importation into their country, which lies to the northward and westward of Bonny, of a kind of European-made brass pans, known in the trade by the name of neptunes, and used for the making of palm oil and salt, with which last the countries in the interior have been supplied by the coast from the earliest times on record. The article is now largely imported from Liverpool, both to Bonny and Calabar. The Eboes, who are also from a neighbouring country, have already been spoken of as a superior race, and the inhabitants, generally, are a fair dealing people, and much inclined to a friendly traffic with Europeans, who humour their peculiarities. Their general honesty, when the loose nature of their laws, as respects Europeans, and the almost entire absence of the moral influence of religion amongst them, are considered, affords a favourable prognostic of what the negro character would be if placed under the restraints and precepts of an enlightened system of jurisdiction.

It is probable (and this opinion is entertained by Captain Adams and others) that Bonny, and the towns on the low line of the coast on either side of it were originally peopled from the Eboe country, and that before the commencement of the slave trade, if it then existed; the inhabitants employed themselves in the making of salt, by evaporation from sea water. The country, says Adams, for many miles into the interior is "a vast morass, heavily timbered, and unfit, without excessive labour, to produce sufficient food for a very scanty population; and as the trade in slaves increased, these towns, particularly Bonny, grew into importance. The king of New Calabar, in the neighbourhood, and Pepple, king of Bonny, were both of Eboe descent, of which also are the mass of the natives; and the number of the slaves from the Eboe country, which, throughout the existence of the British trade were taken from Bonny, amounted to perhaps three-fourths of the whole export. It is calculated that no fewer than 16,000 of these people alone were annually exported from Bonny within the twenty years ending in 1820; so that, including 50,000 taken within the same period from New and Old Calabar, the aggregate export of Eboes alone was not short of 370,000."

The Eboes, tho' not generally a robust, are a well-formed people, of the middle stature: many of their women are of remarkably symmetrical shape, and if white, would in Europe be deemed beautiful. This race is, as has been already remarked, of a more mild and engaging disposition than the other tribes, particularly the Quaws, and though less suited for the severe manual labour of the field, they are preferred in the West India colonies for their fidelity and utility, as domestic servants, particularly if taken there when young, as they then become the most industrious of any of the tribes taken to the colonies. Their skin is generally of a yellowish tinge, but varying to a jet black; of the same tribe, and speaking the same language, are the Brechés, so called from the word Breehé, signifying gentleman, or, like Hidalgo in Spanish, son of a gentleman. As these had seen better days, and were more liable than their countrymen, who are inclined to despond when sent on board ship, to take some desperate means of relieving themselves, and encouraging others to shake off their bondage, the masters of the slave ships were generally averse to purchasing them. The Breehés informed us, that in their country every seventh child of their class, when about six or seven years of age, undergoes the operation, to distinguish its rank, of having the skin of the forehead brought down from the hair, so as to form a ridge or line from temple to temple. This disfigurement gives them a very disagreeable appearance, and the custom

CHAPTER X

is chiefly confined to the sons of great men, and our author never saw but one female so marked. But the Eboes and Brechés are tatooed with their country and family marks. The national tatoo of the commonalty consists of small thickly placed perpendicular incisions, or cuts on each temple, as if done with a cupping apparatus. These people are kind and inoffensive in their manners, but so fearful of the whites when first brought amongst them, that they imagine they are to be eaten by them; and while under this impression they would sometimes attempt to jump overboard, or destroy themselves in some other way, so that it was necessary to watch them narrowly. Their apprehensions, however, were to be overcome by mild treatment, and they soon became reconciled to their lot. Their mutual affection is unbounded, and, says our author, I have seen them, when their allowance happened to be short, divide the last morsel of meat amongst each other thread by thread.

Besides the Eboes and Brechés, we received at Bonny negroes of several other nations, named Quaws, Appas, Ottams, and Brasses. The Quaws, (or Moscoes of the West Indies) are an ill-disposed people, whom the Eboes regard with great aversion, as they consider them cannibals in their own country; an assumption which their desperate and ferocious looks would seem to warrant. Their skins are blacker than those of the Eboes, and their teeth are sharpened with files, so as to resemble those of a saw. These men were ever the foremost in any mischief or insurrection amongst the slaves, and from time to time many whites fell victims to their fury at Bonny. They are mortal enemies to the Eboes, of whom, such is their masculine superiority, and desperate courage, they would beat three times their own number. The slave ships were always obliged to provide separate rooms for these men between decks, and the captains were careful to have as few of them as possible amongst their cargoes.

The females of this tribe are fully as ferocious and vindictive as the men.

The Appas are a race of people so slothfully inclined, that they trust for a subsistence to the spontaneous productions of the earth, and rather than betake themselves to cultivation, will even eat grass and soil. The few of them whom our author knew were extremely indolent in their habits; and probably owing to this, and the coarseness of their usual food, their flesh was loose and soft, and their bodies feeble. They are however of a harmless disposition, and the Eboes take a great delight in tantalizing them.

The Ottam tribe are stout and robust, and of a deeper black than any of the other tribes at Bonny. Their bodies and faces are carved and tatooed in a frightful manner; they seem nevertheless to be a well-disposed good-tempered race, and are much liked by the Eboes. Besides these we sometimes got a few natives of Benin, which is about 160 or 170 miles from Bonny. These resemble the Eboes, and it is probable were partly of the same nation. They are the most orderly and well-behaved of all the blacks. In their own country they are famous for the manufacture of a beautiful sort of table-cloth.

"I will here," says our author, "state the price which we usually gave for a single negro at Bonny, because I believe that two-thirds of the people of England thought we stole them, or got them for nothing.

"Paid for a negro man at Bonny in 1801 :—
One piece of chintz, eighteen yards long;
One piece of baft, eighteen yards long;
One piece of chilloe, eighteen yards long;
One piece of bandanoe, seven handkerchiefs;
One piece of neccanee, fourteen yards long;
One piece of cashtoe, fourteen yards long;
One piece of photoe, fourteen yards long;
Three pieces of ramatts, forty-five handkerchiefs;
One large brass pan, two muskets;
Twenty-five kegs of powder, one hundred flints;
Two bags of shots, twenty knives;
Four iron pots, four hats, four caps;
Four cutlasses, six bunches of beads, fourteen gallons of brandy.

"These articles cost about £25, so that the reader will see we did not procure negroes (as many have supposed) for nothing.

"Next to the king, the priests of Bonny exercise an almost arbitrary power over the people. Indeed they sometimes appeared to pay very little respect to their royal masters; as the following instance of their impudent intrusion will testify. One day, as I was dining with king Holiday, a number of priests rushed in just as we had taken our seats, and before we had time to look about us, they swept every thing off the table. The decks could not have been more quickly cleared by a magician. Here a scuffle took place between them and me; for the king, such are their customs, could not, or durst not, meddle with them, and, for myself, I was unwilling to relinquish my share of the feast without resistance. I accordingly commenced action, and after a hard battle succeeded in beating them off, and regaining a portion of the spoil. Although I handled them rather roughly, such was

CHAPTER X

the favour in which I stood amongst them, that they never offered to revenge themselves upon me for my reprisal."

The manners and customs of the inhabitants of Bonny, as well as their religion, (which is a sort of Polytheism) resemble those of the different nations along the coast of Guinea. Our author was led to think that they believe that there is a God attached to every tribe, and that there is a Supreme Being, who rules over all. In this opinion he is confirmed by all the travellers who have visited the country. One writer (Leyden) assumes, that in order to fix their ideas of a true deity, they require some definite figure, and generally invest him with human form, as being the most perfect. This assumption is not however to be considered as of universal application; for Bosman, who was a strict observer of the negro character, remarks, with allusion to their fetiches, (that is, their charms or idols) "It is really the more to be lamented, that the negroes idolize such worthless nothings, by reason that many amongst them have no very unjust idea of the Deity, for they ascribe to God the attributes of omnipresence, omniscience, omnipotence, and invisibility, besides which they believe that he governs things by providence. By reason that God is invisible, they say it would be absurd to make any corporeal representation of him; for it is impossible to make any image of what we never saw; therefore they have such multitudes of images for their idol gods, which they take to be subordinate deities to the supreme God, without considering what sort of trifles they are, and only believe they are mediatory between God and men. They know enough of the devil to call all that is evil by that name, and believe themselves obliged to worship and serve him to prevent him from mischieving them." The Africans are also believers in two principles, the evil and the good; but their notions on the subject are crude and inconsistent. They seem originally to have represented their good deity as black; but they have been told, that this black deity is the devil of the whites, and essentially evil, and they now frequently conceive the good one to be white. A tradition is also extant amongst them, that the Great Being in the beginning having created black and white men, gave the former the choice of two gifts, gold and the knowledge of the arts and sciences; the blacks having chosen the gold, and left learning to the whites, He, offended at their avarice, condemned them to be slaves. They have various opinions of the creation of man; for besides those who ascribe his origin to the Deity, there are others who attribute his formation to the *Anæsie*, an enormous spider,[26] and others entertain the scarcely less ridiculous notion that he emerged from caves and holes in the earth.

Our author, the subject of these memoirs, was further of opinion, that the negroes of the western coast believe themselves endowed with a spirit or soul, and that every one after death shall be punished by an evil spirit, according to his crimes in this world. The notion, however, of a future state is not universal, for some avowedly obey their chiefs and their priests, never troubling themselves about what is above them. "Not a few," according to Dr. Leyden, "suppose the deceased are immediately conveyed to a famous river, named Bosmanque, in the interior of Africa, where their deity examines their past lives, and enquires whether they have observed their religious festivals, abstained from forbidden food, and kept their oaths inviolably ? If the result of this be favourable, they are gently wafted over the river, to a land of pure happiness, resembling the Paradise of Mahomet; if unfavourable, the deity plunges them into the river, where they are drowned, and buried in eternal oblivion. This is obviously an imperfect representation of the Mahometan doctrine." The belief in ghosts is common, and the supposition that the unexpiated crimes of the deceased cause their souls to wander after death. Others believe in the transmigration of souls, and the idea, that after death they shall for their crimes be made to inhabit the bodies of animals, and particularly that of the monkey or ape, fills them with frequent apprehension. The existence of this notion receives some confirmation from the assertion of Bosman, that they believe that apes could speak if they chose, but that they wisely remain silent lest they should be domesticated and put to work, to which they have an utter aversion. Whatever influence such terrors, however, might otherwise have on their moral conduct is neutralized by their erroneous conceptions of good and evil; for while their human sacrifices, their cold-blooded executions, their cruel wars, and their vending of their fellow-beings, continue to be considered just and proper, or to be regarded, from familiarity, without abhorrence, these barbarities will continue to be practised without pity or remorse.

Amongst the whole population of Western Africa the worship of idols, or rather the belief in charms, is general. To whatever is chosen, whether animate or inanimate, for this purpose, is given the name of *fetiche*, a corruption of the Portuguese word feitisso or feitico, signifying a charm, magic, witchcraft, &c., and known in the West Indies as the Obi of the Africans. These are not, according to Loyer, worshipped as Deities, but regarded merely as charms. The devotees are directed in their

CHAPTER X

choice of these fetiches solely by their own caprice or fancy, or by the advice of their fetisseros, or priests. In honor of these idols or charms, they deprive themselves of some pleasure, commonly abstaining from some particular food or drink; and this custom of fasting has induced some writers to believe that the Catholic faith would be more likely to gain ground amongst them than any other Christian persuasion. Every one has his fetiche, and many a considerable number. Some choose the tooth of a dog, tiger, or civet cat, an egg, or a bone of a bird; others select a piece of wood, a branch of a tree, the head of a goat or parrot. In fine, as stated by the ill-fated Captain Tuckey, "any thing vile serves for a fetiche, the horn, hoof, heads and skins of snakes,[27] shells and fins, pieces of old iron, copper, wood, seeds of plants, or a mixture of all." A plate of one of these fetiches, seen by Captain Tuckey, appears in the volume quoted. It represents an European padlock, in the iron of which they had contrived to bury a cowrie, shell, and various other matters. The bill of a bird, and the head of a snake, appear as if caught between the outside edges of the two plates that form the front and back of the lock. The whole is suspended to a necklace or rosary composed of a sort of bean intermixed with smaller seeds. Such a fetiche is considered a protection against thunder and lightning, the attacks of wild animals, and other evils. Should the possessor be unsuccessful in the desired object, or some misfortune befal him, the failure is attributed to the weakness of the fetiche, and he has recourse to another, or applies to the priest for one more powerful. Should the wearer, in spite of his protecting fetiche, or talisman, be devoured, the calamity is, by others, ascribed to his having given it some offence.

Besides these private or household fetiches, there are others, whose influence extends over whole nations or tribes. These are frequently mountains, rocks, trees, rivers, or lakes, but more frequently animals and reptiles. The Widanese, who believe in one supreme God, worship a species of serpent, of a large size, as the most powerful fetiche. The idol of the Dahomians is the leopard; that of Popo the alligator. The people of New Calabar worship the shark; the Lagos people, the canine race; and the natives of Bonny, as before noticed, the iguana, a sort of large lizard. It is remarkable, that these tribes evince their religious animosities, one to the other, by devouring each other's animal fetiches. Thus at Benin, the iguana is devoured; at Old Calabar, the dog; on the Fantee coast, the shark; yet neither the difference of religious opinions amongst these tribes, nor these reciprocal affronts, appear to excite them to fight, although they are fond of war. In Bonny the natives attach the greatest confidence to their fetiches, believing that they not only protect and direct them, but that they animate them to fight, with greater courage, and they therefore carry them with them when about to face any danger. Their chiefs, in particular, when going to war, carry several of these about their persons, believing that they are thus rendered invincible in battle. These baubles are, our author thought, purchased at a dear rate from the priests, who cunningly keep alive these superstitious hopes and fears of the populace for the purposes of gain. The people will sometimes talk to their fetiches with great earnestness, and touch themselves with them on various parts of the body, for they believe that they see and watch all their actions.

In Tuckey's journal there is a brief description of a fetiche rock, accompanied by a fine engraving. This rock rises abruptly from the river Congo, and has a romantic appearance, being partly bare, and precipitous, and partly covered with trees and verdure. On the face of it, on one side, are a number of figures or emblems, formed apparently of sand and ashes laid on wet, and which being indurated appear like stone sculpture, and at a little distance, judging from the plate, not unlike Egyptian hieroglyphics. On examination, some of them are evidently representations, of the rudest description, of gentlemen borne by their slaves, men shooting birds, or killing alligators, &c.; but the subject of some of them it was found impossible to define. "One day some of the persons of the expedition showed to one of the chief men a magnet; upon which, the latter (who probably understood the use of the mariner's compass) remarked it was very bad fetiche for black man. He was (says the narrator) too lively, and had too much savey." When any thing is stolen, it is not unusual on the Coast of Guinea and Congo for the priest to hang up a fetiche in the market place, with a view to detect the thief. If the offender do not come voluntarily forward, make restitution, and purchase a pardon, the populace is summoned, and the trial or test called bolongo is put in practice upon those whom the priests chose to suspect. This consists in causing the suspected person to drink the prepared juice of certain herbs, which, if he be innocent, proves harmless; but if guilty, produces faintings, convulsions, and death. There can be little doubt, as Merolla remarks, but the priest modifies the draught according to his good or ill will to the individual under trial. Captain Tuckey remarks, that one of his coolies, a fine strong young man, was supposed to be poisoned at this barbarous ordeal, merely that the fetiche might have its effects. In this

CHAPTER X

manner the most wanton murders may be committed; but though our author witnessed several human sacrifices at Bonny, it does not appear that this mode of trial was put into practice during his stay on the island.

There are, says our author, two high priests, who reside near Bonny. One of them occupies a small village, called Jue Jue Town, three or four miles from the capital. The great Jue Jue Man, as he is called, is invested with the care of the great idol, the iguana, commonly called the guana. The second grand Jue Jue Man lives at a place called Fish Town, between three and four miles from Bonny, on the opposite side of the river. There the tiger is worshipped as the chief idol, and the priests there affirm that one of these animals comes into the town every night and sleeps till morning in a house in which they perform their ceremonies, called the Jue Jue house; at which time he will not offer to molest any one, young or old. This assertion is nothing, in my opinion, but a contrivance of the priests to keep the people in awe of their authority and power. It is however of some moral effect, for the fear it produces operates on the people instead of a police, so that very few thefts are committed amongst them. These Jue Jue Men, the high priests, by these and other devices, hold the populace in the most absolute awe and subjection : such, indeed, is their influence, that they will even persuade them they can arrest the flowing of the tide.

Fish Town has the privilege of being considered a sanctuary for those who are in danger, whether of high or low degree. When king Pepple (since dead) and Holiday disagreed, I have known the latter, who was the weaker party, obliged to fly with his friends to Fish Town for protection, and there remain until the dispute was adjusted by the intervention of the priests. The Bonnians have likewise a priest of some consequence at Peterside, or Trade-bays Town, two or three miles above Bonny, on the opposite side of the river. Here also they worship the tiger. Although I have been in both places, I never saw that animal, nor any one like it; and I am led to believe, that the crafty priests, to give a colouring to their assertions, train up boys to imitate tigers, by dressing them in skins; and occasionally permit them to be imperfectly seen in the twilight, thus to keep the people in awe during the night.

The iguana is, as a matter of course, treated with great respect at Bonny, no one being suffered to molest it. It is about four or five feet long, and resembles the lizard in shape, but is of a less agreeable colour, and has a long forked tongue, which it shoots out, two or three inches at every step it takes in walking about the streets, so that its appearance is very formidable, although it is perfectly innoxious. The greatest care is taken of them by the priests, and a house of rest is built and kept in order for them in the town. Their weapon is their tail, with which they will knock down poultry and small animals with ease, and afterwards devour them, no one daring to interfere with or molest them. They swim remarkably well. "I happened one day," continues our author, "to pick up a guana that was making its way across the river, and sent it carefully on shore in a clean cloth. As soon as this circumstance became known the whole town was in a state of commotion, and the people united in thanking me for my attention to their idol. The young females of the town actually composed a song in my praise on the occasion, which they sung strewing flowers in the streets as they preceded me." The abstinence occasionally observed out of respect for their fetiches has been already noticed, and our author thus records a singular instance of penance in one of their kings. "I one day saw king Holiday under the influence of deep remorse, arising out of some breach of religious duty. He had permitted his beard to grow for some time, and after shaving his head and face, a mixture was made by the priests of something resembling fine earth and water, with which they besmeared him all over.[28] He then lay for some time prostrate on the ground, lamenting and moaning grievously, as if doing penance. Indeed, I have reason to think the practice of doing penance is not uncommon amongst them. It is usual, also, by way of atonement, to hang up a dog by the hind legs[29] on a pole, and in this situation the poor animal hangs until death relieves him from his sufferings. On other occasions a brace of fowls are suspended with the same view. It is also their custom, once a year, to make an offering of a great number of fowls to their gods. When the time of offering approaches, the country people bring in great numbers of fowls, which, with certain ceremonies, are tied by the feet, and deposited in a thicket about three miles below the town. We generally contrived to save their gods the trouble of carrying off these fowls, by securing them for our own coppers on board, and, strange as it may appear, we were suffered to do so with impunity, so that it would not have grieved us had they made such offerings every day in the year."

CHAPTER XI

THE kings of Bonny (there were two during our author's intercourse with the natives) although in many respects they appeared to exercise an absolute power, unrestrained by any fixed principles, may be properly termed the heads of an aristocratic government. This is evinced by their having a grand Palaver-house, in which they themselves presided, but the members of which, composed of the chiefs or great men, were convened and consulted on all matters of state emergency, and sometimes (as appears in the case of the illness of king Holiday's wife) in matters relating to the domestic affairs of the kings themselves. The government, indeed, may be said to combine three estates, the kings, the great men, and the feticheros, or priests; the last being probably considered as instruments of popular subjection, whose influence over the people the two first consider it politic to tolerate, if not to encourage. In some of the great kingdoms of the in terior, as Ashantee, Aquambo, and Dahomy, the kings are absolute; but at Bonny, and many other parts of the coast, the monarchs appear to hold a very mild and popular sway over their subjects; and whatever we find of apparent cruelty or barbarity in their conduct, or that of their head men, is attributable not to any wanton or uncontrolled indulgence in a savage disposition, but to an accordance with those superstitious customs and ceremonies, sometimes ridiculous, and often horrible in the eyes of Europeans, which they have been taught, in common with their countrymen, to consider as fit and necessary either for the purposes of justice, or the conciliation of their gods.

The revenues of the kings are derived from the duties on shipping and trade, contributions drawn from their subjects of all necessaries for their household, fines adjudged in criminal and civil cases, presents from Europeans, and from other less honorable sources. When paying for the negroes (says our author) the kings are sure to have two men on board to take the customs from the traders, which amounts to the tenth part, or "bar," as they call it. Besides the usual payment for firewood, water, yams, palm oil, and even for burying ground, whether we made use of it or not, we were obliged to pay customs' duties on all these. With respect to the slaves, we had to pay for them a second time, for after the payment of the first purchase-money, we were called upon to pay what were called "work bars," a few days before the vessel sailed.

The body dress of the kings consists of shirts and trowsers, and like all the kings on the coast, they generally wear gold-laced hats. They are attended, when they board a ship, by a large retinue of servants, one of whom carries a gold-headed cane, which, when sent off to a vessel by the king, serves as a note, or authority, when he is in want of any thing. "It is rather singular," says our author, "that although the two chiefs, Pepple and Holiday, were relations and copartners in the throne, they could never agree : and I do not recollect having ever seen them together on board of any ship. Pepple was the superior, and maintained the ascendant over Holiday in a high degree." Their houses were only distinguished from those of their subjects by their being somewhat larger, detached, and more numerous, and being furnished in a superior manner, as many articles are imported for them from Europe. Bonny has long been celebrated for the size and construction of her canoes; and those of the king deserve notice. They are formed out of a single log of the capot, a species of cotton tree, which attains so enormous a size, that it is said that one was seen at Akim, which ten men could scarcely grasp. The canoes in general use, have about fifteen paddles on a side; but those of the king, which are superior vessels of the sort, carry, besides the rowers, as many as a hundred and fifty warriors, well furnished with small arms. They have also a long nine-pounder at each end of the canoe; and when they are equipped for war, with drums beating, horns blowing, and colours flying, they make a very dashing and formidable appearance. The kings often take excursions in their canoes, attended by about thirty stout men paddling, and a steersman. Several others are employed in playing some musical instrument, while others dance in the middle of the canoe. The rowers keep admirable time with their paddles, so that they drive through the water at a rapid rate, and appear to great advantage. Whenever king Pepple came off in his state canoe to the ship, all the traders, rich and poor, precipitately betook themselves to their canoes; and, on his coming on board, we always manned the side, and hoisted the colours.

Our author was not perhaps aware that Bonny owes its sovereignty

CHAPTER XI

to Benin, otherwise he would naturally have attributed the visit, which he records in the following passage, to that circumstance. " While I lay," he remarks, "at Bonny, on my last voyage, two large canoes arrived from Benin, full of presents, consisting of the manufactures and produce of the country, and with these came two remarkably fine looking men of from thirty to forty years of age, well formed, and about six feet high. Their look and manner were of a superior order, and they walked in a majestic style, followed by a retinue, of servants. They were robed in a loose flowing dress; I found they spoke pretty good English, and I conversed with them on several occasions, particularly on the subject of the slave trade. They expressed their conviction that so long as there were lands to cultivate, and seas for ships to sail on, slavery would continue to exist. These men were near relations of king Pepple, and had been sent to Bonny, as ambassadors by the king of Benin. They remained about a month feasting in their way, and then returned with their large canoes laden with presents. I never met with any black princes so sensible and well-informed as these men, or who had so noble and commanding an appearance."

The men and women at Bonny dress much alike, and with more simplicity than decorum. A piece of cloth is, in their way, invariably tied round the waist. This is rolled up in a small compass, and made fast, so that it hangs from the naval downwards, covering the legs half way. The chiefs' wives have sometimes five, six, or more pieces of different kinds of cloth tied about them, especially when going to any of their festivals, so that the body looks like a roll, or truss of yarn, tied at both ends. On these occasions the ladies always use paint, daubing their faces in a remarkable manner. They also make up their hair to a great height above their heads, and show by the use of various ornaments, that they are not altogether ignorant of the arts of the toilette. Both men and women are represented as cleanly, and fond of bathing and washing; but the heat, and the use of palm oil as a cosmetic, give them a rather disagreeable odour. They are extremely fond of any thing gaudy or uncommon amongst them in dress, and if they get hold of a showy article of European clothing, such as a coat or vest, will strut about in it with all imaginable consequence, as if it constituted an entire suit. A ludicrous example has been furnished by our author of this taste in king Pepple, with his red morocco boots; and captain Adams gives a droll account of some negroes at Majumba, on the more southern coast, on whom an English captain had practised a joke. "On landing," says he, "we were not a little surprized and amused at the grotesque figures which many of the natives made, who had on their heads large wigs, made apparently of the bristles of pigs, not a hair of which had a curve in it, and at the extremity of each stood a dew-drop, (for it was a misling rain) with now and then a dash of sunshine. At this time the wigs made a very brilliant appearance; they were of all colours, though red and white were the predominant ones, which, contrasted with the black visages and naked bodies of the wearers, gave them a most ludicrous appearance."

The inhabitants of Bonny, like their brethren along the coast, do not appear to have formed any notion of the resources their country is capable of, if elicited by art and industry. In this respect they are like children, who, having fallen upon a mine, pick up the bits of glittering ore on the surface, without thinking of the treasures that may be below. The greater portion of what they derive from the soil is the spontaneous gift of nature; and so little do they turn their attention to husbandry, that if the crops on the small spots of land near their towns, into which they have rudely cast their seeds, and the wild fruits chance to fall short, they are frequently exposed to such privations that many of them sell themselves as slaves to their more fortunate or more provident neighbours or chiefs, in order to save themselves from starvation. All this might be obviated with a little industry and economy. The negroes are of quick apprehension, of good memories, robust in person, and capable of enduring great bodily labour and fatigue; but their want of a knowledge of the comforts and elegancies of life, and their consequent indifference to make any effort to obtain them, together with the probable influence of the climate, which disinclines them for any exertion beyond that of pleasurable exercise, present a bar to their melioration which it may be difficult to surmount. Where there is much idleness there must be much sensuality, and the negro freely indulges in those desires which indolence and a state of nature cannot fail to produce. He is immoderately addicted to women, and Europeans have taught him to be a lover of intoxicating spirits. He moreover yields himself to the superstitious notions of his priests. Notwithstanding all this barbarity is not so characteristic of the negroes as gentleness and docility, several instances of which our author has adduced, and his opinion accords with the generality of those writers, who have visited the coast. The state of society in Africa does not arise from any peculiarity in the race, but from the situations in which the natives are placed, their want of those advantages which more favoured countries enjoy, and other causes that

CHAPTER XI

operate upon the human mind. To dispel the tedium of inertion, they have recourse to amusements, and spend the greater part of their time in ceremonies, feasting, dancing, and celebrations. Murray, with reference to the character of the inhabitants of those regions, remarks, "Improvidence, gentleness, and the abandon of thoughtless gaiety, appear to compose the leading features of the negro character. In a fertile soil which supplies the necessaries of life with little labour, with few natural wants, and strangers to artificial ones, they devote themselves wholly to pleasure. Music and dancing are indulged in with passion throughout all native Africa." "From the period of sunset," says Golbery, " all Africa dances."

The principal employments of the men of Bonny are fishing, navigating the rivers inland, in the prosecution of trade, hunting wild animals, or procuring palm-wine, &c. in the forests, while the more wealthy are engaged in trafficking with the Europeans. The principal labour of the fields, as well as the entire management and duties of their household affairs, entirely devolve upon their wives. They have no knowledge of the plough, nor do they attempt to apply the services of animals to any machine for the cultivation of the soil. The hand, aided by the rudest implements, is the only power employed, and the crops they receive in return for so small a quantum of labour and skill is an ample proof of the fertility of the soil, which is not however generally so productive as that of the windward coast, Sierra Leone, and Cameroons, owing probably to the admixture of sand in the alluvial soil. On occasion of planting the yam, which is a principal article of food, and also when it is dug up, a grand ceremony is performed, intended as an expression of thankfulness to Providence for its bountiful supply of the fruits of the earth. Amusement is however the principal business of life, and dancing is the most popular recreation after the heat of the day. Their dances are attended by young and old, who enter alike into the spirit of the entertainment, and strive to outvie each other in those laborious motions and postures of the limbs and body, which in their eyes constitute the excellence of the art, and which are more expressive, if not so delicate as those exhibited in our English ballrooms. Their dancing requires much muscular strength, particularly in the knees, for when the dancer stoops the knees are required to be kept in perpetual motion. Their music in Bonny, says our author, is extremely simple: two or three men, musical amateurs, sit on the ground, and with a small stick in each hand beat time on three small billets of wood laid across their legs. Here however, as in other parts of the coast of Guinea, they have sometimes musical instruments of a somewhat higher claim to ingenuity, particularly those used in war. These consist of drums, horns, a rude species of guitar, and sometimes calabashes filled with small stones, which serve as castanets. "The horns," says Bosman, "are made of elephants' teeth, cut and adorned with several images of men and beasts, and that so finely that it seems to be done literally in obedience to the second commandment, for it is difficult to discover whether they are most like men or beasts. At the small end of these horns is a square hole, at which, by blowing, they produce a sort of extravagant noise, which they reduce to a sort of tune and measure, and vary at pleasure, seeming to blow upon these horns so well, that though it is not agreeable, yet it is not so horrid as to require a whole bale of cotton annually to stop one's ears, as Focquenbrog has it." The drums are made from the stem of a tree, hollowed out and covered with a skin of some animal, or, when it can be procured, the ears of an elephant.

"The inhabitants of Bonny," says our author, "rich as well as poor, are very great beggars, especially when they come on board of a ship, so much so that it is very difficult to resist their solicitations. As to their honesty, I wish I could speak so favourably of some of my white brethren as I can of the more respectable of the Bonnians, amongst whom I have on some voyage sold goods on credit to the extent of £600 or £800, for which, when I reminded them of payment by merely giving them notice by signal, in the course of three or four days the whole of their debts would be punctually liquidated. To pass a general condemnation on the blacks would therefore be unjust, although I must admit they will overreach if it lies in their power."

It is remarkable, that although the country is unwholesome for Europeans generally, and particularly if they expose themselves to the rain, or to the chilly air and the dews of night, some foreigners have been known to retain their wonted health during a residence of many months, and others of years, and the natives are subject to few diseases, and often attain a good old age. The common disorders are syphilis, the country fever, flesh worms, cholic, flux, head ache, and occasionally the small pox. Although they apply certain remedies, chiefly decoctions of herbs and cupping, which they perform with a small calabash, after having made incisions, they depend upon charms, in a great measure, for relief. The flesh worms are peculiar to the coast, and do not so often attack strangers as they do the natives, who assign various causes for their appearance,

CHAPTER XI

amongst which the chief is the badness of the water. Villault, an intelligent French physician who visited the country, ascribes them not so much to this cause as to the nipping winds and rain that fall on the coast, and which he conjectures breed these worms. They are most apt to be engendered in the beginning of the rainy season. "Every drop of rain (he writes) is bigger than a pea, and if one be ever so little wet in a shower, and let his clothes dry on his back, besides their rotting in three days, he may be sure of worms or some dangerous distemper."[30] He was confirmed in this opinion by laying a piece of flesh in the rain, or in the evening dew, and he found that as soon as the beams of the sun glanced upon it the next day it turned all into worms. The flesh worms are of various sizes, the smallest being as slender as a hair and a foot long; the largest have been known to be three times that length, and some writers affirm even considerably longer. They disclose themselves in various ways, and generally make their way through the skin by a tumour. They are then fastened to a stick, upon which they are carefully wound as they protrude, until they are entirely extracted. Should they break, the swelling grows dangerous and often mortal. The pain these worms occasion is so intolerable, that the patient can neither stand, walk, nor rest in any position, and some who are seized by them are even driven mad!

Our author observed the attempts of the Oboe doctors, or Dibbeah, to cure diseases by charms. "One of these, who seem to partake of the priestly character," he remarks, "whom I had on board during a sickness in the ship, begged very strenuously for a male fowl, and on receiving it he killed it by cutting its throat. He then threw himself into many strange postures, and while muttering some incantations over the sick men, he sprinkled the blood on their heads. They were mightily pleased with this ceremony, although they were in a dying state. The Eboes were very subject to head ache, and in order to relieve them we sometimes resorted to cupping. They were not strangers to the operation, but told us it was a remedy often had recourse to in their own country. They make much use of pod pepper, palm oil and various kinds of herbs for the cure of diseases, and they will eat foo-foo and palm oil when almost dying. Foo-foo is boiled yam beat up in a wooden mortar of their own making until it becomes a paste."

The principal trade of Bonny, in our author's time, was in slaves; but since its abolition amongst the British they have happily turned their attention to procuring and exporting palm oil. Ivory is rarely offered for sale, and only in small quantities and at dear rates, the elephants being probably fewer in the neighbourhood than on other parts of the coast. The slaves are procured from the interior, and much bustle takes place when the inhabitants are preparing their canoes for the trade. These vessels, which are large of the kind, are stored for the voyage with merchandise and provisions. "Evening," says Adams, "is the period chosen for the time of departure, when they proceed in a body accompanied by the noise of drums, horns, and gongs. At the expiration of the sixth day they generally return, bringing with them 1500 or 2000 slaves, who are sold to Europeans the evening after their arrival, and taken on board the ships." The Africans become domestic slaves, or are sold to Europeans, by losing their liberty in war, resigning it in famine, or forfeiting it by insolvency, or the crimes of murder, adultery, or sorcery. It may be inferred, too, without libelling the character of the Africans, that European cupidity has often led them to hunt their unoffending fellowbeings for the sole purpose of enriching themselves by the sale of their bodies! "The traders," our author further remarks, "have, in general, good memories, and some of them can reckon their accounts with as much expedition as most Europeans can with the aid of pen and ink. If they know the captain with whom they are dealing to be particular, they will generally calculate with accuracy; but, like many amongst ourselves, they will frequently overreach if they can, and although I have had occasion to remark upon their honesty, I must say, that many of them were in general restrained only by the dread of detection. Most of them, I must in strict justice add, are addicted to lying, and whatever be their probity amongst themselves, they do not make it a matter of conscience to take an advantage of strangers.

The Bonnians being chiefly Eboes, or descended from that tribe, speak their language, or probably a corruption of it, or an admixture with that of others. The languages on the coast are as various as the tribes, few of whom understand each other. They are all represented as soft and harmonious, and abounding in vowels, but never having been reduced to writing, or analytically studied, it is impossible to pronounce upon their respective qualities, though from the quickness of the natives in their communications amongst themselves, and the regularity of their public debates, it may be inferred that they are sufficient for all the purposes of intercourse in a simple state of society. Our author, who seems to have contracted a sort of affection for the Eboes, owing to the docility of their dispositions, took considerable pains on his several voyages to make

CHAPTER XI

himself acquainted with their soft and pleasing language, of which he has furnished the following brief vocabulary.

English	Eboe.
Man	wocoe
Woman	wana
husband	ecoey
wife	ecuiana
child	watacree
an old person	okeebery
a white person	andoucha
head	eshey
eye	ana
belly	affo
smell	senney
master or captain	nammacoe
doctor	dibbea
cook	osheeta
my friend	onenim
a large ship	owba coocoo
a small boat	ewba wanta
pig	asa
goat	agoe
monkey	waka
fowl	ocuccoe
parrot	eacha
fish	assoe
dog	ecotta
beef	annoe
bread	achecha
yam	gee
water	menney
spirits	myabeeca
cocoa nut	accobecca
palm oil	mano
salt	ownoe
pepper	ussoe
cold	oyee
death	awawo
surprise	awamea

English	Eboe.
tub	athasa
a severe beating	pem pem coocoo
a moderate beating	pem pem wanta
sleep	owry
large	coocoo
small or little	wanta
bad	gorranjoe
good	adeema
warm	oeo
no	ofurry
look	laguana
get up	lecota
go below	gemalla
give me	wetta
come here	beea
my god!	howitshem!
shake hands	brakey
make haste	geyen gwango
what is your name?	awagey?
be moderate	beecoe
to steal	oche
to sweep	pra pra
to eat	aney
wash with water	sau sau menney
hold your noise	domona
what is the matter?	ginnemegay
one	oly
Two	aboo
Three	athoo
Four	anoo
five	esee
six	esei
seven	esa
eight	sato
nine	egetee
ten	eree

There appears to be no affinity between this language and that spoken on the banks of the Congo, of which Captain Tuckey gives the following specimen, and which he remarks, as a curious fact, strongly resembles that spoken at Mosambique, on the far distant opposite coast of Africa.

English	Congo
Three	tatoo
Ten	coemy
Four	me-sana
Man	momtoe
Woman	maikaintu
Foot	cooloo
Day	booboo
Dead	cofoy
Water	maza

The language of the Quaws, says our author, like the character of the people, is harsh and disagreeable. The Ottam and Brass languages are more pleasing, though both are excelled by that of the Appas.

The female names among the Eboes are such as follow: Adda, Beera, Bory, Tilly, Acco, Lolo, Ocoba, Glass, Adeema, Orawarry and Caffey. Adda is very common. The usual names amongst the men are Geeta, Eeka, Howatcha, Adasoba, Agee, Opob-bo, Hyama and Ocory.

The Eboe country, from which Bonny draws a great portion of her supplies, possesses, says our author, abundance of every thing in the way of food that nature can desire. Fairs are occasionally held among the Eboes for vending the produce of the country. Their business is chiefly done in the way of barter. The clothing of the lower orders is made of a kind of thread, manufactured from grass. A superior kind of cloth is also made from cotton, which there grows spontaneously. Their dyes are pretty good, particularly the blue, from which circumstance, as well as from my having frequently seen the king's wives painted with that colour, I conjecture indigo must be abundant in the country.

Of his favourite Eboes Captain Crow gives us the following anecdote. On board of his ship, as before remarked, they were accustomed to amuse themselves at the expense of the more simple Appas. One day a party of them, observing some Appas near them, drew a line on the deck with chalk, to represent the boundary between the Eboe and Appa countries. One of them then got a piece of boiled yam, and passing to the Appa side of the line, turned his back on the Appas, holding the yam behind him, and retreated slowly towards the Eboe side. As anticipated, a simple Appa, lured by the bait, followed him to obtain it; but as soon as he got on the Eboe side, the Eboes, uttering a loud yell of triumph, grappled the poor fellow as their prisoner of war; thus good-naturedly exemplifying the respective situation of the two countries.

The Bonnians compute time by observing the moon, and it is surprising

CHAPTER XI

with what accuracy they will calculate the ebbing and flowing of the tides. The rivers here are flooded from May to December, and the height of the inundation is in July and August. Though the dry season terminates in July heavy rains fall till towards the end of the year. The first of the rains are thought to be peculiarly unhealthy. Even the natives run from them for shelter. Some authors contend that they are impregnated with a poisonous matter, which arises from the noisome vapours from low lands, reptiles, &c. The wet season is generally preceded by tremendous tornadoes and thunder storms, during which trees are blighted, and ships frequently struck by lightning. The heat is considered the greatest during the months of October and March.

The ceremony of marriage in Bonny, as throughout the coast of Guinea, is somewhat singular. Polygamy being general, and a man being the more esteemed for the multiplicity of his wives, few young women remain long unmarried. It is usual, says our author, amongst friends in Bonny to contract marriages before even the intended wife be in being. Should, for instance, the wife of one of two friends be enceinte, the husband and his friend will agree that the child, if it prove a daughter, shall be the wife of the latter when she is of age. With this view, if a daughter be born, the intended husband takes the infant home to him after she has been nursed, and keeps her ever after. When she has arrived at what is considered womanhood, a grand feast takes place, presents are exchanged between the two families, and the young bride takes her place amongst the other wives (if any) of her husband. This singular custom, though it leaves no free will to the female, tends much to promote concord amongst the friends of the young woman and her husband, who is perhaps old enough to be her grandfather. However, habit is every thing, and I have seen these old blockheads kiss, and fondle with, these young creatures with great ardour. What is still more extraordinary, every kindness is shown by the old wives to the young ones—a circumstance that might be a lesson to jealous ladies in England.

If one chief fixes his affections upon the daughter of another who resides in the up-country, the contract is done by proxy. After an exchange of presents, the female, on arriving at age, is sent home to her husband, when great rejoicings and feasting take place. Marriages are generally solemnized when the female is yet of tender years, for such is the constitutional precocity of the sex in that country, that many of them become mothers before they have attained the age of twelve.

These marriage customs, with some variations, prevail along the whole coast,—every man maintaining as many wives as his means or inclination allow, and as these generally provide in a great measure for their own subsistence, and contribute to that of their husband, wives are a desirable possession. A father who sees that his son is able to get his living, says Bosman, seeks out a wife for him, provided the son does not save him the trouble. When the parties are agreed, the fetichir is sent for to administer the oaths. He obliges the wife to promise she will love her husband, and be faithful to him. The husband, on his part, promises to love her. The parents then make mutual presents, and at night the husband leads his wife home. The daughters frequently receive a small portion, seldom exceeding an ounce of gold or its value, from their parents, and wherewith to purchase palm wine for the wedding. The marriage expences are but trifling, and include new clothes for the bride, who is dressed very fine on the occasion, and adorned with gold and other ornaments, either bought by the bridegroom or borrowed. She is attended to his house by some young women, of her acquaintance, who remain with her a week.

All the wives, who seldom exceed twenty, (except amongst the princes) till the ground, sow maize, and plant yams, except two, or sometimes one. The first or principal wife (so called) has the care of the family, and is exempt from labour. The second, who is privileged, is called on the gold coast the bossam, because she is consecrated to their deity. The husband is always more jealous of these favourites, who are generally handsome and beautiful. The first wife has also the keeping of her husband's money, and in some parts the husband must obtain her consent, or conciliate her by a present, before he can take another. There is much emulation among the wives, each practising all her charms to secure the preference of her husband's love; yet it does not appear that this competition disturbs the harmony that usually prevails amongst them.

The women of Bonny, says our author, are generally faithful to their husbands. The pride of family descent, which operates as a moral control, is carried quite as high among the Africans as with us in England, and those who are ignobly born are subject to the continual mortifying remarks of their more fortunate neighbours. If a wife break the marriage vow, the husband may put her away, and take another, and the seducer is severely fined, or perhaps reduced to slavery. In the inland countries this crime is still more severely visited, the offenders being frequently ruined, and in some cases both parties suffer death. Bosman remarks, that there

CHAPTER XI

are some mercenary negroes who marry many wives only to obtain a good living by them; and, our author on this subject says, the Eboe chiefs have a scandalous custom, when they come down to Bonny to trade, of bringing with them a number of their fine young wives, whom they suffer to parade the town at night and to intrigue with any black man of property they can fall in with. After accomplishing their designs, they acquaint their husbands, who are generally on the watch on such occasions. The detected individual is obliged to pay perhaps the price of three or four slaves to the husband, and if he be poor, and unable to raise the amount required, is sold as a slave, and the proceeds are pocketed by the designing knave of a husband. Bosman quaintly remarks, that "notwithstanding all the severity of the marriage laws, their women will take liberties, and indeed, considering that ten or twelve are confined to one man, it is no such mighty wonder if they are continually intriguing. The men being awed by the fear of punishment, the women leave no acts untried to allure." After some curious account of the manner in which these female seducers accomplish their designs, and how they are in the end discovered with their paramours, the same author, in his usual quaint style, expresses his concern for the rigour of the law, and his pity for the men who by this means come to their end, as he terms it. It is remarkable, that the husbands and wives never eat together.

Some negroes, but very few, live unmarried. Our author records, that it is customary with the Bonnians to beat and abuse their wives when newly married, and gives an example in high life. "King Pepple married a fine young woman named Tilly, from the up-country, whom, from the respectability of her family, he styled his queen. On her first coming home I happened to be in the river, in the Will, and I was repeatedly sent for, sometimes in the middle of the night, to come on shore and reconcile the royal couple. The cruel treatment the poor creature suffered, and her cries and lamentations were truly distressing. I always on these occasions spoke very candidly to Pepple, and expostulated with him on his conduct, but all the reply he would make me was, that he loved her too much, and that it was their country fash. It was certainly not the most agreeable way of spending the honey moon. In a short time however these squalls blew over; they became very happy together, and a very kind husband he made to her. The queen ever afterwards showed much gratitude for my interference in her behalf—fruitless as it was."

"A horrid custom", says our author, "prevails amongst these people in the case of a woman happening to be the mother of more than one child at a birth. Both herself and her offspring are immediately put to death! I have repeatedly reasoned with the priests and chiefs about this practice, but to no purpose, so stubbornly will they adhere to their country customs, however much they may outrage humanity." The caprice of opinion in such a state of society is exemplified by the existence of a contrary custom in some parts, and its existence in other parts of Benin, which is probably not more than one hundred and thirty miles from Bonny. There we learn from Bosman, that "If a woman bear two children at a birth it is believed to be a good omen, and the king is immediately informed thereof, who causes public joy to be expressed by all sorts of their music." The father even provides a wet-nurse for one of the infants as a relief to the mother, "In all parts of the Benin territories twin brothers," it is added, "are esteemed good omens, except at Arebo, where they are of a contrary opinion, and beat the twin-bearing woman very barbarously,—for they actually kill both mother and infants."

The rights of inheritance in Guinea are somewhat various, though it appears that either the brother's or the sister's children are the usual heirs. This custom appears to be similar to that of some parts of the East, where king's educate their sister's son as their own, and frequently appoint him to succeed them. The son, it would appear, inherits in Bonny, unless the father wills it otherwise. Our author says, "They have a curious custom, which I consider to be tolerably good. Should a man who is rich and has a large family by his wives doubt the ability of his eldest son to the taking care of the property and family, he will fix on one of his men slaves who is of good understanding and character as his successor. This man, accordingly, after the death of his master takes the whole charge of the establishment and family, and marries the wives and perhaps some of the daughters of the deceased. I have known several rich men, who died at Bonny, leave their eldest sons without any tie whatever to support the family; and these young men having squandered all their father's property, would afterwards be constrained to sell themselves to the kings for support—and thus become their slaves."

Here, as in other parts of Guinea, the lamentations over the dead, and their manner of burial, are peculiar. The relations, friends, and neighbours, of the deceased gather round the body, which is laid out, and the females begin to sing mournfully: some of them occasionally address questions to the corpse, as, "Why he died ?" "What reason he had for leaving life?"

CHAPTER XI

They also go round the body, crying, leaping, clapping their hands, and making a terrible noise. An ox or some animal is killed, and the fetish of the deceased is sprinkled with the blood as a propitiatory offering by the priest, to whom a sum of money is paid, that he may, by his conjurations, obtain repose for the departed, and assistance and protection in his journey to the other world. Several other ceremonies are gone through by the priest, in which the blood of a fowl is used, and it is customary to put into the coffins of great men some articles of value. These are buried, after two or three days, under the ground floors of their houses, sometimes under the floor of the palaver house; and it is revolting to see the land-crabs creeping up and down from holes in the floor over the graves. Although there is no doubt these ugly creatures consume the bodies, the inhabitants eat them with a great deal of relish.[31] After the interment, their friends and servants continue to cry and roar almost incessantly for several days, if not weeks, the duration of mourning being regulated by the wealth and respectability of the deceased. On these occasions, if we are to credit Bosman, (and he is corroborated by others who have recently visited the coast) grief is not the only passion which is displayed; for some are silent, others crying and shrieking, whilst others are laughing as loud as they can. As soon as the corpse is interred, every one goes where he pleases, but most to the house of the deceased, to drink and be merry, for they seem to think that the soul of the departed delights in merriment. This festival lasts for several days, so that this part of the mourning looks more like a wedding than a burying. The bodies of kings have been known to be kept a year above ground, whilst a continual funeral ceremony was going on. And it appears from the following passage of our author, that even disinterment of the dead has been resorted to, that renewed ceremonies might be performed over their remains.

"I happened, says our author, to be at Bonny in 1801, when a grand ceremony took place. King Pepple wishing to honour the memory of his father, who died about ten years before, got his remains disinterred, and invited his friends from all parts to be present on the occasion. All the town was in an uproar for five or six days, playing, feasting and drinking. In every corner were to be seen puncheons of brandy, palm wine and tumboe, of which every one was at liberty to partake without cost, and there was no end to the slaughter of goats, pigs and poultry. A carcass of an elephant having been sent down from the Eboe country, as a present for this grand feast, was left to lie in the corner of a street amongst the mud, for eight or ten days, exposed to the sun, until it became quite putrid. The stinking flesh, when cooked, was, however, considered by the natives as a treat.[32] All the women of fashion were invited to the fête. They appeared in their best dresses, with their hair tastefully made up, and their faces and part of their bodies ornamented with paint and adorned with beads. Some of them wore large brass rings[33] round their legs, of about a pound weight each, and I observed many with holes bored through the cartilage of the nose, from which ornaments of various kinds were suspended. Several short plays, or dramatic pieces, were performed on the occasion; and the merriment that took place I am not adequate to describe. To give effect to the whole, King Pepple would have some great white man's name given to his brother, the present king of Bonny; and as I happened to be the senior captain in the river, it devolved upon me to baptise the young man. His Royal Highness the Duke of Clarence being a favourite, I christened him, with all the solemnity I could muster, by his name.[34] My performance of the ceremony gave great satisfaction to the multitude who witnessed it, and especially when they learned that the name given was that of an English prince. The feasting being at an end, to work went the priests to bury the remains of the old king over again, and, as was customary on such occasions, several articles of great value were deposited with him in the grave."

At the funerals of kings, and of grandees, or great men, at Bonny, human sacrifices are offered up. Our author, as related in a previous chapter, was present on two occasions when such sacrifices were made, and endeavoured, in vain, to avert them. The slaves sacrificed were some of those of the deceased, generally his principal servants; but it appears from Artus, that in other parts of Guinea each of the grandees, on the death of a king, makes a present of a slave to the deceased. Some give him one of their wives to dress his victuals, others their slaves to serve him, and even their children, so that a considerable number are sacrificed before they are aware of it, for they are sent on some errand while people lie in wait to dispatch them. The bodies are carried with the royal corpse to the grave. The king's favourite wives, in some parts, also seek to die, that they may accompany their lord and master to the other world, and along with him are buried his clothes, fetiches, and whatever he was fondest of—and meat and drink are for some time supplied in vessels left round the place of interment.

Atkins gives the following brief account of the funerals of the common people at Cape Corse (or Coast):—"At a death the relatives and neighbours keep a noise and howling till the day of interment, always at their own houses, where the corpse being put into a trunk and carried a small circuit on men's heads, the town's folk attend with wild noise and firing of guns; till finding the deceased does not awake, they drink and make merry, and bury with the corpse a portion of liquor, pipes, &c."

In the following passage our author refers to the burying of the poorer classes:—"The Eboes, when employed at any kind of labour, continually talk to their tools, and that in an earnest manner, as if they were addressing a human being. Other inanimate objects they will address in the same manner, even to their canoes and the ground on which they tread; and I have repeatedly heard them at buryings of their countrymen address the corpse on family affairs, and shout and beat the coffin, giving it their final injunctions when it was about to be lowered into the grave."

Bonny is not without its busy bodies or duennas. Our author says, that every man of consequence has an old woman in his pay, to talk, and collect all the news she can in the course of her gossiping— so that hardly a word can be spoken or an act performed but these women carry an account of it, with their own exaggerations, to their employers. When they can find no scandal to pick up, their invention serves their turn to show their industry, and incalculable trouble and mischief are occasioned by the lying stories of these despicable babblers.

CHAPTER XII

At Bonny, as on the whole coast, the natives have a custom of swearing by the fetiche. This is done by the party, whose veracity is put to the test, taking his favourite fetiche, and drinking what is termed the oath-draught, which is followed by an imprecation, that the fetiche may kill him, if he do not perform the obligation he has promised. This custom, ridiculous in itself, has the good effect of keeping them faithful to each other, for they firmly believe that if they perjure themselves they will not live an hour. The ordeal drink is composed of simple ingredients, which have no malignity in themselves. The faith of these people in fetiches is so great, that a number of them on the Gold Coast stood amazed at Villault, when they saw him destroy several of their wooden gods, without being overtaken by immediate death from the hand of their Deity.

The laws are administered without the aid of counsel. The parties appear before the judges, who are composed of some of the first citizens, and of the priests, and each being allowed fairly to state his case, a decision is immediately pronounced. Poisoning, which is an offence of frequent occurrence along the coast, adultery, sorcery, and man-stealing are punishable with heavy fines, and sometimes with the loss of life. "In Bonny," says our author, "such is the abhorrence in which poisoning and witchcraft are held, that persons suspected of either of these crimes are decapitated without any ceremony." Beheading, indeed, is the usual way of despatching criminals who cannot be sold. Flogging is inflicted for minor offences, and, in some cases, offenders are deprived of a part of their ears, a punishment which is considered ignominious. All trials, continues our author, take place in the Palaver-house. In this building, running round the interior of the walls, are a number of shelves, on which are deposited the skulls of chiefs taken in war. These relics, which are considered as martial trophies, are painted with different colours, and adorned with feathers indicating the rank of the deceased warrior. The person who had the charge of this place of skulls in Bonny pretended, that he knew to what

CHAPTER XII

particular chief each skull belonged, and could recount the several battles in which they had fallen, or were captured. Most offences committed in these countries may be compounded for, notwithstanding the declared severity of the laws in some cases : and if the offender be unable to pay the fine imposed upon him, he is sold as a slave. In all cases of injury the relations of the criminal are considered responsible, if he cannot himself pay the fine, and are obliged to make up the required sum amongst them, or suffer him to be condemned to death, or slavery, as the sentence may be. Every one is also liable to make good the injuries done by their slaves. In Bonny the jurisdiction is almost entirely in the hands of the priests. Here, too, the suitors have often occasion to complain of the "law's delay"—suits being frequently removed from court to court, at a great expense to the parties. Of this our author furnishes an instance : "A friend of mine," he remarks, "a very clever Eboe man, named Tom Taylor, from being a slave to a rich man, named Brave Boy, had been appointed by him his heir, in pursuance of a custom already noticed. On the death of his master he had some difference with King Pepple respecting the property left to him in trust, and was therefore obliged to contest the matter at law. The defendant removed the cause from one court to another, until it was at length transferred to a supreme court far up the country. It cost my friend a great deal of money to carry on the suit, for among the other articles which he took with him in his large canoe, with which to pay the law expenses, were five puncheons of brandy. After being absent for some weeks he returned with flying colours, having gained his cause. I requested him to tell me some particulars respecting the court at which the affair had been finally decided, and those who presided over it. He spoke in the highest terms of the wisdom and impartiality of the judges before whom he appeared, and added that they were all eunuchs, an assertion in which he strenuously persisted, on my expressing some doubts of the authenticity of his information."

One of the municipal regulations of Bonny is, that should a person be unable to secure his property under cover before night, he must apply to some priest of consequence, and request him to put "his mark" upon the goods. When this is done, all is safe from theft, none daring to meddle with the articles while the mark is upon them. Such too is the regard in which this custom is held, that should the mark be put upon a ship, owing to any misunderstanding between her captain and the chiefs, no intercourse whatever can take place between the vessel and the shore, until the difference be adjusted by the intervention of friends, in which case the mark is removed, and matters go on as before. This measure however is never put in force until all other methods of reconciling the parties have been resorted to without effect.

In Bonny, as on the whole coast, the inhabitants generally keep their fires burning during the night, not only to counteract the effects of the chilly damp air that often succeeds a day of intense heat, but to expel, by the smoke, the musquitoes, sand flies, and other annoying insects, that swarm on these shores. During our author's time the people slept on mats, on the damp floors of their houses, through which, and the oily nature of their food, their bodies were almost constantly in a state of relaxation; yet, as before noticed, longevity was frequent. In this respect, as well as others, some improvements have since crept in amongst the Bonnians, and many of them have procured couches, or sleeping places, elevated from the ground, some of which may be dignified by the name of bedsteads. Here, as at Cameroons, and generally on the coast, the use of knives and forks is scarcely known, except to the kings and chiefs, some of whom, when not entertaining an European, still dispense with them, using their hands, even to sup up their soup, with an agility and ladle-like convenience, which sufficiently demonstrate that fingers have a higher claim to antiquity of usage, than those fashionable instruments. The salt made at Bonny, like that about Benin, is beautifully white, and of fine flavour. "It is made," says our author, "from the green mangrove bushes, which are burned in large brass pans, brought out from England for the purpose, and thus manufactured into salt.

The manner in which property is preserved in Bonny is such as would naturally suggest itself to a people who are almost wholly destitute of the security doors and locks. Most of the hard articles, such as lead and iron bars, chests of beads, and marcelas, (a kind of coin) they bury under the floors of their houses. Much valuable property is secreted in this way. The chiefs and more wealthy classes have store houses at some distance from the town, in which they deposit their dry goods. They are in general very careless in storing their gunpowder, and I have seen thousands of kegs piled up in the rafters under the roofs of their houses, and sometimes even over their fire places. Owing to this carelessness, I have seen the town twice burned down, with the loss of many lives by the explosion. It was to no purpose that I reasoned with their priests and chiefs on this culpable neglect. They insisted that the consequent destruction was the

CHAPTER XII

will of the grand idol, the Iguana, which it was not for them to arraign, or controvert."

The use of gold as a currency in the towns on the coast from Whidah to Bonny, inclusive, is almost unknown, little of that metal being found so far to the south. At the last place the money is called "bars," which maybe termed a nominal value, each bar varying from two to three shillings sterling. The name is derived from small bars of copper or brass, not unlike small crooked stair-rods, being occasionally, and probably originally, the medium of exchange. Here however trade is usually carried on in the way of barter. A piece of silk bandanoes will be rated at four and a half bars, a bunch of beads at one bar, and so on. Although Bonny now exports a considerable quantity of palm oil, slaves were, during our author's time, and still, unhappily, are, the principal articles of export and exchange. In this respect Bonny may be likened to Loanda, a Portuguese city on the more southern coast—of the currency of which, so far back as the year 1666, Angelo and Carli, two voyagers, give the following account, which is curious so far as it relates to the classing of the slaves with pieces of cloth: "There is little money passes in that country, but instead of it they buy and sell maccutes, birames, and Indian pieces, or muleches. The maccutes are pieces of cloth made up of straw and a yard long, ten of which are worth a hundred reys. The birames are pieces of coarse cloth made in the Indies, five ells long, and cost two hundred reys the piece. The Indian pieces, or muleches, are young blacks, about twenty years of age, worth twenty milreys each; if they are younger they are valued by the people who have judgment in them. Young women are of the same value as young men."

The principal food of the inhabitants of Bonny consists of casavi and Indian corn bread, yams, and other roots, fowls, fish, and palm oil or butter. Besides these the neighbourhood produces plantains, bananas, sweet potatoes, punipions, &c. The palm tree is common throughout Africa, and is perhaps more useful than any other that grows in those climates. Four or five species of this tree are mentioned by Europeans, and several more by the natives. The principal of these are the date tree and the cocoa-nut tree. All the species are not often found in one district or country, as some parts of the coast abound with one and some with another, the rest being only partially, or not at all known. On the western coast the wine palm is the most common. Wine may be drawn from all the sorts, but the date and cocoa tree, owing to the goodness of their fruit, are generally spared, and the liquor is extracted from the other species, the fruit of which is of less value. The first is a small sort of spurious date. The flowers are red, with five leaves and a round pistil in the centre. Its fruit, each the size of a small egg, grows in large prickly clusters, one of which contains eighty to a hundred fruits or nuts, according to the goodness of the tree. The skin, says Barbot, is of a light red or orange colour, the pulp is white, inclining to red, of a good consistence, a violet smell, and bitter in taste like an olive. They have a stone as big as a peach, and when ripe their orange colour changes to a pale yellow. When gathered, they are bruised gently in a kind of wooden mortar, and put into a large pot or copper pan covered with water. When they begin to boil they stir them with a flat stick to separate the pulp from the stones, which sink to the bottom. They are then strained, and when cold form a substance like butter, especially when newly made. This they call palm oil, though palm butter would be a more proper name for it. The negroes use it as butter or lard, and the Europeans find it in their sauces equally as good as fresh butter or lard, if new. Our author considered it a good substitute for butter, and also used it for the lamp. A large quantity of this oil is now usually imported into Liverpool from Bonny. It is chiefly used in the manufacture of soap. Bosnian remarks, that "palm oil is naturally red, but if kept some years becomes white. It is a little nauseous at first to new comers, but to those who have been accustomed to use it, it is no despicable sauce, besides that it is very strengthening and healthful."

A Mr. Grant, (now of Liverpool) who has been many voyages to Africa, in capacities that gave him an opportunity of much observation, states, that the Cameroons palm oil and wine are esteemed the best; that the oil, when newly made, is as thin as wine, of a reddish colour, like Port, and that it is a fine refreshing and enlivening drink, but rather heady.

The next kind of palm (from which wine is drawn) is called *hondier*. The leaves, which compose a trunk at the top, and the trunk itself, are covered with strong prickles, regularly dispersed, as if to defend it from attack or injury. The leaves are broad and indented, like those of the artichoke. It shoots out three round stems, about four feet long, loaded with white flowers, the pistils of which change into a round fruit, like a green walnut. This fruit or nut is covered with green husks, thin and tough, and is flattish, white, oily, and of the consistency of a horse chesnut. From this the oil is extracted by boiling, but of a quality that soon becomes rancid, and is then fit only for lamps. This tree is called in America the prickle palm.

CHAPTER XII

The wine or cypress palm is the largest of the species, and grows to the height of fifty, sixty, or one hundred feet. Its flowers are like those of the last. It produces a nut which is never eaten, and the tree would be useless, but fox the celebrated wine which it produces, and which is esteemed the Malmsey of Africa. The wine is obtained by making incisions round the stem, just below the top or crown, or by cutting out a branch, where the whole of the branches diverge, and it is caught in calabashes, which are left till filled by exudation. The negroes are extremely expert in mounting these tall trees, which they do by means of a hoop or band of cloth, with which they encircle the tree, swathing themselves loosely to it. This band supports them behind, and by placing their feet against the stem of the tree, and shifting it as they advance, they propel themselves upward.

The wine, we learn from Sabot and others, is of the colour and consistency of whey. It sparkles and is sweet, with a pleasant tartness. For a day or two it ferments, growing hard and strong, like Rhenish wine. It is a powerful diuretic. Bosman says, "it is delicious and agreeable, but withal so strong that it unexpectedly steals to the head, and may speedily intoxicate." Thus it may be said, that in Africa all-bountiful Nature supplies even wine to the inhabitants, setting up, as it were, her alembics in the woods, and placing her store casks on the tops of trees, which have only to be tapped by the votaries of Bacchus, when they would sacrifice to the rosy god.

The manioc, or sweet casavi, an American plant, is much cultivated on the coast. This root when ripe, and after the juice, which is reckoned unwholesome if not poisonous, has been squeezed from it, is ground into a sort of meal, of which cakes are made, of a white colour, but so coarse that they seem to be made of saw-dust. This bread is, however, sweet and palatable, and has a slight effect in promoting salivation during mastication. The country abounds with yams of all kinds, which when boiled with meat, peeled and dressed with salt and oil, are considered good and nourishing. It is remarkable, that the yam partakes of the colour of its skin; some being purple, others white; others of a mixed colour, according to the exterior dye or tinge. They are the common substitute for bread. When roasted they taste like an English potatoe. There is also a species of potatoe (particularly at Whidah) of an oval shape, large and superior to yams. These two roots, it is said, constituted the principal food of the negroes, until the Portuguese introduced milho, or millet, of which they have both kinds. The large kind, or maize, affords two crops annually. The small millet, or Guinea corn, produces a grain resembling coriander seed. Both are good as bread—of the art of making which, however, in a proper manner, the natives are yet ignorant. Villault says of the western coast, "Their best and pleasantest bread is of maize and millet mixed together." In the interior, particularly northward of the Gold Coast, rice is grown in abundance in some parts, but in Bonny it is scarcely known.

There are beans and peas of various colours and kinds, and of one kind our author remarks, "I hapened in 1801 to procure some very fine calavancies, and some Guinea corn, which it appeared had been brought from Benin. The calavancies were the first of the kind I had seen at Bonny, but they are plentiful in the up-countries. The negroes are particularly fond of this bean. Pod-pepper, or Cayenne," he adds, "is found in great abundance; but I never saw any of the Malagetta pepper, the *Gratia Paradisi*, or cardamoms. The latter, which grows on shrubs in red shells or husks, is often procured from canoes on the windward coast, and we could not give the negroes, especially those of Benin, a greater treat than a few grains of this pepper in a morning. Some of them told me that their doctors made great use of it as a medicine." Bosman remarks, in corroboratioin of this fact, "That in desperate cases lime juice and Malagetta are often administered with success, even to Europeans, when other remedies of their own doctors have failed."

Cocoa-nuts grow, says our author, in great abundance about Bonny. Their native oranges, for want of cultivation, are rather sour, but Seville oranges, pine-apples, and limes, of fine flavour, are very plentiful. There are also some vegetables of the Calilue kind (which are much like spinach), and there is no want of ocra, well known in the West Indies as a good ingredient in making soup. The fig-banana, one of the most useful, nourishing and delicious fruits of a tropical country, and the plantain, are also abundantly supplied in the market. Tobacco of a good quality is found in the adjacent country, but as the natives manufacture it in an unskilful manner, without any moisture, it is weak and insipid. Their honey is good. The bees are the same as those of Europe. Their nests are found in the woods, attached to the branches of trees, and in some parts their wax is an article of considerable export. The forests produce a sort of cotton tree, the capots before noticed, as used for the making of canoes. These trees are prodigiously thick, being enlarged by numerous sprouts or branches. The wood is soft and porous. They have been known to exceed sixty feet in girth, and are certainly the largest trees in the world. Bosman

CHAPTER XII

quaintly remarks of them, "If we had any Romish priests in this country, we could give them some of the branches to build their small oratories, and the thorny prickles, with which the tree is abundantly stored, would serve to correct and chastise their unruly flesh, and save the charge of buying whips!"

The negroes in some parts consecrate particular trees, under which they hold their religious and other meetings, and these are generally such as, in the greatest degree, display the perfection of nature. The mangrove trees are also remarkable: they grow (as in the West Indies) only in the water, or on banks daily covered by the tides, making as it were a marine forest, through the glades of which a boat or canoe may be propelled. Their lower branches throw down shoots or suckers, which strike root at the bottom, so that each covers a large area, and forms a verdant arcade, impervious to the sun. To the roots adhere vast numbers of oysters. Barbot remarks, "It is good pastime to eat oysters on the spot, for the under bows serve to walk on the surface of the water, the middle ones for seats or resting places, and the upper for shade and shelter." The oysters are very flat, some of them large and good; others of a sharpish taste, not so much esteemed.

Bonny, being insulated, is little infested with beasts of prey, and our author remarks, that he never saw there a tiger, or any other ferocious animal, though the towns on the main are sometimes visited by them. The inland inhabitants often told him, that to prevent them from taking their children in the night, they always, when an alarm was given, made large fires, which served to keep them off. Elephants, he adds, are not numerous in this part of Africa, as is manifest by the low state of the ivory trade, the article being scarce, and sold at so dear a rate as to allow little or no profit to the purchaser. The vulgar opinion, that the wild animals of Africa are extremely ferocious to man, and prone to attack him, is not borne out by the best authorities. On the contrary, even the lion has been known to suffer persons who had no means of defence to pass unmolested; and the elephants are universally represented as docile, an instance of which our author has furnished.

Carli and Merolla, who travelled on the Congo coast in 1666 as missionaries, were of a different opinion, and seem to have afforded much merriment to the natives by their trepidation when the wild beasts appeared. The negroes would then betake themselves to the trees, and the worthy fathers being less nimble, were glad to be pulled up after them. "Carli," says the compiler of 'African Discoveries,'[35] "When lying in his hammock in one of the libattes, heard on the other side of the hedge three great lions, roaring so loud, that they made the earth shake." Happily the hedge was too high for them; and Carli, in the morning, finding that his companion's rest had been undisturbed, warmly congratulated him on his escape, since otherwise, he observed, " he might have gone to heaven without knowing which way." Soon after, as they were travelling, a still more serious alarm arose. A conflagration kindled at some distance, drove towards them all the wild beasts of the district. The negroes immediately sprang to the tops of the trees, and the missionaries, little accustomed to such feats of agility, were with difficulty dragged up by ropes. There was no time to be lost, for such a host immediately arrived that the whole party "would scarcely have made a good meal for them." The same author enumerates tigers, lions, wolves, pocasses, and rhinoceroses. "These all looked upon and eyed them very earnestly; but the fire behind, and the arrows which the negroes shot down upon them, speedily induced them to forbear any further pause."

The elephant seems to regard mankind with kindness, or, if threatened, with generous disdain; but when wantonly attacked, he resorts to a fearful retaliation. There are immense herds of these animals in the interior of the Ivory coast, and also at Cameroons and other parts. They are hunted and shot with iron bullets, their hides being in most parts impenetrable by leaden balls, which fall off flattened by the contact. At Acra, a tooth of one of these huge animals has been known to weigh two hundred and twenty pounds. The elephant is said to live one hundred and fifty years.

Of the amphibious animals, the principal is the crocodile, which abounds in all the rivers,— amongst the reeds of which they lie basking in the sun, or float down the sluggish stream, on the surface, the head and part of the back only appearing, so that, being of a muddy dark colour, they resemble the trunks of trees floating on the water. Their mouths reach from ear to ear. The male, it is said, throws back, when thus floating, the upper jaw upon his neck, and when a sufficient quantity of insects, fish, or any other prey, alight on either jaw, he closes down the upper one like a lid, and thus devours them. They are sometimes alert in seizing the prey, for which they watch, dragging it into the water, and bringing it on shore to devour it piecemeal, as hunger may press them. They have seldom been known to attack a man, unless he fall in their way, or strike them in the water, when they will pull him under and kill him. Some of the negroes wade into the little bays of the rivers and fight them, though they are often severely lacerated for their temerity. They are generally from twelve to fifteen feet in length, and have been known to reach even twenty. Their scales are impervious to shot, and the negroes kill them by a blow or wound in the back of the neck—or by drowning, which is done by distending their jaws with a stick, so that they cannot close them. The priests frequently keep some of these creatures in food, privately, in the pools or lakes near the towns, and thus obtain a command over them, which they turn to good account with their ignorant and superstitious countrymen; for it is the nature of this creature to leave the pools, and go to those who have been accustomed to feed them at a certain call, and when they receive whatever food is given them, to return to their holes or corners with grateful alacrity. Mr. Grant (before alluded to) tells a pleasant story of one of them, which shows the discipline to which they may be brought by good treatment. Having occasion to land with a boat's crew to procure water at Dix Cove, they proceeded to the spring by the side of the river, but were scared away in alarm by a huge staring alligator. He immediately went to the castle, and represented to the governor that a sentinel whom he did not at all approve of, was posted at the wateringplace, and that unless something was done to dislodge him, they would be unable to procure the required supply, adding that, for his own part, he did not relish so dangerous a service. The governor smiled at his fears, and instantly sent a servantman to treat with the enemy. Grant was surprized at the temerity of the attempt, and kept aloof, in some trepidation for the safety of this ambassador to the scaly monarch of the river. The man, who carried a fowl in his hand, boldly approached the spot, and uttering some strange words, up came the alligator with all submissiveness, and taking the fowl from his hand, walked quietly into the water, and disappeared, leaving the coast clear for Grant and his companions. They did not however fill their casks without keeping a sharp look out upon the deep water, lest the alligator, notwithstanding his politeness, should again exhibit before them his awfully portentous jaws.

Abundance of fine fish, says our author, are found in Bonny river. They are of all colours, and many of them of delicious flavour. Amongst them may be numbered sole, ray, flukes, mullet, plaice, and a fish not unlike our trout, bream, jack fish, swordfish, and baracouta. There is also a fine fish, called the jue jue fish, with a black spot on either cheek, resembling a haddock. The shark is eaten at Bonny, with great rejoicing, on account of its being the grand idol at New Calabar, the inhabitants of which retaliate by feasting on the iguana. The latter have the best of the bargain, for noxious as the creature looks, its flesh is admitted to be good and delicate, like that of a chicken.

Bonny river, continues our author, swarms with sharks, so that it is dangerous even to wash one's hands over the boat's side.[36] I have been an eye-witness to several unfortunate persons being destroyed by this voracious fish. It is well, however, that these formidable enemies of mankind are matched in their own element, otherwise they would probably be still more numerous and destructive. There is a large fish in these rivers, called the saw-fish, whose weapon is a hard, flat, bony snout, sometimes a yard in length, the edges of which are furnished with sharp teeth, of about a finger's length each, set considerably apart. With this denticulated horn, which is fixed in their upper jaw, the sawfish fights, and often kills the shark, which is a clumsy fish in the water, and which, by reason of its mouth being half way down the neck, can do no mischief without first turning on its side, or partly on its back. When at Bonny, I one day saw a large shark spring out of the water, and fall into the boat. It had been engaged in fighting with a sawfish, and having the worst of the battle, took a desperate leap to make its escape; I have caught several sawfish with the seines. They are of an excellent flavour, and much relished by the natives. It is stated, that they are also bitter enemies even to whales, when such appear on the coast, which they cut and lacerate in such a manner that they take to the shore and bleed to death.

The shark, which is a viviparous animal, was known to the earliest navigators, and soon became distinguished for his insatiable appetite. In the voyage to Africa of Denis de Carli, (1666) the narrator remarks, "There is another fish in the seas called the shark, very greedy of man's flesh. They catch it with a rope and a chain at the end of it, to which is fastened a strong hook, baited with a piece of flesh. The shark perceiving it, swallows the flesh, hook and most of the chain. Then the sailors draw the head above water and batter it with clubs; after which they bind the tail, where its greatest strength lies, and bringing it on board, cut it to pieces." The strength of this fish in his tail is such that it is dangerous to approach him, even after he is brought upon deck, until he be either maimed or stunned. The modern way in which the sailors dispatch him is often not very merciful, as they probably consider his sufferings as some retaliation for his voracity. They sometimes cram a handspike down his throat, and cut off his tail with a hatchet. They have also been known to cut out his eyes

CHAPTER XII

and turn him adrift again, thus leaving him to a darkened and miserable existence, exposed to the attacks of other monsters of the deep, from which his loss of sight precludes alike a chance of escape or retribution. He has a large mouth, and a triple row of teeth, and such is his tenacity of life, that Merolla (a voyager of 1682) remarks of him—"Observing that his heart beat long after being torn from his entrails, I took it up and kept it till next day, when going to view it again, to my great wonder it still panted." It is said that the brain of the shark when dried becomes as hard as stone, and is a good medicine for females in child-birth. Not a year passes but these ravenous fish make a prey of numbers of human beings who have the misfortune to fall in their way; and they have been known to follow vessels across the ocean, that they might devour the bodies of the dead when thrown overboard. They have also been noticed to tear to pieces the hammocks in which the dead were committed to the waves, not suffering them to sink, although heavily loaded, and devouring the whole, cloth and all! A shark of extraordinary dimensions used to be fed at Port Royal, in our author's time, from the flagship, to prevent the men from deserting; and for a man to go over the side to swim on shore was to throw himself into the jaws of death. A circumstance which occurred in the autumn of 1826, and which is recorded in Beaufoy's Mexican Illustrations, will serve to close these reminiscences of the merciless character of the shark.

A British sloop of war, containing a lieutenant, two midshipmen, and thirtytwo sailors, was capsized off the coast of Cuba. The poor fellows hung about the wreck until the sharks collected and began to fight for their prey. The first bitten was the lieutenant, whose leg was taken off above the knee. He observed the horror of his crew, and, regardless of pain, cheered them with—"Never mind, my brave boys, old England will furnish me with a good wooden substitute." He was soon torn to pieces, and others quickly shared the same fate. A young midshipman was pushed up on a part of the wreck where the sharks could not reach : one seaman swam off, and thinks he frightened the voracious animals by splashing the water; but most probably they remained where their victims were more numerous. The seaman was picked up by an American vessel, which also put about and saved the midshipman. On this horrible occasion thirty-three human beings were dragged off one by one and devoured.

Atkins relates, that at Whidah a canoe attempting to land with goods, upset in the surf: a shark seized one of the men in the water; and by the swell of the sea they were both cast on shore; but the shark never quitted his hold, and with the next rise of the sea carried him clear off.

The cattle, says our author, are generally of a small size, and for some reason, which I could never learn, are never slaughtered; nor are they eaten until they die a natural death. I believe this practice has its origin in some superstitious notion emanating from their priests, for King Pepple seldom made any scruple to permit the English captains to kill a beeve when they wanted it, only making it a condition that they should send the head and offal on shore for his own use. No attention is paid to breeding of cattle, in consequence of which their number is but small about Bonny, although there is excellent pasturage of fine Guinea grass in the neighbourhood. Their flesh is moreover greatly inferior to that of European cattle, being loose and spongy. A similar disregard is observable in the breeding of pigs, goats, sheep, and poultry, which might be raised in great numbers. In the interior of the Eboe country live stock is said to be abundant. The sheep on the coast are covered with hair like a dog, and their flesh is somewhat dry and insipid. The goats are more fleshy and fat, and are therefore preferred. The hogs are also neglected, except at Whidah, where they are said to equal those of Europe in delicacy and firmness. Dogs are sometimes here, as in Calabar, and other parts, killed for food. The European dogs here alter strangely: their ears become stiff like those of a fox, and their barking degenerates to a sort of howl.[37]

The most common fowls are cocks and hens; and the interior produces a variety of birds suitable for the table. Eggs are never eaten in Bonny; they are all used up by the priests on religious occasions, particularly when the chicken is formed. I have sometimes seen, says our author, the priests come to the king's house : having muttered some invocation, they would break an egg, and after touching the king all over with the chicken it contained, immediately kill it. The meaning of this ceremony I could never learn, as they keep such matters a a profound secret.

Parrots are esteemed the most valuable birds, less on account of their plumage than their adaptation to talk; they are of the blue or grey kind. There are plenty of these, though they are not so common on the coast as inland. The natives do not however scruple to ask a good price for them; and to be presented with one is considered a compliment of the highest order. In the interior are found wild and tame ducks, geese, pigeons, partridges, pheasants, doves, woodcocks, sparrows like those of Europe, swallows and a variety of birds of bright and beautiful plumage. An uncommonly fine bird was frequently seen at Opam by Bosman, which

CHAPTER XII

he describes as having a bill like a parrot, of a dark yellow, the breast and underpart of the body of a brilliant green, the upper part grey, red, sky colour, and deep blue agreeably intermixed, and the head, neck and tail of a fine green. "The feathers of this bird," he remarks, "rise on the head like a comb, it has large eyes, above and below which are the most beautiful red rays that can be imagined.

CHAPTER XIII

IT does not appear that our author visited Old Calabar, and as it is only a day's sail from Bonny, and is a port of equal or of perhaps greater importance, the following brief particulars respecting it, obtained from Mr. Grant, before mentioned, may not here be irrelevant.

The entrance to the river, or rather estuary, is between a point called the Bluff Head, on the east, and another called Tom Shott's point on the west; the channel being a little more than a league westward from the former. There are five fathoms of water on the bar. Shott's point took its name from a king or chief who possessed that part of the coast, and who, with his people, used to seize, kill, roast and devour all the whites he could lay hold of, until his sanguinary career was arrested by Duke Ephraim of Calabar, whose people, assisted by some English seamen, had a desperate conflict with the outlaw and his satellites.

About seven leagues up, on the right-hand, is Fish-town, above which the estuary widens out to the northward, in an oval form; its greatest breadth being about ten leagues. This large sheet of water is however in many places shallow, particularly on the westward; and it is interrupted by several banks and swamps, which are dry at low water. Nine or ten miles from Fish-town, on the west of the estuary, is Parrot's island, which is entirely inhabited by parrots and monkeys.[38] From this island European ships frequently procure their fire wood. To the west of it on the main land is Hickery Cock-town, a place of considerable importance, where nearly all the palm oil exported from Calabar is manufactured. The country, back from that town, is prolific in the palm-tree, which grows most luxuriantly on the banks of the rivers, creeks, and swamps, where it is nourished by the periodical inundations. To the east of Parrot island lies James's island, about ten miles north of which is the entrance of Calabar river, which runs from the E. N. E. At its mouth there are seventeen fathoms of water. A town, called Jamie Henshaw's town, lies about nine miles further up on the right bank, and on the opposite shore are the ragged trees, a

CHAPTER XIII

conspicuous wood of irregular appearance. Above Henshaw's town, about four miles, is Duke's town; next, about three and a half miles, is Willy Tom Robin's town, and next, at about an equal distance higher, is Old Calabar, on the south side of the river.

Calabar consists of a great number of low thatched houses, or huts, like those common on the coast, and so irregularly scattered amongst trees that a stranger may easily lose his way. There are a number of large guns, which form a sort of fort along the shore; but these are so ill mounted and in such bad condition, that they are not used for any purpose but an occasional salute, and cannot be fired with safety. The streets are covered with sand, which, by the sun, is rendered so hot that at times it will burn the feet. One main street, called Duke-street, runs from the shore direct to the market place, and terminates at the duke's house.

Duke Ephraim, now between forty and fifty years of age, is one of the most powerful chiefs on the western coast of Africa; and though he holds several kings of the interior in subjection, he whimsically adheres to the title of "duke," which he considers higher and more expressive of power than that of "king." It is usual for foreigners to pay their first visit to this chief, by whom they are generally courteously received and hospitably entertained. The duke has a good wooden house, which was built in Liverpool and sent out in the frame, in the vessel to which the narrator then belonged. It is a frame house of considerable size, raised on pillars from the ground, and the original structure has been of late years much enlarged. It is finished and ornamented in a manner which in Africa is considered complex, sumptuous and extraordinary. The narrator, on one voyage, resided many months at a time in the town; the captain and crew of the vessel to which he belonged having all died except himself and another. He had then an opportunity of becoming not only an acquaintance, but even a favourite of the duke, of whom he was a long time the intimate guest. This house or place is stocked with numerous clocks, watches and other articles of mechanism, sofas, tables, pictures, beds, procelain cabinets, &c. of European manufacture; most of which are huddled together, in confusion, amongst numerous fetiches, and in a state of decay, from disuse, carelessness and want of cleaning. Articles of table crockery, knives, forks, spoons, plate, &c. appear at the king's table, which is set out with considerable taste and splendour, although here and there a calabash presents its less assuming appearance; and unless the guests be "great men," and strangers much thought of, the fingers are sometimes used, even at the ducal board, as the more convenient purveyors for the mouth.

Here, as it appears is now the practice at Bonny, one or other of the king's wives prepares a lunch, in her way, at her own domicile, having the table neatly laid out for the reception of the English and other captains in the port. The principal dish of which the natives are fond is what is called a "yam chop"—the word "chop" being also applied to substantial eating generally. This dish consists of boiled yams and boiled fowl—for here every thing is boiled—served up with sweet palm oil and pepper, and forms a repast which the narrator (who enjoyed remarkably good health) often ate with a good relish. His good health he attributes to his abstinence from intoxicating liquor, and other excesses, as well as to not sleeping in the dew, during the night; which those who attended the nightly dances on shore usually did, after being heated with spirits, and were consequently soon carried off.

The duke has above two hundred wives, who reside each in a separate house—the whole surrounded by a high mud wall, within which no one has access without his especial permission. The duke has several children, but it does not appear that he or his chiefs in general show any greater affection for their own offspring than that which they entertain for those of others. The children indeed are little caressed, and they do not, from the nature of the climate require the same nursing as in Europe. The women who have children, and amongst these are many under fourteen years of age, do not carry them in their arms, but resting astride on one haunch, which is thrust out, the arm being employed to prevent them from falling.

The narrator noticed as remarkable, that mothers here wash their children every day from head to foot, from a vessel, at the bottom of which is a black eel, or some species of snail, about four inches in length, and which will bite if it be touched. They attribute some particular virtue to this snail; and, during the time of washing the child, water is every now and then ladled, with the hand, into its mouth; much against the will of the poor thing, but, it is believed, very much to its advantage.

Duke Ephraim is remarkably keen in trade, and will haggle in the making of a bargain in a manner that shows how perfectly he understands the doctrine of self-interest.

The duke's dress is generally very simple, consisting of a *paan*, or mantle, with a sash formed of a white handkerchief, or piece of cloth.

CHAPTER XIII

He, however, on some occasions, displays a taste for a costume of a more gaudy and imposing description; and will wear a sort of robe or mantle reaching to the knee, and composed of several colours, with a silk, sash thrown over the shoulder. He always appears in a gold-laced round hat, like those worn by gentlemen's servants, which is sometimes set off with plumes of feathers. His apparel and decorations it is however impossible to describe, as they change with every new caprice, or are regulated by the presents he may receive, or the articles he may purchase from captains of vessels; but when he does not affect the general nudity of his countrymen, it may be said to be a sort of showy Anglo-Turkish costume. He usually wears, as well as his chief men, sandals of home manufacture.

When the duke parades about, he is preceded by thirty or forty attendants, and followed by as many more. On visiting the vessels in the roadstead, in his state canoe, he is accompanied by a numerous retinue; and amongst his regalia is a human skull mounted on a baton, and carried before him by a boy.

At Calabar, probably from the want of other and better employment, one town in the estuary or neighbourhood is frequently at war with another, and a fighting day is regarded as a sort of pleasurable festival. As at Bonny, guns are mounted in the bows of their war canoes, which are full of armed warriors; and when they start off, with bangees, or drums beating, and colours flying, they present the appearance of an armament with which it would be no child's work to cope.

Here, as at Bonny and other places on the coast, before Europeans can "break trade," as it is called, or, in other words, commence dealing with the natives, a present is required for the duke, called a *dash, dashê,* or *cumé*: this is never in money, but generally consists of a puncheon of rum, a quantity of tobacco, or an assortment of several marketable articles. On first landing at Calabar strangers are struck with the indolent, careless, yet cheerful appearance of the men, who saunter about the streets; sometimes strumming a musical instrument made like a child's money box with holes in the top, over which pieces of thin bamboo cane are fixed at one end, so that they vibrate on being touched, and send forth a sober monotonous tink-tink sort of jingle. The men at Calabar dress as in Bonny, but in both places considerable approaches have been made to a better taste than that exhibited during our author's visit to the latter place. A lady of Liverpool made an attempt, some years ago, to introduce a more decorous costume amongst the numerous wives of the king—and which, it was hoped, would, from their example, lead to a national improvement. She sent out, as presents, a number of petticoats, chemises, and what were known as "curricle bed gowns," with frills and ornaments. These were viewed with curious eyes by the royal ladies, who exhibited themselves in them for a day or so, and thus caused no small merriment amongst themselves: but their appropriation was only the freak of the time, and the wearers soon returned to their former simplicity of apparel. The women of Calabar are, however, very grand in their own way on holidays, when they wear dresses of variegated colours, and have their hair tightly made up in the form of a cone, a foot or two above their crowns—a fashion which gives them a remarkable and somewhat dignified appearance. Here, as at Bonny, the women wear large copper rings on their legs and arms called "mancelas"— although on any excoriation of the skin they produce canker. These rings are every day burnished, and are truly a massive sort of jewellery. The national mark, or tattoo, is three or four stripes on each temple, and also a number of stripes, (made by incision) in parallel lines, down the arms.

The customs of the people are, with some few variations, similar to those at Bonny. The men of the town call themselves freemen, in contradistinction to the slaves; and the women go to the plantations, and do all the work of agriculture and house-keeping. The productions of the soil are those common to the coast, and the quantity of palm oil which may now be procured here and at Bonny is unlimited. The trade in oil is chiefly carried on by Liverpool vessels, which have, in the last season, imported no less than eight thousand tons. There are no shops at Calabar. The market-place is the grand mart, and is well supplied with all kinds of provisions. Here articles of every description, African and European, are constantly on sale in the open air.

Our narrator observed some customs consequent on the death of a great man, which were either unknown in Bonny, or not remarked by our author; although in other parts of the coast similar observances have been witnessed by various travellers. In addition to human sacrifice, in such cases (the notion being that the slaves and others sacrificed will accompany and serve the deceased in the other world) they here construct on the shore, at low-water mark, a small house or hut of bamboos thatched with palm leaves, say two feet long, and two and a half in height. They then go to the house of the deceased, and take a number of articles, his property, such as cloth, old bones, pieces of iron, jugs and other small articles; and, having cut the cloth in pieces, driven a hole into the bottom of the jug,

CHAPTER XIII

and otherwise broken or mutilated most of the articles, they kill a goat, sprinkle the blood all over the small house, and deposit them in it; and, after some ceremonies, leave them as a monument or offering to the departed. The narrator remarked, that although they held these little tombs sacred amongst themselves, they were not offended if Europeans disturbed them. They seldom, indeed, lasted long, for being without a door, and open at one end for the inspection of the curious, sailors generally carried off any thing worth the taking; and generally made prize of the boxes, which they converted into parrot cages. Our informant states, that he had the misfortune to witness several human sacrifices during his stay at Calabar, the only part of the coast which he visited, where he was horrified by such barbarous exhibitions. To his credit for humanity, (although he candidly confesses that he has, by fortuitous circumstances, been engaged, as was the author of the foregoing pages, in the slave trade) he on several occasions interfered, but in vain, to save the lives of the innocent victims thus consigned to a fearful destruction. On seeing a beautiful young female brought down to the beach for execution, he became deeply interested in her fate; and, after all arguments to forbear were found to be unavailing, although he was then poor, he eagerly inquired if the girl might be purchased; in hopes of concluding a bargain, and thus saving her life. The Duke and the populace were, however, headstrong in their purpose, telling him, "No can sell—you no savey we country fash." The poor creature was instantly decapitated. At these executions the sufferers are pinioned, and tied in a sitting posture to a stake driven in the ground; and round their heads, so as to cross their eyes, is fixed a rope, the end of which is held by some bystanders who participate in the sacrifice. The executioner comes up with a leaden-handled sword, and generally at one blow severs the head from the body; when it is instantaneously pulled away by the rope, and, while yet warm, is tossed up in the air, and played with like a ball. If the executioner fail to strike off the head at a blow, the spectators set up a laugh of scorn and disappointment. On another occasion, he witnessed the inhumation of two men alive, and two women from the up-country. They were put in couples, male and female, into separate holes, and covered with earth. "These terrible sights," he remarks, "put me in a horrible state of feeling. I was nearly fainting. I thought I should have died, and was not myself again for a long time." When old King Hio, of Croo-town, near Calabar, died, (in 1820) he saw, he believes, not fewer than a hundred human beings sacrificed in one day. They were taken down to the beach, and their heads cut off; after which the bodies were thrown into the sea, and the heads buried and left until the flesh decayed; when the skulls were taken up, and deposited in the fetiche, or *devil*-house, of which there is one in every town. These unfortunate victims submit to their fate with a comparative degree of resignation, or, rather, without betraying any extraordinary degree of terror. This apathy arises from the impression that they will, on being sacrificed, be transformed into white men, and enjoy all the felicity of another distant and delightful country.

There is here a custom, which, if it existed at Bonny, escaped the observation of our author. Every month or "moon," (for by such the Africans compute their time) a personage, who is known by the name of "Great Egbo," and whose authority, it appears, the inhabitants are compelled to respect, though they do not know, or will not reveal, the secret of its origin, parades the streets, in the character of a national bailiff and executioner. He is dressed up in a fantastic and rather frightful manner, with long artificial hair, and his face muffled up, so that he cannot be recognised by those with whom he comes in contact. He is armed with a naked sword in one hand, and a cow-skin whip in the other; and, thus equipped, sallies forth into the streets, followed by a crowd of men and boys; being authorized to flagellate and even destroy those whom he meets or overtakes who have not paid up certain tributes to the chiefs.

He is known and dreaded, being considered as a sort of avenging demon. Most of the natives being aware of the day of his periodical visit, secure themselves in their houses, or fly for refuge on seeing him approach, or on hearing the sound of the bell which he carries fastened to his back to announce his coming. He is always upon the run, and some of those he comes upon, who have not paid the tribute, he instantly kills by cutting off their heads at a blow. On others, probably minor offenders, he inflicts only stripes. His authority does not, it appears, last long; so that all who barricade themselves within doors are safe from this avenging minister of despotism. The narrator saw this personage go up to a fisherman, (having first stopped his bell, that his approach might not be known) and, before the poor fellow could, after starting round on hearing his footsteps, make his escape to his canoe, his head rolled upon the beach. The dread in which he is held is such, that fishermen and others will even leap into the water, and swim across the river, though endangered by the sharks, to escape him.

There is also a little or "picaneeny" Egbo, personated by a lad, who exercises a jurisdiction over the younger portion of the community;

CHAPTER XIII

but with this redeeming difference from the elder fiend, that he is not permitted to carry a sword, being simply armed with a cow-skin whip. "To blow Egbo" upon any one who is a European, has a similar effect with the mark put on ships at Bonny, in cases of disagreement between the chiefs and the captains, as it causes a suspension of intercourse until the parties come to an understanding.

On the death of a man of consequence at Calabar, his wives clip and shave off their hair in rings round their heads; some describing circles round from the forehead, others segments of circles, or curves, according to fancy. After the funeral, and on other occasions of festivity, the men who assemble to drink dance a wild fandango round a table, on which abundance of brandy, rum, and other liquors is placed. This dance they accompany with singing and bellowing; and one of the party every now and then makes a stop, as a signal, when all the others stop also, and every one drinks. Even Europeans who happen to be in the way must conform to this custom.

The currency is copper; and the palm oil, a principal commodity, is sold at so many coppers, say at the rate of from eight to twelve for a *croo*, which is about twelve gallons. The coppers are generally a nominal value, though they are represented occasionally by copper rods. The manner of carrying on trade does not appear to be always regulated by those niceties which are known in Europe; each party often appearing equally eager to take advantage of the other. The first object of a captain is to get possession of the oil as it comes in canoes and jars from Hickery Cock-town and other places. The duke exercises a sort of jurisdiction in awarding to what captain each successive importation shall be sold; and as it is always an object to load a vessel as quickly as possible, and some, after all their exertions, are detained for months waiting for the completion of a cargo—many manœuvres are put into practice, and many presents made to obtain an undue partiality. The narrator, on whom, owing to the mortality of the crew of the ship to which he belonged, devolved the command, states, that to obtain a cargo, so as to leave the country, is sometimes attended with a struggle as it were for life and fortune; and he relates a laughable incident in which he thought himself justified in out-jockeying a Liverpool captain. A small canoe, with oil, having arrived, Grant considered that it was his turn to obtain the purchase; the other: as strenuously held out, and a quarrel ensued, during which Grant declared that if he did not get the oil he should sink the canoe. The other went to the duke, and Grant intended to follow him and to insist upon his claim; but just as he was starting for that purpose, he descried a *large* canoe, loaded with oil, coming up the river. He hastened to the duke's, where he found the captain declaiming against him. After stating that he considered he had the best right to the oil in the canoe in question, he added, that, since his contemporary was so much put out of the way about it, he would relinquish it on the duke's promise that he should have the next load that arrived. This was readily agreed to, and he and the captain shook hands. He lost no time in returning to the beach, and immediately possessed himself of the cargo of the large canoe which had just come in, to the great mortification of the captain. The oil thus collected is carried to the oil-house of the ship on shore—a place constructed for the purpose— where it is measured and put into casks. It is agreed to give the market price in goods; but this is not always done with the strictest regard to accuracy. The goods from European ships are here stored in a warehouse belonging to the duke, where they are perfectly safe from pillage, and when the oil is received, the vender is asked what he wants. His general reply is, "Me want gun, me want powder, cloth, me want ebery ting," some even add, in their simplicity, "Me want de *ship* too." The matter is settled by an order given to the duke to deliver so many muskets, so many yards of cloth, and so forth—the value of which however is, in not a few cases, considerably short of the actual amount as a barter. Our informant is extremely candid on these matters. It is admitted on all hands, that *Blackey* will overreach if he finds an opportunity; but the probability is, that his rogueries are often but apt imitations of *Mr. Whitey*, who would fain always be thought to be a pattern of honesty. It is not however assumed that dishonest practices are frequent; on the contrary, it appears, by our author's account, and all others, that, with some exceptions, the captains engaged in the African trade were men of integrity, and, it may be added, of humanity.

At Calabar, the duke and a considerable number of his men can speak tolerably good broken English, and even write mercantile letters, sufficiently explicit and intelligible, on ordinary affairs. Several of these have been addressed to gentlemen of Liverpool, as well as epistles of a more private and confidential nature, accompanied by presents, in return for others transmitted to the writers. These documents, particularly those of Duke Ephraim, are concise in diction, and exhibit a mixture of seriousness and of drollery, which render them curiosities of their kind.

Such are the particulars obtained from Mr. Grant relative to Calabar; and we may conclude by remarking, that the customs and manners of the

CHAPTER XIII

inhabitants not noticed in this sketch resemble those of Bonny and other parts of the coast.[39] In addition to what has already been stated relative to fetiches, it may not be improper (the fact, in its proper place, having been accidentally omitted) to supply a fact from Bosman, which will render the account given of the superstition of the natives, with respect to these household idols, somewhat more complete. That author states, that when they are inclined to their idols, or desire to be informed of something by them, they cry out, "Let us make fetiche;" meaning, "Let us perform our religious worship, and see what our God saith." If injured by another, they make fetiche to destroy him, by causing some food to be exorcised by the priest, and placed where their enemy is wont to pass, believing that if he touch it he will die. Those who are afraid of this, cause themselves to be carried over the spot, when no harm ensures. The same quaint author adds, that they consider their reward (in this life) from their gods to be in the number of their wives and slaves, and their punishment in the want of them; and that they believe in the devil, who does them much mischief, and who is annually banished their towns; the ceremony of his banishment being preceded by eight days' feasting and revelry.

As an addendum to the notice given of the sharks, which are as numerous at Calabar as at Bonny, it may be remarked, (from several authorities) that they are generally attended by two, three, or more pretty coloured little fish, the size of herrings, which are called pilots. These go in and out at the shark's maw, and fasten on his back in a familiar manner. They are supposed to be, as the jackal is to the lion, instrumental in procuring the shark his prey, and warning him of dangerous shoals; in return for which they receive food and protection from their patron.

We now return to our author, CAPTAIN CROW, who concludes his narrative in the following words: "Thus have I endeavoured to communicate for the information of the reader such facts as my memory, aided by occasional memoranda, enables me to furnish, relative to Bonny and its inhabitants, the correctness of which may be relied upon. I trust they will be found to be worthy of notice, when it is considered that they relate to a people respecting whom little information has been obtained in this country, and that little generally of an erroneous or, at least, more unfavourable nature than is warranted by existing circumstances. Could I flatter myself that any thing I have said would tend to place the poor blackey's character in a more favourable point of view than it has been generally represented, and thus obtained for him a more kindly consideration from my countrymen, I should feel that I had not in vain employed the leisure hours spent in committing these sketches to paper. In the sincere hope that they may be of some benefit in this respect, I now cordially bid the reader farewell."

The benevolent sentiments here expressed, together with our author's kindness, often acknowledged by those under his charge, sufficiently evince the regard in which he held the poor Africans. He has furnished numerous instances, in accordance with the opinions of many intelligent writers on the western coast, that the general negro character is full of gentleness, mingled with a sprightliness and good humour which incline their possessors to innocent mirth and mutual good offices. There is nothing intrinsically barbarous or inhuman in the disposition of the blacks: much of what is objectionable or even abhorrent in their character to Europeans is to be attributed to ignorance and superstition, to the baneful influence of intestine wars, and to the practice of trafficking in their fellow men; in which last they have probably been first initiated, and are yet unhappily abetted and encouraged, by Europeans. Certain it is, that if slavery existed amongst themselves before the latter visited their shores, it was always, as it is now, in the more civilized parts of Africa, of a character, so far as regards actual servitude or labour, far more mild than that existing in the colonies, where the object often is to extract from the bondsman the utmost possible quantum of labour, consistently with his health and preservation. Our author adduces no one instance of severe labour, or grievous privation, endured by the slaves in their own country, although he admits that they are frequently the victims of barbarous customs; and his idea that the condition of the West India slave was preferable to that of the African, is clearly to be attributed to the scope of his observations having been confined to peculiar parts of the coast.

The grounds on which he reasoned may be thus assumed. First:— Most of the slaves whom he saw in Africa were not domestics, but prisoners of war, criminals, and such as had forfeited their freedom by laws (barbarous it must be allowed); or who had been trepanned and brought down in gangs from the interior for sale, by men whose interest in their comfort and good condition extended only to the casual period of their sale. Secondly:—The frequency of human sacrifices and sanguinary punishments, with which he was frequently horrified, (an evil from which colonial slaves are exempt) he placed to the account of African slavery. And Thirdly:—In comparing the condition of the Africans with

CHAPTER XIII

that of the West India slaves, he drew his conclusions (as has already been mentioned) from what he had observed at the seaports of Jamaica and other islands; where the slaves, who are either domestics, artizans, or labourers connected with commerce, experience a treatment very different from that of their fellow blacks on the plantations : the former have no field labour, no toil, beyond what falls to the lot of home servants in England, to endure; and, if they be owned by generous masters, they are decently clad, and even provided with weekly pocket money. In fine, the domestic slaves of these towns, no one who has resided in the country will hesitate to admit, are generally well-treated and happy; and for these to be transferred to plantations where they must work with a general gang, be subject to a severe taskmaster, and kept almost destitute of that clothing and those comforts which decency and respectability demand at the hands of the masters in the towns, would be truly a "leading into captivity" of the most grievous kind. But whatever were our author's opinions of slavery, certain it is that the negro was a being to whom he felt a warmth of attachment which, under such circumstances, could be the offspring only of a generous mind; and it is but fair, therefore, to assume, that had he seen the possibility of ameliorating his condition with safety, and a regard to what he considered to be the interests of his country, he would have gladly stepped forward to assist in promoting so desirable an object.

The tractability of the African, and his susceptibility of gratitude for favours received, he has often exemplified; and it is now doubted by but few individuals that he has a capacity to receive such instruction as may fit him to be, if not a brilliant, at least a useful member of society. Without, therefore, wishing to cast any reflection on those who were engaged in the African slave trade, and amongst whom were many men of integrity and worth, who were probably ignorant of its more objectionable details, it may be suggested that there is now a wide field for the philanthropist and mercantile adventurer to make some reparation to Africa for the wrongs which England may have inflicted upon her, in participating in the sale of her natives—and that is, by an increased commercial communication with her sea-ports. Among the means which have been resorted to for the improvement of the Africans the abolition of the slave-trade, and the employment of artizans on the coast, have already done much good; and it is to be hoped, that the traffic of every succeeding year will tend more and more to render the productions of Africa—her oil—her ivory—her gold —her timber—and not her people—the principal articles of merchantable value: so that the chiefs and native princes may at length be induced to turn their attention to the produce of the soil. An increased intercourse with strangers would also in course of time assist in effecting a moral improvement among the natives; and the lights of knowledge and the spread of religion would dispel the gloomy clouds of superstition that now unhappily hang over them. The foregoing sketches may, it is hoped, be of some service in a commercial as well as a philanthropic point of view. The author's generous wishes will also be thus accomplished, should the account of Africa contained in the preceding pages aid those who may visit that country in forming a correct judgment of the character of the blacks; so that they may hence be the more induced and the better enabled to communicate to them, in a friendly and acceptable manner, such information on the arts of civilized life, and on the principles of our common Christianity, as may conduce to their elevation in the scale of humanity.

The following few anecdotes, some of which are unknown to the public, will serve further to illustrate the character of "poor blackey," as he is emphatically denominated by our author.

A vessel belonging to Messrs. Fisher, of Liverpool, having been lost on the coast, after receiving at Gaboon her homeward cargo, it became necessary, in order to prove the loss, and recover the insurance, to bring home to England, as evidence, one of the natives who had witnessed the accident. The case was tried in London, before Lord Ellenborough; and the counsel for the plaintiff was the present Lord Chancellor, then Sergeant Copley. The witness being placed in the box, was asked if he acknowledged the existence of a God, and understood the nature and obligations of an oath; but neither the bench nor the counsel could make him comprehend their meaning, or obtain a satisfactory reply. At length a gentleman present, who was well acquainted with the negro character, suggested to the counsel to put the question in a different form, which he did by asking, "Suppose you do good, where you go ? and suppose you do bad, where you go ?" At these words the negro's countenance brightened up in a manner which showed that he fully understood the inquiry. He instantly answered, "Me savey if me do good, me go up dere—fine country—fine peoples; if me do bad" (he continued after a pause) "or tell lie, me go down *dere*—to bad place—devilly hole:" a declaration which he emphatically enforced by pointing portentously down to the hollow or pit of the court, in which all the gentlemen of the long robe were complacently seated, who little thought that blackey should, unwittingly, by his last act, call forth the laughter of the audience at their expense. When the merriment had subsided, he was asked what he knew of the ship and cargo in question : he replied, "Ship for Cappy Young come for Gaboon, him stop dere till him ship bellyfull;" (suiting the action to the word by extending his hands in a sweep from his stomach, to indicate a paunch) "and after he go away—come too much wind—blow he ashore—he all break—all loss! neber see he ship more."

In the "Life" of our late townsman, Mr. Rushton, father of the present Mr. Edw. Rushton, is recorded the following instance of negro magnanimity:—

> "Rushton was naturally kind-hearted—he could not witness the distresses of human beings without feeling strong emotions of compassion, and the following incident had prepared his mind to regard with pity the sufferings of the negro race. In one of his voyages to the West Indies he had contracted an acquaintance with a black man of the name of Quamina, whom he kindly taught to read. On some occasion he was despatched to the shore with a boat's crew, of which Quamina was one. On its return to the ship, the boat was upset in the surf, and the sailors were soon swept by the billows from the keel, to which, in the first confusion, they had all clung. In this extremity Rushton swam towards a small water cask, which he saw floating at a distance. Quamina had gained this point of safety before him; and, when the generous negro saw his friend was too much exhausted to reach the cask, he pushed it towards him—bade him good bye— and sunk to rise no more. This anecdote Mr. Rushton has often related in the hearing of the author of these memoirs,[40] and never without dropping a grateful tear to the memory of Quarnina."

The following anecdote, illustrative of the good-humoured *fourberies* of the blacks, was a few years ago furnished to the *Liverpool Mercury* by a gentleman who had lived in Trinidad:—

"After the fire which some years ago destroyed a great portion of Port of Spain, (the chief town of Trinidad) the merchants whose houses were consumed, or rendered uninhabitable, resorted, for mutual convenience, to an hotel, where they formed themselves into a society; and, when the town was rebuilt, they continued to meet occasionally, to cultivate the good fellowship to which their association had given rise. On one of these occasions, the negro servant of one of the members (a merchant of high respect) bethought him that as all the massas were about to devote themselves, abroad, to feasting and conviviality, it would be but fair that their men should enjoy themselves at home; and having assigned to each of his fellow servants his respective part, he availed himself, as keeper of the keys, of the advantages of the larder and the wine cellar; plenished the hospitable board in the dining-room; and, by special invitation, assembled all the black servants of the gentlemen who had gone to the dinner. The guests, who came dressed in their Sunday clothes, did ample justice to the entertainment; and each assuming, as it were, his master's identity, talked of the prices of the several articles of trade, of the expected arrival of 'My brig, the Mary,' or 'my ship, the John;' and with proper gravity, bought, sold, and bartered, with so much spirit, that the colony was in a fair way of witnessing an astounding briskness in the mutation of property. On the removal of the cloth the usual general toasts were drunk; after which the president rose, and announced, that the toast he was about to give demanded a bumper. The guests obeyed, and blackey had just risen to announce his pledge, when his master, who, feeling himself unwell, had left his party, caught from the end of the hall, a full view of the sable assemblage, with their glasses elevated, listening for the toast. He, at first, naturally looked very *black* himself; but being yet unobserved, and unexpected, he stepped on one side the outer door, where he could observe, unseen, their further proceedings, before attempting to disturb their conviviality. His servant, placing his hand upon his heart, with honest sincerity, now exclaimed, 'Gemmen, I *give you my massa—he one d—d good fellow!*' This testimony of a servant's regard, though evinced at rather too great a cost, was worth something: the good-natured master, disarmed of his resentment, returned, unobserved, to the party he had left; leaving blackey to entertain his guests as he pleased; and, when he returned home at a late hour, the room was cleared, the table, plate, &c. (not the wine) arranged in their usual places—and of the feast—'like the baseless fabric of a vision—not a wreck was left behind.'"

Our author's individual kindness to the blacks, and his intimacy with their chiefs, lead us to infer, that, had he cast his eye upon the following

CHAPTER XIII

anecdote, he would have given it a place amongst his memoranda. It is taken from a valuable and scarce work, "The official Report of the Lords of the Committee of Council, appointed for the investigation of matters relating to Trade and Foreign Plantations :"

"The late Sir Charles Price having purchased twenty newly-imported negroes, had them brought before him to be reviewed, soon after their arrival, at the plantation where he intended to settle them. As soon as they were all collected and arranged for this purpose, he could not help being particularly struck with the appearance of one man, whose looks bespoke a mind that was labouring under some severe affliction. An irresistible curiosity prompted him to inquire, among the plantation slaves, for one of the same country, who might perform the office of interpreter. A female linguist was soon found, who put several questions to the African, dictated by her master, but to which no answer was returned. The man turned a deaf ear to her expostulations, and seemed to maintain a sullen silence. In the mean time, Sir Charles, surveying the rest of them, remarked another man, whose air of cheerfulness promised better success. The proper inquiries were therefore addressed to him, and from his replies it was understood, that his disconsolate companion had been a Cabocero, or chief of a village, in his own country, possessed of a great many slaves; 'and myself,' continued he, 'was one of the number, and used to wait upon him every day.' When this explanation was conveyed to Sir Charles, he was sensibly touched with the vicissitude of fortune, which had reduced the chief from a state of such elevation and authority in his own country, to be the companion in servitude of his own slave. He immediately withdrew, sent far the Cabocero to his house, and having, by means of a trusty interpreter, received a confirmation of the story from his own mouth, he executed a manumission, the purport of which was explained to him, and accompanied with a declaration to this effect: 'You are now no longer a slave, but at full liberty to go wherever you please. If it be your choice to return to your own country, I will endeavour to have you safely reconveyed. But, if you prefer remaining here, your condition shall be as comfortable as I can possibly render it.' The astonished negro, in a transport of delight, fell on his knees, and, embracing the hands and feet of his benefactor, bedewed them with tears of gratitude; then, thanking him in terms the most expressive of his feelings, said, that as it was so kindly left to his own option whether to revisit Africa, or remain where he was, he would freely confess, there was among his companions a young negress, whom be wished to have for his wife; and if she would but consent, he should prefer staying in Jamaica, and ending his days with her. Sir Charles consulted the girl—she made no objection; a spot was assigned for their habitation upon a part of his estate. Here they lived together very comfortably for many years; in the course of which their felicity was heightened by the birth of several children. Sir Charles's bounty did not terminate with his life; for in his last will he bequeathed freedom to the wife and children. Nor was his former liberality ill bestowed, for the poor fellow conceived an inviolable attachment to the person and interest of his friend, and was of very great service in the rebellion of negroes which happened in 1769; when, by his influence over those belonging to Sir Charles's plantation, most of whom were Coromantees, he effectually restrained them from joining with their mutinous countrymen."

From the same authorities, namely, the witnesses who appeared before, or transmitted their written opinions to, the Committee of the House of Lords in 1788, and amongst whose names frequently appears that of our late townsman, Mr. Penny, then the partner of a gentleman to whom we are indebted for some of the information in the preceding pages relative to Calabar, we find that our author is borne out in his supposition that the minds of the Africans are probably as capable of cultivation as those of the whites. Unfortunately, however, the education of those of them who have come to this country has, it appears, been confined to reading, writing, and a little arithmetic. In the above-mentioned year there were about fifty mulattoes and negro children in this town and neighbourhood under instruction; and that number was short of that of former years, from the circumstance of a black, Mr. Philip Quakoo, a native of Cape Coast, who had been educated at Oxford, and was appointed chaplain to the fort of his native town, having undertaken the education of children at that settlement. "The influence," says one of these documents, "which European education seems to have upon Africans, after their return to their native country, appears chiefly in their more civilized manner of life. They endeavour to live and dress in the European stile, to erect their houses in a comfortable and convenient manner, and evince a fondness for society. Few of the females return to their native country; such as have, retain the dress and outward behaviour of their sex in Europe." It is added, "It has always been the practice of merchants and commanders, of ships to Africa, to encourage the natives to send their children to England; as it not only conciliates their friendship, and softens their manners, but adds

CHAPTER XIII

greatly to the security of the trader, which answers the purpose both of interest and humanity."

These official papers furnish many instances of negroes and negresses becoming intelligent members of society through English education. But one of the most brilliant examples of negro intellect, magnanimity, and perseverance, is to be found in the life and character of Captain Paul Cuffee, who visited Liverpool in the year 1811. Mr. E. Smith, published at the time, in the *Liverpool Mercury*, a very interesting memoir of this extraordinary man, written by a gentleman of Liverpool; and from that publication, with the use of which, together with others illustrative of negro character and intellect, that gentleman has kindly favoured the editors, we supply the following sketch, premising, that it is necessarily much more limited and unsatisfactory than the ably drawn-out and authentic original.

The father of Paul Cuffee was an African, who had been brought up as a slave in Massachusetts, but through industry and economy was, while yet a young man, enabled to purchase his personal liberty. Paul, his son, was born in one of the Elizabeth Isles in the year 1759; and, at the age of fourteen, was left, in conjunction with his brother, with the care of supporting his mother and six sisters from the produce of a small piece of unproductive land. Conceiving that commerce was more lucrative than agriculture, he, at sixteen, entered as a common seaman on board of a vessel bound on a whaling expedition to the bay of Mexico. He afterwards went to the West Indies, and during the American war was, in 1776, taken prisoner and carried to New York, but was soon after released. A personal tax being demanded from him and his elder brother, he resisted the claim, on the plea that it was unjust, unless the payers were allowed a share in the representation; but being compelled to pay it, they presented a petition to the legislature to grant to all the blacks, who paid taxes, the same privileges, in proportion to the imposts upon them, as those enjoyed by the whites. This spirited appeal was warmly and indignantly opposed by some of the members; but, to the honour of the two brothers, as well as of the legislature, it was finally carried. After this, Paul and his brother built a small boat, and proceeded to sea on a mercantile excursion; but his brother being intimidated by the dangers to which they were exposed, they made for their native isle, and retired to their little farm. Paul, however, was of an intrepid and resolute spirit; and collecting the materials for another expedition, he again pushed out upon the ocean, and lost all his little treasure in a storm. But his resolution was not to be crushed by these repeated misfortunes; and he commenced and amidst numerous difficulties completed, with his own hands, an open boat, in which he sailed for another of the Elizabeth Islands. On the passage he was captured by pirates, who robbed him of his vessel, and all that he possessed. He then joined one of his brothers in building another vessel, and succeeded in procuring a small cargo, with which he arrived safely at Nantucket, where he succeeded in disposing of it to advantage. On a second voyage he was again deprived by pirates of all but his boat; but still undaunted he resolved to persevere. He had not received the benefit of education during his father's life; but this deficiency he supplied by self-instruction; and, at the time of his marriage (to a native of the country, a descendant of the Indian tribe to whom his mother belonged), while he was yet young, he could not only read and write, but was a quick arithmetician. When he had attained his twenty-fifth year, he had a covered boat of twelve tons burthen. He hired a person to assist him, and made many advantageous voyages to different parts of the state of Connecticut. His next vessel was of eighteen tons burthen, and with this he sailed from Westport to the banks of St. George in quest of cod-fish, and returned with a large cargo. This adventure was the foundation of an extensive and profitable fishing establishment from Westport river, which was long the source of an honest and comfortable living to many of the inhabitants of that district. At this period he formed a connexion with his brother-in-law, Michael Wainer, who had several sons well qualified for the sea service; four of whom have since laudably filled responsible situations as captains and first mates. As his circumstances improved, each successive vessel he navigated was larger than the former, till, in 1797, he was owner of one of forty-two tons. In this year, knowing the disadvantages of a limited education, having himself several sons, and there being no school in the neighbourhood, he effected a meeting of the inhabitants to establish one: but a difference of opinion amongst those convened having raised an obstacle, he constructed a suitable house on his own ground, which he freely gave up to the use of the public, and the school was opened to all who pleased to send their children. He next made a whaling voyage in 1793, and such was his skill and perseverance, that out of seven whales taken at the fishing ground that season, six fell to his share, and he returned home with a valuable cargo of oil. In 1795 he built a schooner of sixty-nine tons burthen, and was also owner of several fishing-boats. On one occasion, directed by a spirit of

CHAPTER XIII

mercantile adventure, he sailed from Norfolk to Vienna, on the Nantioke river. His appearance there filled the people with alarm. The sight of a vessel well equipped, owned and commanded by a black man, and manned by a crew of the same complexion, was surprising and unprecedented. The white inhabitants were apprehensive of the effects of their appearance on the minds of their slaves; but the good behaviour, candour, and modesty, of Paul and his crew soon dispelled their fears, and he was treated with kindness and respect. He sold his cargo to advantage, and took in corn, by which, on his return to Norfolk, he realized a thousand dollars. After several other successful trips, he purchased the house in which he lived (at Westport), and the farm adjoining for 3500 dollars, and placed it under the management of his brother, who was a farmer. He afterwards commanded the ship Alpha, of 268 tons burthen, of which he owned three-fourths, and his crew consisted of men of colour. This ship performed voyages under him from Westport to Savannah, to Gottenburgh, and to Philadelphia. In 1806 he built a fine brig called the Traveller, and in 1811, having often turned his attention to Sierra Leone, with a view to contribute to the welfare of his fellow blacks in that settlement, he sailed thither in his new vessel. He arrived there after a two months' passage, and resided in the colony about the same length of time. "The African Institution," says his biographer, "having been apprized of his benevolent designs, applied for and obtained a license, which being forwarded to Paul Cuffee, induced him to come to this country with a cargo of African produce." For the more effectual promotion of his primary object, he left his nephew, Thomas Wainer, in the colony, and, with the most disinterested views, brought with him to England Aaron Richards, a native of Sierra Leone, with the intention of educating him, and particularly of instructing him in the art of navigation. He arrived at Liverpool in September, 1811, consigned to Messrs. W. & R. Rathbone; his vessel being navigated by eight men of colour, and an apprentice boy; and, says our biographer, "It is but justice to the crew to say, that during their stay, their conduct was extremely praiseworthy, and the greatest cordiality prevailed amongst them." He twice visited London, the last time at the request of the Board of the African Institution, who were desirous of consulting with him as to the best means of carrying their benevolent views respecting Africa into effect. He afterwards, it appears, made two other voyages to Sierra Leone.

A sound understanding, united with great energy and unconquerable perseverance, seem to have rendered him capable of surmounting difficulties which would have discouraged an ordinary mind; whilst the failures which attended his well concerted plans appear to have resulted rather from casualties, than any error in judgment.

The death of this remarkable individual is thus recorded in the National Intelligencer, September 25th, 1817 :—

"Died, at Westport, on the 7th of September, Paul Cuffee, a very respectable man of colour, in the 59th year of his age. A descendant of Africa, he overcame, by native strength of mind and firm adherence to principle, the prejudice with which her descendants are too generally viewed. Industrious, temperate and prudent, his means of acquiring property, small at first, were gradually increased; and the strict integrity of his conduct gained him numerous friends, to whom he never gave occasion to regret the confidence they had placed in him. His mercantile pursuits were generally successful; and blessed with competence, if not wealth, the enlarged benevolence of his mind was manifested, not only in acts of charity to individuals, and in the promotion of objects of great general utility, but more particularly in the deep interest which he felt for the welfare of his brethren of the African race. He was concerned, not only to set them a good example by his own correct conduct, to admonish and counsel them against the vices and habits to which he found them most prone, but more extensively to promote their welfare, and that at a considerable sacrifice of property. He three times visited Sierra Leone, and after his first voyaye thither, went to England, where he was much noticed by the African Institution, who conferred with him on the best means of extending civilization to the people of Africa; and some of whom have since expressed their satisfaction of his pious labours in the colony, believing them to have been productive of much usefulness to that settlement."

Such was Paul Cuffee: a man whose perseverance, gentleness, and acquirements, under every disadvantage, rendered him an honor to his race.

But the most remarkable instance of negro intellect which has fallen under the observation of the editors is to be found in the writings of the Baron de Vastley, secretary, to king Henry, of Hayti. A translation of a pamphlet, written in Hayti, by this talented and spirited individual, and published in this town in 1817, is well worthy a perusal. It is entitled, "Remarks upon a Letter addressed by M. Mazeres, a French Excolonist, to J. C. L. Sismonde de Sismondi; containing Observations on the Blacks and Whites, the Civilization of Africa, the Kingdom of Hayti, &c." This,

CHAPTER XIII

as the translator remarks, is perhaps the first work by a negro in which the energies of the mind have had a free scope; and it may be added, that the author supports the cause of Haytian independence with considerable powers of reasoning, and in language energetic and even elegant. As a specimen of the style we select the following passage, which strikingly corroborates our author's opinion of the capacity of the negroes:—

"The opinion of Sismonde respecting Hayti, far from being founded upon hypothetical or false grounds, rests upon the most certain facts, correct truth, and living examples. We appeal to strangers who frequent our ports, and visit the interior, to decide whether we are not organised upon the model of the most civilized nations of Europe ? Have we not a firm monarchical government, constitutional charter, laws, and regulations ? Is not justice impartially administered ? Are not our troops numerous and orderly; are they not in point of discipline equal to the first in the world? Have we not built impregnable citadels, constructed according to the strictest rules of art, in inaccessible places, where the greatest obstacles were to be surmounted in completing works worthy of the Romans ? Have we not erected palaces and public edifices, which are at once the glory of our country, and the admiration of strangers ? Have we not manufactories of saltpetre and gunpowder? Is not the mass of our population devoted to agriculture and commerce ? Are not our sailors able to cross the vast expanse of ocean, and do they not navigate with ease the largest ships along our coast ?

"We write; we print: while yet in infancy, our nation can already boast her writers and her poets, who have defended her cause and celebrated her glory. There will not indeed be found among them the pen of a Voltaire, a Rousseau, or a De Lille; but then we have not, like their nation, been civilized upwards of a thousand years. Have we not then every reason not to despair? We have also made essays in the fine arts, and are convinced that proper masters are alone wanting to enable us shortly to produce our Lepoussins, our Mignards, our Rameaux, and our Gretrys. In a word, experience has demonstrated to the world, by the astonishing progress we have made in learning and in civilization, that the capacity of blacks and whites for acquiring the arts and sciences is equal. Read the history of man: never was a similar prodigy seen in the world. Let the enemies of the blacks show a single instance of a people, situated as we found ourselves, who have achieved greater things, and this in less than a quarter of a century. Not only have the Haytians acquired along with their immortal rights the admiration of the universe and of posterity; but they have acquired still stronger claims to glory by raising themselves from ignorance and slavery to that height of splendour and prosperity which they have already attained."

The following instance of negro intrepidity, which has already been published, is perhaps worthy of repetition:—

"Four black officers were arrested on a charge of plotting the assassination of the president of Haiti, and the expulsion of the Europeans—a charge which they denied, but admitted a desire to alter the government, and to break off all connexion with France. They were condemned, and their execution is thus described by Mr. Mackenzie in his *Notes on Haiiti*: "They moved on without the slightest hesitation, until they arrived at the fatal spot close to a dead wall. On reaching it, they still remained pinioned; but the policeman retired, and the shooting party advanced with evident reluctance. At the word being given the firing commenced, and instead of the wretched scene being closed by one, or at most by two well-directed fires, there was absolutely a succession of discharges resembling a *feu-de-joie*. I am sure that not less than one hundred discharges must have taken place before the execution was ended. On reaching the ground, the whole four refused to be bandaged, threw off their hats, and exclaimed to their executioners, 'Ne craignez pas!' The first volley only slightly wounded Captain Francois, who stood at the extreme left; a second brought him down though still alive. Michel was shot through the body in several places, and had both his arms broken before he fell. Lieutenant Lion fell next, after having been severely wounded. During the whole of this revolting exhibition, Sergeant Lion Courchoise was standing on the extreme right of the party calmly smoking a cigar, without moving a limb, or a muscle of his face. A ball through his body brought him to the ground, and as he touched it, he spat the cigar from his mouth, and calmly discharged a volume of smoke from his lungs. The firing party then advanced, and putting the muzzles of their pieces to the bodies of these unhappy men, ended their sufferings by blowing them literally to pieces. They dreamt not," adds Mr. Mackenzie, "of future immortality, nor that a record should ever be made of a firmness and courage which would have done honour to any Roman."

Were further testimony wanted that negroes are as susceptible of mental improvement as any other race of men, it would be found in the recent observations of the celebrated traveller, Dr. Walsh. That gentleman

CHAPTER XIII

had scarcely set his foot on shore at Rio de Janeiro than he had a remarkable opportunity of putting this opinion to the test, by observing the negro under four different aspects of society, clearly demonstrating that his character in each depended on the state in which he was placed, and "the estimation in which he was held." He saw the negro first as a slave, despised, and "far lower than other animals around him." Next, the poor African appeared advanced to the grade of a soldier, "clean and neat in his person, amenable to discipline, expert at his exercises, and showing the port and bearing of a white man similarly placed." Thirdly, our author had occasion to respect the negro as a citizen, remarkable for the respectability of his appearance, and the decorum of his manners. And fourthly, to admire him as a priest of the living God; and, says Dr. Walsh, "in a grade in which moral and intellectual fitness is required, and a certain degree of superiority is expected, he seemed even more devout in his impressions, and more correct in his manners, than his white associates." This is valuable testimony in favour of the negro character.

CONCLUSION

It only remains to perform the mournful duty of stating some particulars relative to the last illness and decease of our author. During the last few years of his life, his health, owing to various causes, and among the rest, to the injuries sustained by his constitution from the extreme hardships he had undergone, and the bodily injuries he had suffered, began sensibly to decline. Still, however, he persevered in following his usual daily routine, as described in a previous part of this work. The News Room still found him at his post, and his friends continued to enjoy the pleasure of his company. Although conscious of a diminution of his wonted strength and vigour, he still exhibited the same contempt of wind and weather as when in perfect health. Often would he be seen in his perambulations, in the depth of our severe northern winters, clothed in his usual garb, and without that indispensable requisite, a top-coat. To the latter article of dress he had a settled antipathy; and when remonstrated with on this subject by his friends, he would remark, " That our modern dandies might wear their top-coats and dominoes for him—that he considered it as a sure mark of effeminacy, and unworthy of a British sailor; and that their use, instead of protecting the wearer, only made him the more susceptible of the effects of our changeable atmosphere." It was therefore only some two or three years previous to his decease that he could be induced to wear this obnoxious appendage, and when he did so it was with considerable reluctance.

In the course of the year 1827 he removed to Preston, and found it necessary to resort to surgical advice, for the removal of a complaint which had caused him much suffering, but of the existence of which few of his nearest friends had previously been aware. He there underwent an operation of a dangerous nature, which was attended with excruciating pain, and much loss of blood; and from which, although at the time he experienced the desired relief, it is believed he never recovered. It reduced him to a state of debility, which rendered the occurrence of any fresh attack of indisposition almost necessarily fatal. During his residence at Preston he corresponded with an intimate friend in Liverpool, and, amongst other letters, wrote one immediately on his recovery, of which the following is an extract:—

"Preston, June 26th, 1827.

"My dear sir—Your welcome and kind letter came to hand in due course. A thousand thanks for the information it contains, and for your kind attention, which, I assure you, I shall not forget. I am still, thank God, in a fair way of recovery, and, from the nature of the painful operation I have undergone, much better than I could have expected; and the doctor will have it that my getting on so well is little short of a miracle. Certainly I must say, that a good and great Providence has always been kind to me. I am most comfortably settled in lodgings; and if the great poet Milton named the abode of our first parents "Paradise *Lost*," I must call this "Paradise *Found*." After a walk of two or three minutes from leaving my lodgings, I find myself on one of the most beautiful walks, I suppose, in the kingdom. The river runs close by, and the fields, covered with verdure, are to be seen as far as the eye can reach. The view from my bedroom window, too, is very beautiful; and I have a nice room to myself, in which to study and write whenever I think proper. Even now I lose no time in making memoranda. In order to complete my book, I think I cannot do better, with your good advice, than come over to Liverpool, to arrange with you respecting the best way of doing so; and then retire here for three or four months, where I can go on without interruption. I could send you my book from hence by a safe hand every other month or six weeks, just as you please, to receive your corrections. Indeed I shall be a slave to it until I get it done to my satisfaction; for I expect it will be one of the first things of the kind ever got up by a Manksman."

In the spring of 1829 he began to exhibit symptoms of debility, which justly alarmed his friends. These unfavourable appearances were quickly aggravated by a severe cold, which compelled him to keep his room. It was only after much entreaty that he was induced to call in medical aid, and through the unremitting attention of our townsman, Dr. Carson, his disorder was so far checked as to afford hopes of his speedy convalescence. Unfortunately, however, so strong was his desire to revisit his favourite haunt, the News Room, that, contrary to the advice of his medical attendant, he would venture out when in a state which demanded confinement to his chamber. The consequence of this imprudence may be easily imagined. His disorder recurred with redoubled force, and, after a lapse of a few days, nature sank under the struggle, and he, who had conquered many enemies, was, in his turn, vanquished by the fell destroyer, death. His last hours were marked by that same kindness and urbanity of manner which distinguished him throughout life. Two of his most intimate friends visited him a few hours before his decease. He was grateful for the little attentions paid to him, and on their leaving him, to see him no more, he very affectionately expressed his thanks for their visits, and implored blessings on them for the kindness which they had manifested.

He died on the afternoon of Wednesday, the 13th of May, 1829, in the 64th year of his age.

His remains were, at his particular desire, conveyed for interment to his native island. The concourse of attendants at his funeral was immense, and all seemed eager to evince their respect for the memory of their esteemed countryman. It might appear ostentatious to particularize the attendance on the occasion. Suffice it to say, that almost every individual of rank and respectability in the island was present. The funeral procession consisted of about twenty coaches.

His remains were interred in the burial ground of his ancestors, in Maugbold church-yard, where he lies entombed with his venerable parents, to whom his attachment knew no bounds; and for whom, throughout his eventful life, he had exhibited the strongest tokens of filial regard and affection.

THE END.

Notes

1. This was a feat which was thought very adventurous; but our author was a good pilot on the coast.
2. The beating of the rain probably elicited those phosphoric particles which are sometimes observable on the dipping of an oar into the sea in calm weather. A similar luminous appearance is often seen in fish placed in the dark.
3. One of the ropes that reach from the masthead to the end of the yard, and serve to steady it, &c.
4. This gentleman was killed, when full colonel, at the taking of Guadeloupe.
5. A General long since.
6. If the wages of men-of-war's men were made equal to those given in the merchant service, and if small bounties were granted for volunteers for a certain number of years' service only, there can be no doubt but the navy would be more sufficiently manned than by the present

NOTES

system of coercion; and the expense of the impress service, with all its oppressions, would be saved to the country. The abolition of corporal punishments would also favour this object.

7   Perhaps his majesty's choler was excited by the small items of money that followed the "dittos" of the invoice!

8   Seizing the leg is there considered a very great mark of condencension and favour.

9   Or Heebos.

10 Six of the number afterwards died.

11 The word "pills" means the large shot taken out of the ship's bottom.

12 Mrs. Mann was a white woman who kept a turtle crawl at Port Royal.

13 A man of the name of Goodall kept a famous house there for a good beef steak; and as Captain Mann and myself were constantly together we were called by the blacks "the two partners."

14 "Fum fum" means flogging.

15 Wars.

16 What silly talk.

17 Whether these trees have grown up to realize the benevolent purpose of those who planted them is not known, or whether indeed the island still remains in existence, or has again sunk into its parent ocean, which is not improbable. Perhaps some recent voyager to that coast may favour the public with some account of it through the newspapers.

18 These are generally pieces of young branches of the common lime, or of the citron of sweet lime tree, the skin of which is smooth, green, and pleasantly aromatic. They are used about the thickness of a quill, and the end being chewed the white fine fibre of the wood soon forms a brush with which the teeth may be effectually cleaned by rubbing them up and down. These sticks impart an agreeable flavour to the mouth, and are sold in the public markets of the West Indies, in little bundles, for a mere trifle.

19 This cruel mode of punishment has also been resorted to in Holland, but is now abolished.

20 Gunpowder formed a staple article of trade in the African vessels.

21 With respect to the mortality amongst the crews of African ships it must be taken into account that many of the individuals composing them were the very dregs of the community: some of them had escaped from jails; others were undiscovered offenders, who sought to withdraw themselves from their country lest they should fall into the hands of the officers of justice. These wretched beings used to flock to Liverpool when the ships were fitting out, and after acquiring a few sea-phrases from some crimp or other, they were shipped as ordinary seamen, though they had never been at sea in their lives. If, when at sea, they became saucy and insubordinate, which was generally the case, the officers were compelled to treat them with severity: and, having never been in a warm climate before, if they took ill, they seldom recovered, though every attention was paid to them. Amongst these wretched beings I have known many gentlemen's sons of desperate character and abandoned habits, who had either fled for some offence, or had involved themselves in pecuniary embarrassments, as to have become outcasts unable to procure the necessaries of life. For my own part I was always very lucky in procuring good crews, and consequently the charge of great mortality could not apply to my ships. The deaths in the Kitty's Amelia were attributable to the culpable neglect of others, the consequences of which we could neither foresee nor control.

22 Capt. Brown, R. N. had, a short time before, written to me the particulars of my son's death.

23 M'Queen.

24 M'Queen.

25 Might not our author's little island, the N. B. Head, have been a formation of alluvial matter?

26　Bosman saw one of these hideous spiders, which he describes as having a long body, sharp head, and legs as large as a man's finger.

27　A supposition somewhat analogous to this still exists in many country places in Europe, where the skin of an eel, or snake, tied round the wrist, is considered as a preventative against a sprain. An old horse-shoe nailed to a mast or barn-door is also considered as a charm, as well as the placing of a particular bone of a fowl in the shoe, by virtue of which children expect to find what they have lost. We have also our lucky days, as well as the Africans, and even many captains of vessels are known to entertain a strong aversion to putting to sea on a Friday.

28　It is not uncommon at some of the ports in Guinea for the natives, when a ship gets under weigh, to smear their bodies with the silt or mud that may be brought up on the nukes of the anchor; a custom which may probably be also amongst the catalogue of penances.

29　"Male dogs," says Adams in describing Lagos, "are banished to the town opposite to Lagos, for if any are caught there, they are immediately strangled, split, and trimmed, like sheep, and hung up at some great man's door, where rows of putrid carcases of their canine brethren are frequently to be seen. They are fetiche, and intended to countervail the machinations of the evil spirit." The variety and confusion of opinions amongst the Africans, within a few days' sail of each other, are here exemplified.

30　He probably meant it to be inferred, that the rain was impregnated with animalcules, which deposited their eggs in the pores of the skin.

31　A negro, on being asked why his countrymen could think of eating land-crabs, seeing that they devoured the remains of the dead, replied, that he thought the custom reasonable and just; for, said he, "crab eat black man—black man eat he!"

32　This taste is akin to the fashionable penchant for moor and other game in England, when it is so far decayed that the cook must look after it lest it should move off!

33　These rings are worn in several parts of the coast, and particularly at Calabar, and frequently in defiance of their producing sores and lameness.

34　The present king has since adopted the name of his mother.

35　Hugh Murray, F. R. S. E.

36　The African shark, says Artus, has been known to be above 20 feet long, and as thick as an ox. They have sharp teeth indented like a saw, with which they will cut off a man's leg or arm as cleanly as if it were done with a hatchet.

37　Artus states, that European dogs are greatly esteemed on account of their barking, the negroes thinking they speak, from which it may be inferred that those of Africa are a different species—probably indigenous.

38　A writer on the western coast remarks, that there are "fifty species of monkeys," which are capable of "fifty thousand mischievous tricks."

39　The present king of Bonny, son of the late King Pepple, takes the name of *Bess* Pepple from his mother. Next to him in power is a chief called Indian Queen, and next is Tom Africa, the first heir to the throne, and a wealthy trader. They are all represented as honourable in their dealings.

40　The Rev. W. Shepherd, of Gateacre.

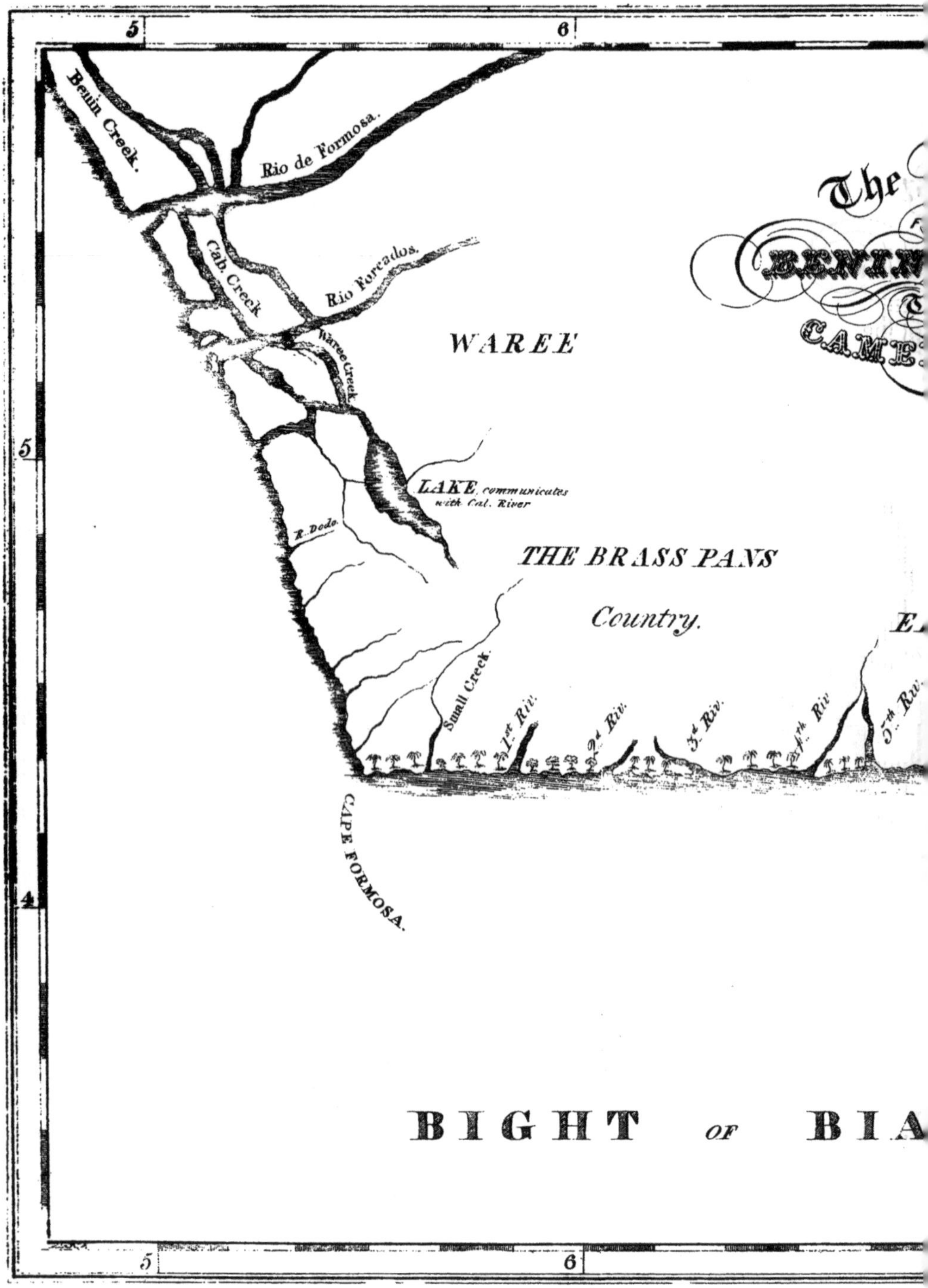

5
6
Benin Creek.
Rio de Formosa.
Cab. Creek
Rio Forcados.
Waree Creek
WAREE
LAKE communicates with Cal. River
R. Dodo
THE BRASS PANS
Country.
Small Creek
1st Riv.
2d Riv.
3d Riv.
4th Riv.
5th Riv.
CAPE FORMOSA.
BIGHT OF BIA
4